Enjoy the Bike
& the Book

[signature]

MW00356162

Eagle With A Badge

The True Story of a State Police Pilot

Paul Creech
and Jack Lawler

EAKIN PRESS ⚑ Fort Worth, Texas
www.EakinPress.com

To my wife, Dolores, without whose love,
understanding, and encouragement
this book would never have been written—
and to Jack's wife, Doodie Lawler,
whose tireless computer work
helped us keep the pages moving . . .
my heartfelt thanks.

—PAUL CREECH

The stories contained within this book are true.
Names of people and cities and dates of events may
have been changed for reasons of privacy.

All photos are property of Paul Creech.

Contents

Paul Creech's devoted partner—
his helicopter, Helo-101.

A Special Dedication

They face danger regularly, without complaining. They work long hours in all kinds of weather, often unable to spend Christmas or other holidays with their families, risking their lives year round for public safety. Some are injured in the line of duty; others have given the ultimate sacrifice. Through it all their spouses worry and pray for their safety, often managing the home and children in their absence.

They are state police pilots, state troopers, Texas Rangers, narcotics agents, DPS special crimes officers, state alcohol beverage agents, sheriffs and their deputies, city police and other law officers, communications operators, EMS technicians, and firemen. They are the "thin blue line" that protects society. Without them, I could not have safely or successfully accomplished what I did. My helicopter, with me as pilot, was only a tool they used to help them make an arrest, save a life, or find a missing person.

To all these unsung heroes of public safety, this book is gratefully dedicated.

—PAUL CREECH

. . . but those who hope in the Lord will renew their strength. They will soar on wings like eagles; they will run and not grow weary; they will walk and not be faint.

—Isaiah 40:31

Introduction

Welcome to my life of adventures in the sky! What you are about to read is not fiction. This is real-life drama as seen through my eyes as a state police pilot.

Climb aboard and sit in the copilot seat of my police helicopter, Helo-101. Fly with me as we patrol the skies of Texas. We will only be a few hundred feet above the ground, because, as police officers, our job is fighting crime on the ground, not 10,000 feet in the sky.

Help me search for dangerous criminals, lost people, and those in danger. There are armed criminals down there, but because we are sworn to uphold the law and protect the weak, you must be brave and steadfast when the shooting starts.

When I was young and a new helicopter pilot, I was sometimes foolhardy and took dangerous risks. But with you aboard, I promise to keep safety at the forefront. Buckle your safety belt and hang on tight! Sometimes in our line of work we may have to plunge into danger as we do our duty in protecting citizens or fellow peace officers. Watch with me as drama unfolds below us. We will feel invincible in our aluminum and plastic helicopter, even though it is not bulletproof. Sometimes we'll fly with the doors off. Feel our friend the wind as she whips the cloth of your flight suit.

If you are willing to become a police helicopter pilot, then you must be willing to devote the best years of your life to protecting and serving in the brightness of day or darkness of night. In so doing, you will have the time of your life. Your spouse must be skilled in last-minute assembly of Christmas toys for your children, because your sworn duty may call you away to an even greater task, perhaps that of saving a child.

Come fly with me and see what I saw. Experience the life of a flying police officer. And don't be surprised if you then view the earth in a different way—as seen through the eyes of an "Eagle With A Badge."

— PAUL CREECH

CHAPTER 1

Threading the needle

The phone roused me from a deep sleep at 3:30 A.M., accompanied by a loud clap of thunder that seemed to rattle my windows. I picked up the phone, still half asleep. Yesterday had been a long and tiring day of flight.

It was the district supervisor, and he sounded tired and sleepy, too. He told me the roads were flooding and that a man and his nine-month pregnant wife were stranded in their car by high water on a bridge. The man had managed to make his way out of the water and call for help for his wife, who was still in the car on the bridge, with the water rising rapidly.

"We need you to get there fast, Paul, and get her out before the water covers the entire bridge," said my supervisor.

I hung up, struggled out of bed, and stepped onto the patio for my personal visual weather check. Rain was coming down steadily, thunder was rumbling, lightning was flashing. Starting a quick cup of instant coffee in the microwave, I called the Denton County sheriff's dispatcher for more information. She verified the highway and bridge flooding and said deputies standing by at the scene warned that rising waters could cover the bridge at any time. She confirmed that the woman was still stranded, and added, "Her husband says she could have the baby at any time."

I called my partner, Kenny Meadows, gave him a short briefing, and asked him to assist me in operating our chopper's searchlight.

With a mental picture of the pregnant woman on the bridge, there was no time for coffee. I had seen the deadly speed of rising floodwaters before. I jumped into my car and quickly drove to the airport.

When I pulled into the complex, Kenny's car was right behind me. *Good man, topnotch partner*, I thought. As we raced for the terminal building, a slashing downpour resumed. Inside, with water dripping off my head and hands, I called the local Aviation Flight Service Station, needing to get some idea as to when the rain might let up. The forecast: thunderstorms throughout the morning, until past dawn.

There was nothing to do but wait for a weather break. The rain was still coming down hard. I called the dispatcher again and told her we couldn't take off in the heavy rains and darkness. Through her silence I could sense her disappointment and urgent concern.

"My helicopter is not instrument certified," I explained, "and we're in the middle of a heavy thunderstorm right here. We'll take off just as soon as possible."

Kenny and I looked at each other, then looked at the big clock on the wall. Kenny walked over to a coffee pot, stagnant with yesterday's coffee. He rummaged below it, but found no coffee. We really needed a cup of coffee!

We paced. We waited. Kenny looked outside. Rain, rain, rain. Finally, at 4:50 A.M., it stopped.

We ran for the hangar, did a quick preflight check on our helicopter, and pushed Helo-101 out. We were airborne about 5:08, headed for the Denton Creek bridge on FM 407, thirty-five miles away. We were both tense, as these were still dangerous flying conditions. We had lost one hazard, the downpour, but still had others—the total darkness and the potential of more storms.

Uppermost in my mind was the thought that a life hung in the balance. No—two lives, I corrected myself.

As we neared the bridge, I contacted the deputy at the scene by radio. "Watch for our searchlight beam and direct me to the bridge," I said.

"Affirmative," he answered.

Kenny turned on our searchlight. The powerful beam

pierced the murky, water-drenched sky. "The beam looks scary, reflecting off all that moisture," I said.

"Want me to turn it off so you won't be scared?" Kenny ventured, with a smirk.

Within my anxiety, I mentally chuckled. *Good old Kenny,* I thought. *I always like a man willing to help his partner in a tough moment.* I began a cautious descent to 400 feet.

The deputy saw our searchlight. "You're close," he said, "turn left and go about 100 yards." Suddenly, there we were, directly over the bridge and the car, with the woman still in it. The searchlight showed it all.

I did a low reconnaissance, circling the scene. Kenny worked diligently to keep the beam on the bridge and the car. Descending and hovering, our rotor blades popping in the humid heavy air, we read the scene. Water covered parts of the bridge; the flooded creek swirled angrily, with debris in it.

Upon seeing and hearing us, the woman had gotten out of her car. I judged there was still enough room on the bridge to land. Suddenly, it seemed that my anxiety and fears were gone. After all, I was a public safety pilot. This was just another "moment of truth" that I had trained for.

"Kenny, I'm going to land on the bridge, in front of the car," I said. "I've got room. Hold the searchlight on the landing area and don't let it move."

I began my approach. My flight path was to be near the end of the bridge, short of where the woman was standing. The rotor blades would have a scant twenty-foot clearance from some tall trees. I descended slowly, carefully . . . between the trees, then down further between the bridge guard railings. It was like threading a needle. I breathed a prayer: *God, this is a human life, and I am the only one who can save her. Please keep my hand steady and the bridge strong, with no heavy debris sweeping over its top.*

I touched down softly.

Kenny got out and hurried to the woman, who was drenched and appeared to be ready to collapse. As he assisted her into Helo-101, water was lapping at their feet on the floor of the bridge. *Hurry, Kenny,* I thought, without speaking the words. Boarding was slow and careful, as she was truly *very* pregnant. She was scared, totally wet and shivering. I suspected she was in shock.

With everybody secured, I came to a hover and took off into the black sky in a 45-degree climb. We had beaten the angry, flooded river—beaten an angry Mother Nature.

I called the ground deputy. "We have the lady. She appears to be suffering from shock and hypothermia. Call the Denton hospital and brief them. Tell them we'll be there in ten minutes."

Doctors and nurses were waiting at the hospital heliport. Kenny hopped out and opened the side door. With little conversation, the attendants began to ease her out to place her on a stretcher. I was still seated at the controls, watching, when she surprised me by suddenly reaching out and clasping my hand. Her grateful eyes met mine. It was a million-dollar moment for me.

The rain had stopped. We took off, back into the black sky toward our airport, and home.

"Great job, Paul," said Kenny. "Gotta admit, I wasn't sure we would have enough room between the trees to land."

"I know. It was tight."

I arrived home at 6:15 A.M., not sleepy at all. I made a real cup of coffee and discovered I was hungry. I watched the morning news and let my adrenaline subside. Getting drowsy, I thought about the squeeze of the woman's hand, the final grateful look in her eyes. I realized, all over again, that this was the only occupation for me.

And I wondered if she would have her baby that day.

Little did I dream as a young boy that in the years to come, other life-saving opportunities—diverse and rewarding—would be mine.

CHAPTER 2

The early days

As a young boy I grew up living in a little house deep within the tall pine trees and dense woods of East Texas. We were three miles from the little town of Colmesneil. We had no electricity or running water. We were very poor, and grocery money was scarce. But at the time I didn't realize we were poor. The thick woods held enchanting beauty and magical mysteries for me. I learned the names of the tall trees that included sweet gum, sassafras, red oak, white oak, beech, hickory, and pine. Wildlife was abundant with deer, squirrels, foxes, raccoons, coyotes, and mink.

My mother and father were faithful Christians, and it was church every Sunday for the Creech family, which included an older brother, four sisters, and me. My father supported his large family by farming in the warm weather months and cutting logs and railroad ties in the winter. With the world in the flames of World War II, my father landed a job at Bethlehem Steel Shipbuilding Company in Beaumont, about seventy-five miles from our home, and the family moved. His job: helping build warships as a welder's helper. He was too old to be a soldier, but he contributed to the war effort, while bettering the Creech family's economic needs.

I was saddened to leave my wooded wonderland, but the move to Beaumont added things to my boyish horizon that would permanently affect my future.

The U.S. Air Force base at Beaumont bristled with World

War II fighter planes and bombers. I watched them fly overhead daily, heard the powerful sound of the radial engines,
and marveled at the speed of the fighter planes. At the local
movie theater, there was always an up-to-date newsreel shown
about the war, and I was spellbound by the scenes of aerial
combat of our planes against the German and Japanese aircraft. Our fighter pilots had a nonchalance about them that
seemed happy-go-lucky and even cocky.

I became fascinated with the fighter airplanes and had
visions of becoming a fighter pilot someday. Even at my young
age of seven, I began learning all I could about the various aircraft systems, weapons, speed, and silhouette identification of
every airplane. We were told the enemy might attack seaport
cities such as Beaumont.

My elementary school was about ten miles from the air-
base. One day, while I was on the playground, a formation of
several P-51 Mustang fighters flew overhead. As I watched
them, one started leaving a trail of smoke. He broke off from
the formation and descended, and I got excited. Later, arriving home and still excited, I told my mother what I had seen.
The next evening my mother showed me the newspaper story
about a P-51 Mustang
with an engine failure
that had crashed near
Beaumont. The pilot
had bailed out safely.
I can still vividly recall
the scene of that sleek
warbird going down.

*Paul Creech as a nine-
year-old in East Texas.*

When the war ended, the wartime footing of the ship-building industry slowed, which ended my father's job. We moved back to the home place in the woods. I was delighted to return. Our house sat atop a hill, and near our back porch was a large red oak tree that seemed to reach for the sky, towering above all the other trees. It became my favorite airplane. Knowing that my mother and dad would not approve of my climbing to such a high and dangerous perch, I would slip away and climb the huge tree to the very top, where I could view the entire countryside. Then I would sit on a fork in the limbs, which became my pilot seat. My control stick was a small adjacent limb. I flew many missions there and shot down many enemy aircraft. No one ever shot me down, and I never had to bail out.

I became skilled at building and flying kites. I built them with wood scraps and covered them with whatever paper I could find.

My first close look at a real airplane came when a military trainer called a Stearman, a biplane used for primary training, developed engine trouble and had to make an emergency landing in a field near our house. The family loaded up into our new 1946 Chevrolet pickup and went to see this curiosity. It was my first look at an airplane up close, and it was a real beauty! There were soldiers there to repair it, and they were friendly, glad to answer our questions. When it was time for us to leave, they gave us a loaf of military bread. This experience thrilled me and deepened my ambition to be a pilot. That night I sat on our porch, listened to the wind sighing through the tall treetops, and dreamed big about flying.

In 1956 I graduated from Colmesneil High School and told my loving parents that I wanted to leave home, move to Beaumont, and seek my fortune. "Hitching" a ride with a friend a few days later, I was so excited, driving away from the home of my youth, that I probably did not see the silent tears in my mother's eyes. As it happens with eighteen-year-old young men, it was the closing of one chapter in my life and the beginning of a new one—an exciting one.

After landing a job in Beaumont as an apprentice machinist building oilfield equipment, I learned that a good friend,

Jimmy Clauder, was taking flying lessons. He soon made his first solo flight as a student pilot. I hung around him steadily, pestering him with questions. It seemed I couldn't ask him enough. He was a good sport and answered me patiently. One day, over lunch, he asked me if I wanted a ride. I immediately said "Yes!" Jimmy had only eight hours' flying time. He had flown solo, but had not yet received his private pilot's license. It didn't matter to me. My heart beat faster as we drove to the airport.

The aircraft was a J-3 Piper Cub. As we approached it, sitting in front of an old Quonset hut metal hangar, I thought it looked so tiny, as delicate as a little bird. I walked around it in awe, then patted it on the fuselage as if it were an old friend.

"Climb in," invited Jimmy. My pilot sat in the rear seat of this two-seater, and the honored passenger, Paul Creech, sat in the front seat. I belted in. Jimmy hand started the engine by spinning the propeller while I held the brake. Then he climbed in, put on his safety belt, and we eased away from the hangar. Soon we were racing down the runway, and almost before I realized what was happening I felt a gentle tug and we lifted off. Airborne! I was *flying!* As the little craft climbed, I was again awestruck.

What a view I had from my front seat. The window swung open and the door swung down. How beautiful was the blue sky, the puffy clouds. The wind blew in my face, my clothes flapped by its fierce gale. Jimmy banked, and I looked down. Houses and cars on the ground appeared to be little toys. No longer was I the little boy sitting in the tall oak tree in the woods, play-acting the pilot. I was a man, and this was the real thing!

All too soon, it was time to land. Jimmy did it smoothly. As we taxied up near the hangar, Jimmy's flight instructor was standing outside it, hands on hips. He had watched our flight and the landing. As we stepped out, he greeted us with a loud and angry verbal blast that included a few choice adjectives. "Jimmy, you're not a pilot yet, and if I ever see you taking anybody riding again before you become a pilot, you will never fly again. I'll see to that."

Undaunted, my friend survived the tongue lashing, continued his flying lessons, and got his private pilot's license. He took me flying with him many more times. Those were balmy summer days, and I couldn't wait to get off work and meet Jimmy at the airport.

Then came another special day. At an altitude of 2,000 feet and with his hands close to the controls, he let me fly the airplane.

It was another superb moment. As I gently turned the little airplane, all the thrills and emotions of my first "passenger" flight came back to me, stronger this time. I was flying an airplane! Soon, with Jimmy as my back seat instructor, I was truly flying the little ship myself, including landing and taking off. I began to wish that I, too, could get my pilot's license. Even now, years and years later, I sharply remember the feelings of exuberance and freedom I felt in those times.

I had the skills but not the money required to pay for the flying lessons and license. I was working in a machine shop, and my pay was very small. Anxious to increase my earnings, and with that pilot's license on my mind, another boyhood memory recurred within me.

A Texas Department of Public Safety (DPS) trooper had come to my high school and made speeches about bicycle and highway walking safety. His sharp uniform, shiny black boots, and positive demeanor had impressed me. Surely, I recalled, he had made a good salary. With a good and steady salary, I decided, I could perform law enforcement duties, afford a pilot's license, and fly in my off-duty hours!

In 1959 I applied with DPS and was accepted for recruit training at Austin. It was sixteen weeks of grueling activities that included tough physical conditioning, instruction in firearms, first aid, and high-speed driving, demanding classroom studies, and much more. In the fall of 1959 I graduated as a Texas DPS trooper and was assigned as a driver license trooper in Beaumont. Later I was transferred to the Highway Patrol in Kirbyville in East Texas. My partner was Bob Hutchins. We pursued and stopped lots of speeders and DWI drivers.

One night on patrol I said, "Bob, I've noticed the highway

*DPS Trooper
Paul Creech, age thirty-one.*

traffic is increasing. I believe that someday it will increase so much that Texas will not be able to supply enough patrolmen and cars to patrol all the highways."

He nodded in agreement, and we discussed it. Then the thought of patrolling with airplanes came to me. I added, "I think that someday traffic law enforcement can and will use airplanes. Bob, I'm gonna get my pilot's license and be ready when that day comes. I can fly and get paid for it, and still be a highway patrolman!"

Bob agreed and decided that he, too, might like to become a flying highway patrolman.

By then I was married and we had two young boys and a daughter. My trooper's salary of $450 per month kept money in short supply.

Bob knew a pilot named Dick Conn, who flew from the Kirbyville Airport. Bob introduced me, and Dick invited me to fly with him. I did so many times. He introduced me to another pilot, Clarence Townsend. I was soon flying again, with these new friends giving me lots of "free" rides.

Soon the local pilots of this airport got together and formed a flying club. One of them, a doctor, bought the club a J-3 Cub for $1,250. The Flying Club agreed to pay him back as we flew the Cub, buying our own gas and paying the doctor a few dollars. It was a real "poor-boy" flying club. There were no club dues, and it was open to anyone. I was still not financially able to pay to fly, and I bummed rides every chance I got.

Inspired and gaining knowledge from this, I soon became determined to take flying lessons. Somehow, I would do it.

Paul (at right) and Kirbyville Flying Club, with J-3 Piper Cub.

With my wife's agreement, I would pay for one hour of flight lessons per month. My training would involve thirty minutes of flying every other week, and I would continue to bum rides with other pilots.

Mr. Elzie Marshall was the nearest flight instructor to my home. He had his own private airport about ten miles from my house. I contacted Mr. Marshall and told him of my financial plight and of the many hours that I had flown with private and commercial pilots. I told him that I could already fly an airplane. I asked if he would be willing to work with me. I'm sure he was probably skeptical, but he agreed. I made an appointment with him to give me my first official flight lesson.

The day arrived, and I took off in the J-3 Cub with Mr. Marshall, who soon realized that I really could fly. We flew for forty-five minutes. He had me do all the aerial maneuvers necessary to solo. I was surprised when he asked me to land to a full stop. He got out, asked for my pilot's logbook, endorsed it to solo, and told me to take off and land three times. I was both excited and scared.

"Are you sure?" I asked.

"Yes," he answered, "but if you bounce when you land, give it the gas, go around and try it again."

I gulped and took off. The little plane felt light without the instructor's weight. *Oh my Lord,* I thought, *I hope I can remember it all.*

My concern about remembering everything and making smooth landings soon subsided. I was in a high concentration mode. As I reached 1,000 feet altitude on the downwind leg of the traffic pattern, a powerful exhilaration came over me. I was flying! And I was all alone up there. It was my ballgame to win or lose.

Soon it was time for my first landing. In my glide path I could see Mr. Marshall standing beside and at the end of the runway on which I would land. I bounced. He motioned and shouted, "Go around!" I could clearly hear his shout through the open window of the Cub. I gave it the gas and went around, then made three nice takeoffs and landings.

I then started taking my occasional flight lessons at Elzie Marshall's airport—the ones that count toward getting a private pilot's license. For student pilots, landings are the most difficult task. Under careful tutelage, I practiced maneuvers, landings, stalls, and takeoffs—in the same type little J-3 Cub in which my Beaumont friend, Jimmy Clauder, had given me rides. It had a 65-HP engine and a maximum cruise speed of about 65 MPH.

After a few basic flight lessons in the Cub, Mr. Marshall told me that the Cub was not acceptable for the Federal Aviation check ride that would qualify me for my private pilot's license. I would need an airplane that had all the necessary flight instruments. I would need to start using his Cessna-150. In the coming weeks, when off-duty and after taking care of family chores, I spent a lot of time hanging around his airport making a pest of myself.

One day my DPS duty station received a bulletin from headquarters stating that DPS would soon be purchasing two helicopters to use in traffic patrol, and that any interested DPS officers with a private pilot's license could apply immediately. My heartbeat accelerated as I read it. I immediately sent a memo stating that I was interested, adding that I only had a student pilot's license.

An immediate answer came back: "No!" I was greatly disappointed.

Mr. Marshall, an observant man who thoroughly enjoyed flying and teaching others to fly, knew that I had missed the chance to be selected as a police helicopter pilot. He had seen the sad look on my face when I told him about it.

I continued a lesson from him "here and there" until one day he said, "Paul, use my airplane, get your license, and pay me when you can." I was in shock. No one had ever done anything like that for me. I asked him if he was kidding. He was not.

I then started serious flying lessons. A few weeks later I finished all required training and passed my FAA private pilot check ride. I was now a private pilot.

With tight money management and the help of God, I repaid Mr. Marshall. His timely and generous help made it possible for me to "soar" like the eagle I had long aspired to be. Everybody, at some point in his or her life, needs a friend like Mr. Elzie Marshall was to me. I shall never forget him.

After receiving my pilot's license, I introduced my two boys, Kenneth, age eight, and Mike, age seven, to the joys of flying. I took them flying in the J-3 Cub. I did not know that these flights would establish a spark that to this day has continued the lineage of my family as state police pilots. Mike is a DPS pilot in Corpus Christi, Texas, flying the Bell Jet Ranger helicopter and Cessna 210 airplane. He and I had the privilege of working together several times before I retired.

A couple of months after receiving my license, my highway patrol office received another memo from DPS headquarters advising all personnel that six additional helicopter pilots were needed. Again, I applied quickly.

This time, I was accepted.

It was another magic moment in the life of a guy whose boyhood involved sitting high in an oak tree and imagining that he was a pilot. And my heart and mind were truly soaring like an eagle as I hurried home to tell my family.

My title in the new job was sergeant pilot. Pilot training was done at DPS/Austin in two Bell 47G-5 helicopters. The

First DPS Jet Ranger, 1969.

two instructors were Roy Swetnam and Carl Mullins, the highway patrolmen who had been picked from the first flight group selected. These instructors and all those early pilots seemed above average and possessed a confident attitude. Many were young highway patrol veterans.

A helicopter could not compare to an airplane. It flew entirely differently. Its rotor blades were its wings. I quickly decided that flight in a helicopter was true flight. It went up, down, forward, backward, and sideways. Ours went forward with a blazing speed of 80 MPH. It was a proud day when, after three weeks of instruction and practice, I finally soloed in the Bell 47G-5 helicopter. At that moment, I knew I had become a flying policeman.

The first DPS helicopters were primarily used for traffic patrol. The highway patrol captains in each of seven DPS regions of Texas evaluated the feasibility of helicopters for traffic use. At least one captain was not favorable toward using them. In his report he stated that the helicopters were too expensive to purchase and maintain (each cost as much as several patrol cars). Also, he wrote, they were not always available due to maintenance problems or bad weather. When I read his appraisal, I thought, *Yeah. They laughed at Edison and his electric light bulb, too.*

My assigned station was Dallas. I'll never forget my first flight from Austin to Dallas. I was riding in the copilot seat, and my flight instructor was the pilot in command. It was a clear day and we arrived at dusk. The city lights were visible in any direction, as far as the eye could see. This country boy had learned to fly in the piney woods of East Texas and had never seen anything like this sea of lights. It was intimidating to me. Until this time I had flown into only three tower-controlled airports in my life. I wondered, *What am I doing here?* To think that the citizens of this area were going to depend on me, a country pilot cop, to keep them safe! I wasn't even sure I could find the airport.

The early days of my police helicopter career were spent in traffic patrol and assisting county sheriffs with criminal searches for escaped felons. My pilot, partner Billy Peace, and I spent a lot of time training and building our confidence. All of the first DPS pilots were young and basically inexperienced. We learned our trade by personal flight experiences, as we developed and shared our knowledge. Much of the training emphasis was placed on auto-rotations, or landing without power. It is simply done by rolling the throttle grip off to the engine idle position. The rotor blades are free to rotate. If this is done properly, it is a normal landing. If not, the pilot rolls the throttle forward, increasing power to the normal range, and stopping the helicopter before touchdown. If one is late rolling in the throttle or shows poor judgment, a hard landing could follow, and possibly damage the aircraft.

We young pilots had the same type of personality as the WWII fighter pilots I had admired as a youth—young, nonchalant, and happy-go-lucky. We gained experience and developed precision in flying the helicopter. It was as if the helicopter and pilot became as one. With a cocky attitude I once hovered under a railroad bridge. In those days, the 1970s, we had few departmental safety rules and regulations. My training and experience would be tested many times in the years to come.

In time, most of us advanced in our helicopter rating from

private pilot to commercial pilot to airline transport pilot rating. As we became more experienced and more time passed, a safety/training officer was appointed by the director of the Texas Department of Public Safety as our aircraft section came to the forefront. A manual was written specifying the do's and don'ts, and all aircraft were configured so that regardless which aircraft we flew, everything was the same.

We soon increased our fleet of helicopters by adding Bell Jet Rangers. As the DPS Aircraft Section grew, we added Aerospatiale A-Star helicopters. They were bigger and faster than the Bell Jet Ranger. By 1998 the DPS Aircraft Section had grown to twenty-six pilots, seven helicopters, six single-engine airplanes, and a multi-engine airplane.

Helicopters had proven themselves in law enforcement. The DPS Aircraft Section had come a long way and had brought me with it. I realized that the boy who had sat in an oak tree "play-acting" a pilot was a real pilot who had reached heights beyond boyhood dreams. And the flying job I had was important. A lot of people had helped me along the way. And because they had, I had also been able, with the helicopter, to help a lot of people.

I also realized that Somebody up high liked me.

CHAPTER 3

A sad win

An expected day off on a summer day can be that extra little pleasure that makes life worth living, I was thinking on that Wednesday. Have a late breakfast, read the paper slowly, then get on my old farm tractor and plow . . . The muddling putt-putt speed of the old tractor plus the smell of the freshly turned earth would be a refreshing 100% contrast to the flights I'd had the past two days. That was in my mind, with no timetable for any of it.

But this pleasant one-day "dream-plan" was not to be for me that day. The phone rang. It was my lieutenant. A man-hunt was starting for a targeted narcotics dealer, Leon Price, in North Texas, about forty miles south of Dallas. All officers in the county, including myself and Helo-101, were needed. "Better get crackin' fast, Paul," the lieutenant said. "And be careful. This guy is big-time . . . may be a bad one."

I alerted my partner, Pilot Investigator Kenny Meadows, by phone. Sighing with a slight self-pity as I rapidly slipped into my flight suit, I said to myself, "Good-bye, tractor. Hello, Helo-101."

Kenny beat me to the hangar, and within twenty-four minutes of my call, DPS Helo-101 and its two pilots were airborne. I described our assignment to Kenny. Kaufman County sheriff's deputies had approached the drug dealer's rural house to serve an arrest warrant. As they had approached, the man had fled out the back door and into a wooded area, pistol in hand. The deputies had given chase on foot, then lost him in the thick woods. Knowing that he was armed, they called for assistance. Among the help requested was the dog-tracking team of the Texas Department of Corrections (state prison).

Our Aerospatiale A-Star chopper, beating the air at 140 MPH, arrived at the scene quickly, with radio guidance from ground officers. A "command post" had been set up on Interstate 20. I brought Helo-101 in low, blades popping loudly, hoping for a lucky early glimpse of the fugitive and to determine how well the officers on the ground had the area surrounded. Banking steeply at 150 feet, Kenny and I watched carefully for power lines, noting thick trees mixed with green cow pastures below. We also noted one area to the north of the ground officers' perimeter that was neither manned nor accessible from any road.

"Thick brush down there," observed Kenny.

"That's why we're here," I grinned. "Watch for anything that looks out of place."

We kept circling, banking steeply and peering carefully through treetops, looking for movement, color, or anything out of nature's ordinary landscape. Nothing. Except we spooked a deer. I remembered that I hadn't finished breakfast or gotten that second cup of coffee, which I wished for now.

Eager for the dog team and its handler to arrive, I hoped that I could keep the "bad guy" pinned down until they got there. I'd worked the chopper/dog routine before; we had been effective teams. The chopper circles over the area of the possible escape path of the fugitive, slowing his progress, while the experienced dogs sniff him out.

Still at low altitude, we swept over several officers at various points along the pasture's edge, all with weapons drawn. Then I heard a familiar voice on my radio: Sgt. Charlie Sparkman, the dog team handler. He was calling for a county deputy but was getting no answer.

I estimated Sparkman was too far away, so I responded to him on the Helo-101 radio. The TDC sergeant advised that his estimated arrival time would be twenty minutes. I gave him the command post location on I-20, then relayed to the officers on the ground Sparkman's location and estimated arrival time.

Sparkman's estimate was accurate, and he came ready for action. His club cab pickup truck was pulling a large horse trailer loaded with horses, tracking dogs, and prison trusties who helped with the animals. There was a reserve team of dogs and horses for back-up use in case the "first teams" became fatigued. The horses were stamping nervously; the dogs were barking. By agreement, I landed near this entourage for the purpose of giving Sparkman a quick airborne look at the search area.

We shook hands with the TDC dog handler sergeant. Sparkman was dressed in a gray uniform, cowboy boots, white Stetson hat, brush country chaps and wore a large .45 pistol. We talked loudly a moment over all the noise, then we all climbed into Helo-101. The dogs seemed to bark even more furiously when the chopper lifted off, as if fearing they would miss the action if their trainer left them.

One of Sparkman's horses, being readied for pursuit.

"Lord," I mused, "if the bad guy knew all this was coming after him, he'd surrender now."

Kenny and I gave the TDC sergeant a quick air tour with brief narrative, at two different altitudes.

"I got it," said Sparkman. "Put me down."

We did. Mounting a big white horse, Sparkman, with his dogs barking excitedly and running around him, headed for the woods at a brisk canter. Kenny and I took off again, noting the direction the tracking dogs were moving. I kept the chopper out in front of the dogs, hoping to see the fugitive as the dogs closed in, and perhaps preventing further evasive flight by him. Circling so as not to get too far ahead, we caught glimpses of Sparkman on his horse, gesturing and shouting to his dogs. I knew the dogs would "sniff and run," "sniff and run," in and out of the thickly wooded area.

Suddenly, a ground officer radioed, "Helo-101, I hear gunshots in the area of the dog team!"

Banking Helo-101 and descending slightly, we saw the fugitive come running out of the woods. Thirty to forty yards ahead of him was one of the dogs running scared at high speed, with his tail between his legs, and forty to fifty yards behind him came Sparkman on his white horse, at a gallop. Adjusting my speed to follow the chase below, Kenny and I clearly saw the fugitive turn and fire at Sparkman, who fired at him in return. At each shot by Sparkman, his horse would buck.

"Shades of the Lone Ranger," I said to Kenny, as both of us peered intently through the Plexiglas window. But this was no movie down below.

The fugitive came to a large fence, scrambled over it, and kept moving. Sparkman's horse couldn't jump it. The sergeant dismounted, got wire cutters from his saddlebags, and began cutting the fence. In a hover mode above the scene, we could easily see that the fleeing drug dealer, who appeared to be large and athletic, was fast getting away. I keyed the radio mike button.

"Helo-101 confirming shots fired. We need a deputy to meet us at the command post, board the chopper, and we'll try to head off the suspect."

We landed. Deputy John Sexton boarded, carrying a shot-

Command post where Pilot Creech has just picked up deputy.

gun. We briefed him on the gunfight and the chase. Our plan: to airdrop the deputy in front of the fleeing fugitive, forcing him back into the direction of converging officers. Airborne again, we quickly overtook the fleeing narcotics dealer, running over an open field, and landed 150 yards ahead of him near a cluster of mesquite trees.

I advised the deputy to use the sparse clump of trees for cover. No sooner had the deputy disembarked and headed for the trees than the suspect appeared within about 100 yards, running straight at us. He paused and pointed his pistol at our chopper. Whether it was my own adrenaline or the fact that I was encased in plastic and aluminum with a 641 horsepower engine at my fingertips, I suddenly felt untouchable.

"Kenny, I gotta do something to give that deputy time to reach cover," I exclaimed to my copilot.

Kenny rolled his eyes at me as if to say, "Whatever it is, partner, you better do it fast!"

I pulled in all engine power at six feet off the ground and headed straight at the man . . . and into the barrel of his pistol. Two tight-lipped pilots could see the shock in the shooter's eyes. I flew straight at him like a charging bull, then pulled up at the last second, turning hard right. The pistol followed the maneuver, pumping bullets at the chopper.

"Helo-101, he's shooting at you," came a ground radio voice.

"Yeah, we know!" yelled Kenny, watching the instrument panel closely.

Looking out my side window, I saw a puff of dust at the fugitive's feet and knew the deputy had fired. In the same view I saw that Sergeant Sparkman, who had evidently made it through the fence, as riding hard, closing the distance on his quarry. Then a royal shootout commenced between the fugitive and the deputy, with the lawman's shotgun spitting fire. Kenny and I saw it all from 200 feet above. Still running hard, the fugitive suddenly went down. Hovering, we watched as the deputy and Sparkman approached the downed man. They kicked the pistol away from his reach. He wasn't moving. Other officers came running. The situation was under control.

We landed and walked over to the fugitive. He was dead. Buckshot from the deputy's shotgun had hit him in the head, killing him instantly. His pistol, a .357 magnum, was lying near him, empty.

"He shot at you three times as you climbed and turned," a deputy told me.

Making small talk, as our adrenaline ran down, none of us had noticed the absence of TDC's Sgt. Charlie Sparkman.

And then we saw him.

He came riding out of the woods on his big white horse, with one of his dogs draped over the saddle. Cradling the dog in his arms, he slowly dismounted and laid him gently on the ground. He looked down at him a long time, then stroked the dog's head. Nobody said anything. Then the big sergeant laid his hat on the ground and looked up at us with tears in his eyes. "It's old Buster—my best dog, the leader of the pack. I raised him from a pup. That scumbag killed him."

Solemn moment. Everyone was quiet. Dead drug dealer. Dead dog. Sad sergeant. Tired and drained, all the law officers had done their jobs.

We flew home, with Kenny at the controls. I relaxed, and closed my eyes. "Well, maybe the drug traffic at Dallas schools will slow a little now. They say this guy was a big-time supplier."

"Nice flying, Paul," said Kenny.

"Thanks. Hope I didn't scare you too badly."

Back at home I got my first meal of the day and finally, my second cup of coffee. I savored it, sitting on my patio, facing a crimson sunset. My son Mike, a high school senior, arrived home from school. I told him of the day's activities. He said, "I'm glad you're okay, Dad. Sorry you lost your day off."

The next day I called the Kaufman County sheriff and asked if officers had found drugs in the criminal's house. "Quite a bit," he said. "We searched it thoroughly after you left and found lots of methamphetamines and marijuana, plus counterfeit stacks of ten, twenty, and hundred dollar bills. This guy was really dealing."

The sheriff continued, "In addition to the counterfeit money, we found plastic engraving plates and a color copying machine, along with equipment for producing phony identification cards and bogus checks. And on his body we found a dozen fake IDs."

"Well, Sheriff, sounds as if we all really took down a big one."

"We really did. This guy was very dangerous. And you pilots did a great job. We appreciate your help. Deputy Sexton sends his thanks."

"Any time, Sheriff," I said. "I'm glad no officers were hurt."

Small wonder, I thought, that this drug dealer ran from us so desperately, carried a powerful handgun, and didn't mind shooting at us. He really was a big-time dealer with a lot to lose. It gave me a good feeling to realize that we had reduced the flow of dangerous drugs in North Texas a few notches with our action.

However, it was a sad win, for I kept remembering Sgt. Charlie Sparkman's tear-stained face, looking up at me over the body of Buster, his best tracking dog.

CHAPTER 4

White danger

Texas is such a large state that three or four types of weather can occur simultaneously during the winter, such as snowstorms, floods, tornadoes, and hurricanes. This is not a Texas brag, just a fact that pilots need to stay aware of. The state's northernmost part is called the "Panhandle," so named because on the map it resembles a bent skillet, with the northern part appearing as the handle of the pan or skillet. This is the plains country of the state, surrounded by New Mexico on the west and Oklahoma on the north.

In the winter the Panhandle has the state's coldest temperatures and the highest winds, which Texans call "northers." Old-time natives and visitors both have a saying that, in the Panhandle in the winter, there's nothing between you and the North Pole except a barbed wire fence. Once you experience this, you believe it. It is a sparsely populated, sometimes lonely country—mostly ranchland and farms. One can fly over it and see few towns and houses. It is the home of tough, friendly, and hardy people, a place where a total stranger will stop and help you change a tire on the highway.

Across these vast plains and great people, on February 21, 1971, blew the coldest, wettest snow blizzard the Panhandle had ever experienced, a fierce Canadian "front." In the northern part, life came to a standstill. Towns ran out of groceries and other essentials as truckers could not reach them. Ranch people were cut off and isolated. Sick people couldn't get to hospitals. Schools were forced to close. Lost cattle began to starve. Everybody and everything living was concentrating on survival. After receiving urgent calls for help from the Panhandle, the Texas Department of Public Safety decided that its Aircraft Section and its helicopters were needed. It was into this tough scene that I was sent.

I was a two-year DPS helicopter pilot with only about 200 hours of helicopter flight time. That's just a little beyond being a "rookie" pilot. On the night of the 21st my chief pilot, George Burnup, called me at home. He said, "Paul, the northeastern part of the Panhandle has been hit hard by a terrible blizzard, leaving icy roads and up to three feet of snow. Nobody is able to get around. The snowplows are trying to clear the roads, but there are not enough snowplows, and the people need our help. I want you to go to Lubbock in the morning in the Bell Jet Ranger and meet with pilot Carl Mullins. The Lubbock Jet Ranger is down for maintenance, and Carl and his partner Bill Meadors have nothing to fly. Pilot Ken Blanchard will also fly to Lubbock in his Bell 47G5 and pick up pilot Meadors. Ken and Bill will work the area around and west of Perryton. You and Carl will work north and east of Perryton. That's the area that was hit the hardest. Nothing is moving up there except a few snowplows. Do whatever needs doing and keep me informed."

Wow, I thought, *that's quite an assignment.* Maybe it was because I was a relatively short-time chopper pilot, but apprehension came over me. I had never flown over those vast plains with snow covering the highways and limited navigational equipment on my helicopter. I would have difficulty navigating. As I got my flying gear together and set my clock for an early morning departure, my mind played tricks with me. What if I got lost? And with jet fuel not available at many snow-covered airports, what if I ran low on fuel?

Doubts plagued me as I looked in on my sleeping children— Kenneth, ten, Mike, nine, and Pam, two. Somehow I hated to leave them more on this mission than I had on others. One thing was certain: I had a strong feeling that this mission would be a learning experience.

As I turned the lights out in my nice warm bedroom, I had

a strong motivating thought. I was only two years off the highway patrol, and some of my highway patrol friends were up
there now, cold and shivering as they battled the blizzard conditions. So get on up there, Paul, and help these guys!

The pilot I would be flying with, Carl Mullins, was top-
grade. He was one of our two helicopter flight instructors and
had helped train me. It was comforting to know that if I could
find my way to Lubbock, a large Panhandle city and Carl's territory, I would not have to worry. I could depend on Carl.

Early the next morning I was cruising at 3,000 feet above
the ground in a Bell Jet Ranger A-Model, headed for Lubbock,
340 miles away. Near Dallas, the weather was 35 degrees
with clear skies. My helicopter had a 317-shaft horsepower
engine and could carry five people. Not much power for a
chopper this size, but it was the hottest model in the civilian
helicopter market at that time. Neither did it have the sophisticated navigational equipment used today. Mine consisted of
one VOR, an electronic homing device with a needle that
directs a pilot to a VOR transmitting ground station when the
proper frequency is set on the dial.

By midmorning I was within 100 miles of Lubbock, and
there was a world of white beneath me—snow everywhere.
The blizzard had blown itself out, but its aftermath was apparent. As I made my landing approach at the Lubbock Airport, I
was surprised to see little snow, but the terrain was shiny,
even glistening. Suddenly, I knew. *Ice!* I would be landing my
chopper, not on snow, but on ice—and it would be my first
landing on ice.

I slowly lowered the sturdy Bell Jet Ranger and gently
touched down on icy concrete. *Not too bad,* I thought as I slowly rolled the throttle to flight idle. But my airship began to
spin! I quickly rolled the throttle back to full power before it
rotated to 45 degrees, and to my relief, that corrected it. The
spinning stopped.

My basic helicopter training had taught me to roll the
throttle off slowly when landing on ice, but since this was my
first actual ice landing, I did not know that it would be this
sensitive. Suddenly, with this slight scare, I was experienced

in landing on ice, and I used this learning experience several times in the days ahead.

I got out and walked across the tarmac where my pilot partner, Carl Mullins, was waiting. It was not snowing, but the north wind had a bite to it. Carl had on a heavy coat with a hood. As we shook hands, he grinned and said, "Glad to see you, Paul. Welcome to Alaska. I see you remembered what I taught you about landing on ice."

"Yeah, it was a thrill," I answered. "Golly, it's cold. What's the temperature?"

"About 23 degrees. It's going to drop to about 10 tonight."

We fueled the Jet Ranger, had a quick lunch with good hot coffee, and talked about people north of us who were in trouble. We knew there was no time to waste. I was to be pilot-in-command. We walked back to the helicopter, slipping and sliding on the ice. I started the engine and remembered my basic flight lessons on how to take off on ice. I had to assume the skids were frozen to the ice. Starting the engine and slow-rolling in the throttle to full power, I increased the pitch of the rotor blades, the helicopter became light on its skids. If I wasn't careful I could roll the helicopter over as I tried to lift off. Gradually I moved the tail rotor pedals gently back and forth with my feet to break the skids loose in case they were frozen to the ice.

For a few seconds, nothing happened. My pilot partner calmly looked sideways at me, winked, and gave me the "thumbs-up" signal, a vote of confidence. Then I felt the skids break loose from the ice, and we came to a hover. The skids truly had been frozen to the ice, and I surely would have rolled the helicopter over had I not used the proper takeoff technique.

We were soon at 1,000 feet above ground. As we headed north we could see, with each passing mile, that the snow was becoming deeper, completely covering all highways and roads. We discerned the roads by following fence posts which were protruding about two feet above the snow. There was little other detail by which to navigate. Although the sky was clear blue over the endless white plains, we relied heavily on our VOR for navigation.

Soon our target town of Perryton appeared in the distance. It would be our base of operations. They had jet fuel there, too. Approaching the airport, we were relieved to see that all the runways, taxiways, and ramp areas had been cleared of snow. After landing I grabbed my insulated coat and we went into the terminal building, the wind still biting our faces. The sheriff met us and, bless him, quickly poured us some hot coffee.

"Boys, we are really glad to see you. We've never had a snowstorm like this one before," he said. Then he began to brief us. "We have big problems. The snow is two to three feet deep . . . all roads are closed. There may be people stranded or lost. The Department of Transportation is working as fast as they can to clear the highways, but they tell me it's slow going. Your helicopters will be the only means of transportation around here for a few days. There may be a few snowmobiles around, but not many. We've asked the governor to send in the National Guard, but it will be at least two days before they arrive."

"Any fatalities yet, Sheriff?" I asked.

"Don't know of any yet, but lots of telephone lines are down and ambulances can't move. We're expecting medical emergencies, and I know you boys can help us out on this. We really don't know what to expect. Lipscomb County east of here has been hit the hardest. I think most of your work will be in that area. Our dispatchers will give you your assignments by radio or telephone. Be sure to stay in close touch with us."

Then the sheriff personally gave us our first assignment. "Two highway maintenance men will be here soon. I need you to take them to a road grader parked on Highway 15 a few miles east of here. They need to start clearing that road as soon as possible. There's a lot of snow there."

As we lingered over a second cup of coffee, not knowing how fast the action would be for us, Carl said, "I have a friend in the Rio Grande Valley. I'll bet he is doing a backyard cookout, wearing sandals and shorts. It's 79 degrees down there."

The highway workers arrived, both wearing heavy coats and gloves. We escorted them into the Jet Ranger and lifted off, heading east with Carl as pilot-in-command. The highway was completely hidden by deep snow, but with Carl keeping our altitude at 600 feet above ground and our passengers spotting for us, we were able to stay over it by following the fence lines. Carl spotted the grader first. It was covered with snow.

Carl, the experienced pilot in whom I had complete confidence, lined up our descent path between the fence lines, knowing that the invisible highway surface would be hard. Our landing flung up a big snow cloud into the air.

"Good luck, guys," I said to the highway workers as they got out and headed for the frozen road grader. Carl kept our engine running as we waited to see if the grader started.

Finally, a puff ball of exhaust and blown snow erupted from the grader's engine, the men waved, and Carl lifted us off. Looking down as we rode, I thought the grader looked like a tiny bug on a white bedsheet. I was entranced with this world of white as far as the eyes could see.

Under way again, Carl called the Perryton Sheriff's Depart-

Panhandle scene after the blizzard.

ment and reported that we had deposited the men safely at the grader, and that the grader was on the move.

"Ten-four," said the dispatcher. "Now we need you to fly across the Oklahoma border about ten miles to the little town of Shattuck, pick up some insulin, and deliver it to a ranch two miles west of Follett, Texas, on State Highway 15. The rancher will be waiting on the highway in front of the house."

We acknowledged, checked our map, and turned southeast to Shattuck. After picking up the insulin we were soon cruising over the border and then over Follett. Carl descended lower to better follow the fencelines bordering the snow-covered highway. We soon saw a house, a tractor on the highway a short distance from it, and a man standing beside it. He was waving to us. Carl made a "slide-on" landing to keep the snow spray behind us; a conventional landing might have blinded us in a cloud of snow.

The cloud of snow "dusted" the rancher who was near us and holding on to his hat. I got out and walked the insulin to the man. Trying to be lighthearted in a serious situation, I quipped, "Special delivery, courtesy of Texas Department of Public Safety."

There may have been tears in his eyes—or it may have been melted snow—as he said, "Officer, thank you. I can't tell you how grateful I am. My wife is a diabetic and needs this desperately. I don't know what we would have done without your help."

The old-timer's handshake was strong and prolonged. It was the kind of moment I will always remember.

No sooner were we airborne than our radio crackled again. "Perryton Sheriff's Office to Helo-101. Another emergency: Amarillo DPS advises you to go to the Hereford Hospital, pick up an injured patient, and fly him to the Amarillo Hospital. It's a highway department worker who had an accident with a tractor."

"Ten-four, Perryton. We'll be en route," I said.

Carl turned toward Hereford, 180 miles away. Amarillo, the largest city in the Panhandle, was on our route. We landed there to refuel, then were quickly on our way to Hereford. It was midafternoon with clear skies, but a world of white lay beneath us. The hospital was easy to spot. We landed on the emergency room parking lot, and Carl shut the engine down. There were no medivac helicopters or hospital heliports in those days, but our Jet Ranger choppers were rigged to carry a litter patient. Compared to today's medical helicopters, our system back then was pretty antiquated.

We retrieved our stretcher from the baggage compartment, laid it on the ground and unfolded it. Nurses rolled the patient to the helicopter on a stretcher. He was bandaged, splinted and immobilized. I asked a nurse, "What happened to him?"

"He was standing beside a large tractor and started it up," she said. "The tractor took off and rolled over him, crushing his legs. He's critical. Get him to Amarillo as soon as possible."

Carl and I helped the nurses transfer him from the hospital stretcher to our stretcher. He was wearing an oxygen mask attached to a portable tank and was in a lot of pain.

In order to load our stretcher into our helicopter, we had to remove the front and rear seat cushions. We then slid the stretcher through the very small back door opening across and on top of the metal tube over the back of the copilot's seat. With a large person this would be almost an impossible task, due to the weight and having to maneuver the injured person through the small rear door opening. Fortunately, our patient was a medium-sized person.

We then stacked the front and rear seat cushions in the right rear passenger seat. We were ready to go, except I had nowhere to sit. Carl was in the pilot's seat, the cushions were in the right rear seat, and the stretcher was lying across and on top of the left front copilot's seat and the left rear passenger area. I said, "Carl, where am I going to sit?" He answered, "I guess you'll have to hunker down under the stretcher on the rear floor." It was tight but I hunkered, face down, and Carl shut the door behind me. We were a real dinosaur of medical transportation. I knew Amarillo was fifty miles away, a thirty-minute flight. I was so cramped and uncomfortable, stuffed under the stretcher in the rear floor, that I began to count the minutes.

About halfway to Amarillo I heard a strange noise above

me, followed by a greenish putrid liquid raining down around me. "Carl, I think he just threw up," I shouted.

"Are you okay?" shouted Carl back to me.

"He missed me, but hurry up 'cause I think I'm gonna be sick."

I curled up into an even smaller ball, staying well under the center of the stretcher above me. I didn't want another baptism of this odorous, slimy liquid. I knew he had messed up his oxygen mask.

Finally, we landed at the Amarillo hospital. Carl opened my door and I quickly bailed out. With the exception of a few secondary splashes of vomit, I had escaped somewhat unscathed, but the sour smell still clung to my nostrils. I said, "Carl, next time *you* are gonna ride under the stretcher."

"I'm the senior man here," he said. "You rookies have to ride there!"

As Carl and the nurses unloaded the patient, I hurried to the nearest hospital restroom to wash my face and clean up. My flight suit had some odor, too. I sincerely hoped our patient survived, but sometimes, I thought, public safety demands a lot.

Carl and I grabbed candy bars from a vending machine, boarded, and took off for our winter wonderland, Lipscomb County, 200 miles away. Nearing Lipscomb, we called our sheriff's office to check for messages, hoping we could get a breather. It was not to be.

"Helo-101," said the dispatcher, "we need you to go to a ranch south of Lipscomb to pick up a man and woman and transport them to Canadian. It's a family emergency. The woman's mother is gravely ill—she may be dying—and we need to get the lady to her mother's bedside as soon as possible. From the intersection of Highway 305 and Highway 213, it's the first ranch house east on 305."

En route to this place of need, at 1,000 feet above the ground and cruising at 115 MPH, we passed over a few slopes where we estimated the snow drifts were ten to twelve feet deep. That's a lot of snow.

Soon we were over the ranch house. We saw the man and woman standing on the snow-covered highway below. A dog and their baggage sat beside them. Carl descended and turned for a short final approach. Apparently startled, the man and woman backed up near a barbed wire fence. Nearing the ground, Carl came to a slow forward hover. Snow boiled up furiously around Helo-101. Landing on the highway, we came closer to the couple. The wind from the rotor blades was whipping their clothes. Suddenly, the woman's hair flew straight up into the air and came to rest, hanging on the barbed wire fence. "Carl, you blew her wig off," I said, laughing. Carl smirked and grinned as the woman ran and retrieved her wig. She hastily placed it on her head in an askew manner. She was visibly embarrassed.

I got out and gestured to our passenger door. The couple approached, leading their dog on a leash. He was a large, furry animal. Carl sighed, leaned toward me, and whispered, "Paul, tell 'em we can't carry two adults, the dog, and all the baggage. We'll be dangerously overloaded."

I told them. The lady's face fell.

"What will we do?" she asked.

"If you can leave the dog here," I replied, "we can carry you, your husband, and all the baggage."

"I'm not leaving my dog here. He'd starve to death."

I looked at the big dog, who appeared well mannered. Held by the leash, he sat down calmly in the snow to await the decision, and looked up at the lady. She looked down at the dog, then looked at her husband. The man said, "You go ahead, dear, and take Champ. I'll stay here and come when the roads clear."

With this decided I helped the woman and her dog aboard. As I got in, I whispered the details to Carl and added, "We know who counts in this family." Carl grinned.

As we landed at the Canadian airport, the sun was dipping low on the snow-covered horizon. Sunsets in the Panhandle—land of the big sky, as its natives say—are nearly always beautiful. This one, over the totally white plains, was breathtaking. I helped the woman with her luggage as she headed for a pay telephone. Before taking off again, Carl and I relaxed in Helo-101 for a moment. We were tired, drained, and hungry after flying all day. We were anxious for a motel room, some hot food, and a good night's sleep. I called the sheriff's dispatcher in Perryton and reported this little mission completed.

As we neared the airport at Perryton the dispatcher called again. "Helo-101, the Highway Department called again. They would like for you to search for a missing bulldozer operator south of Booker on Highway 23. He's been clearing roads there, has not returned, and is not answering his radio. They're afraid he may be in trouble."

"Ten-four," I answered wearily. "We'll search as soon as we fuel up."

Coming in for our landing, we saw our other DPS helicopter on the tarmac. Near it were our fellow pilots Ken Blanchard and Bill Meadors. We chatted with them as we fueled. They had been doing many of the same things we had been doing in the areas west of Perryton. They, too, were weary and were heading for a restaurant and motel. Golly, how we wished we could join them.

As we climbed aboard for takeoff, I shouted, "Ken, keep the dinner hot until we get back!"

Ken acknowledged this with thumbs up.

Darkness was fast approaching, with just a few soft, dying crimson rays of sunset on the white plains below us. With Carl keeping an altitude at 800 feet above ground, we soon saw the little town of Booker, which had a few of its lights on. I turned on our "Night Sun Light" and we quickly spotted State Highway 23. We could see that one lane had been cleared and knew that the dozer had to be on down the road somewhere.

As we followed the highway at slow speed and low altitude, with our searchlight on, I saw a man walking. He was heading toward Booker.

"Carl, there he is," I said.

We landed on the highway. It was eerie watching the cloud of snow around Helo-101, whirled up by our rotor blades in the brilliant glare of our searchlight. The dozer man waved both arms at us. He was obviously glad to see us. As I opened the door for him to get in, he clasped my hand and said, "I hope you fellas came to give me a lift."

"We're your taxicab. Hop in," I said.

He was cold and shivering. It was 10 degrees on that

highway. Even inside our craft, with the heater on, he was still shivering, almost in convulsions. In a shaky voice he said, "I am r-r-really glad to see you g-g-guys. I don't think I would have made it to B-Booker. And I know my wife is worrying."

"What happened?" Carl asked.

"My b-bull-d-dozer engine quit and I ran the battery down trying to s-start it. With a d-dead battery I couldn't use my radio to call for help."

I turned the heater up to its highest setting as we took off. The working warrior of the high plains finally quit shivering. The job he had been doing was important. Again, I reported our successful mission to the Perryton sheriff's dispatcher. I told her we had found our man, that he was safe, and we would land at the airport in ten minutes.

"Ten-four, Helo-101," said the female dispatcher. "I'll call his wife. She's called us several times."

Our thoughtful sheriff had a deputy waiting to drive us as we stepped out of our chopper at the airport. The flashing lights of the motel, with its restaurant next door, looked mighty good to us. I knew Carl was weary; he'd been at the controls a long time.

The sleep was good, but the night was short. By daybreak the next day our assignments director, the sheriff's dispatcher, had us up and at the airport in Helo-101. By early afternoon we had flown a state highway inspector on an aerial inspection, delivered food to stranded oilfield workers near a derrick, and made front-door deliveries to ranchers—landing in their yards. We also carried the U.S. mail from the town of Canadian to Follett and delivered repair parts to road clearing machinery on the highway. It seemed we were taking off and landing every hour. Only a helicopter could have helped us accomplish these things.

About midafternoon the Lipscomb County Sheriff's Office called us with yet another unique assignment. We were to go to a Follett address, pick up a pregnant woman who was in labor, and fly her a few miles across the Texas/Oklahoma border to a hospital in Shattuck. We were already in the air, and as we turned toward Follett I asked Carl, "Does this mean I may have to deliver a baby?"

"Could be. If you do, maybe we could name him Rotor Blade."

We landed at Follett very quickly and loaded the very pregnant woman and her husband. She had already started contractions, and was moaning and occasionally crying out with loud gasps. I had always had steady nerves when flying in tough weather and other crises, but this thing unnerved me. "Carl," I said, "let's break the speed record on this one!"

Carl, superbly calm, did. We made the twenty-five-mile trip in twelve minutes. I was tremendously relieved when we landed. So was the woman's husband. Hospital nurses were waiting for us in the parking lot and took charge of the mother-to-be. As the husband walked away from the noise of the helicopter, I shouted, "Take care of little Rotor Blade!"

As we lifted off, he was looking up at us with a quizzical expression. Of course, Carl and I had not formally discussed with him our name for his coming baby, but I felt good about it all. After all, we had earned a little levity. I said to Carl, "Partner, we shaved that one a little close. Don't ever do that to me again."

Cruising tranquilly over the frozen countryside, our radio was surprisingly quiet. We looked for anyone else who might need our help. Carl began to fly a tight circle.

"Paul," he said, "look at those cows down there, all huddled together. Up to their bellies in snow. They're starving—can't get anything to eat because of the snow. I see some baled hay in a stack. Want to go down and feed some cattle?"

"We might as well. No tracks around them. Looks as if they've been standing in one spot since the snow first fell."

"That's the way they do," said Carl. "Standing in one spot, huddled up to keep warm, they starve to death."

As Carl descended I saw a big reason why the cattle were starving. They were separated from the hay stack by a barbed wire fence. After landing, I got out and saw something dangerous, too—strands of loose hay bailing wire in the snow, lying around the helicopter. Our tail rotor had barely cleared a long wire. If a helicopter tail rotor had gotten into that, it would have been trouble, big time. I voiced my concern to Carl. Slogging around in the snow, I picked up the loose strands, some of which were partly buried in the snow, and moved them a safe distance from the helicopter.

I immediately got snow in my boots as I began loading bales of hay into the helicopter rear seat area. Then Carl lifted off, hovered over the cows, and landed near them. I dragged hay bales over to the cows and broke them up. Shades of my boyhood! Cold but hungry, the cattle just stood in a frozen stupor, looking at me and the chopper, probably too cold to move. I finished and boarded.

We took off, then circled and watched them for three or four minutes. As if a neon light came on, saying "Restaurant Now Open," they began to eat.

Before the day was over we searched and found more cattle in the same predicament, and repeated the same procedures with them.

By the next day, food was running short in grocery stores in the small Panhandle towns. That meant families on short rations and hungry kids. Grocery trucks could not get into the towns, with some marooned on the highway. We were assigned to meet some of the trucks on the road east of Perryton. Again landing on frozen, snow-covered highways, we loaded all the groceries and water possible into our workhorse Bell Jet Ranger. Looking at our load from the copilot's seat, I said, "Carl, we're mighty heavy. Do you think we can lift off and fly with it?"

"Let's find out. We gotta get food to hungry people."

Carl increased engine power and took off, using the high-density altitude method of sliding along the highway on our skids until we became airborne—in short, a running start until we got "lift." As soon as we became airborne, Helo-101 developed a vigorous vertical vibration, a frightening up and down movement. I looked at Carl and rolled my eyes as we bumped along. He said, "I don't think we'll carry this much on the next trip."

"If you do," I said, "you won't be carrying me!"

We set down on Follett's main street. Eager, grateful hands unloaded for us. These people were worried—and hungry. We sprayed main street with snow as we took off for another load, another highway landing near the truckers. We made more trips like this one, and served the little towns of

Darrouzett and Arnet, both totally snowed in. We landed in the streets beside each grocery store with cartons of bread, sacks of potatoes, beans, and other canned goods. We had to make high landing approaches over power lines and trees and hover under electrical wires in order to land and take off.

Carl was superb. His flying skills made it all look easy. We never had a problem or close call. We gave them excellent curb service. Townspeople were elated and voiced their appreciation. On each trip, kids who were shut out of their schools were excited and fascinated with our helicopter landing and sitting in the middle of their town. Was this job satisfaction for Paul Creech and Carl Mullins? You bet!

On that day, we had served as ranchers, grocery delivery boys, medical assistants, and as a highway surveillance airline.

After finishing with the grocery detail, we took a relaxing tour of a few minutes to again drink in the golden-red sunset over the beautiful clean white world below. So breathtaking, it was hard to realize all the public safety dangers it held.

Carl turned toward Perryton Airport to call it a day. Making our approach to the airport, he flew low over the airport's fence. Unbelievably, my eagle's eye saw a bobcat stalking a jackrabbit, slowly but surely closing the distance between them across the snow. I showed the scene to Carl and said, "Turn around and let's break that up. That poor jackrabbit is having a hard time trying to survive without some bobcat trying to eat him."

Carl said, "Hey, partner, that bobcat has gotta survive, too."

He was right. In the Texas Panhandle, with its winter blizzards, spring tornadoes, and summer dust storms, only the strong survive. There was one exception. We had helped those weak, dumb, starving cows survive.

To our relief, we landed without any further radio assignments. In our motel room, anticipating a good night's rest, I plopped on a bed while Carl took a hot shower. Our room telephone rang. It was the dispatcher. "Four highway workers running snowplows on Highway 305 in Lipscomb County south of Darrouzett have not returned. They're way overdue. We need you to try and locate them."

"We'll get right on it," I said.

I filled Carl in on the call, then added, "Looks like a repeat performance from last night, except tonight there are four missing."

It was bitter cold—15 degrees—as we hitched a ride with a deputy to the airport. There was very little wind and a quarter moon—just enough moonlight to reflect off the snow and make it possible to see the ground and the horizon. Had it been a dark, moonless night this would have been a very difficult and dangerous flight, and we would not have attempted it. Moonlight was our friend, for artificial lights from cars and homes were few and far between in the Panhandle.

We took off into the night. With Carl flying the helicopter and me operating the searchlight, we soon flew over Darrouzett and located the right highway. The glare from my "Night Sun Light" lit up the white highway and ground below while casting eerie shadows on certain parts, especially steep snow drifts at slight slopes. The light picked up four men, trudging along. Carl saw them, circled, and again landed on the highway.

I got out as they approached us. The poor guys were shivering but grinning and happy to see us. One had ice crystals on his beard.

"What happened?" I asked.

"Our snowplows got stuck in deep snow drifts," one said. "It was too cold to stay with them, so we decided to walk to Lipscomb."

"We can only carry two at a time," I explained. "Decide who goes first, and we'll be back quickly for the other two. We're only five miles to town, and we can make it back in fifteen minutes." They worked it out, unselfishly, I noticed.

Airborne with the first two men, we called the sheriff's office and reported our success and our procedure. The sheriff himself was waiting when we landed by his office. We let the twosome out and immediately went back for the other two. Then, heavily fatigued, we took off flying at top speed, anxious to get back to our motel and a warm bed.

By the end of the fourth day, all major roads had been cleared, vehicles were able to move about, and people could take care of their own needs. It was our last "goodwill" flight in the Texas Panhandle to combat the blizzard of '71. The next morning the sheriff thanked us profusely for our work.

We had flown missions for four consecutive days. The Texas National Guard had arrived on our third day. It had been a tough and tiring duty tour, with Carl and I flying twelve hours each day. We knew we had done a good job under the toughest of conditions. Doubtless we had saved the lives of several people and hundreds of cattle. And we had taken some of the sting out of the cold aftermath of a severe Texas blizzard.

We got nice letters of appreciation from Panhandle sheriffs and the Texas Highway Department (now Department of Transportation), but the State of Texas didn't give us bonus pay for our work. The extra pay we received was the grateful look in hurting people's eyes, the joyful handshakes, and the appreciative "thank-yous" of the hungry adults and children in the little towns where we delivered groceries. These moments were all thousand-dollar paychecks for Carl and me.

If Carl had listened to me, we could have saved that jackrabbit, too!

CHAPTER 5

The Red Baron strikes again

As a small boy I had read stories of Eddie Rickenbacker, America's first World War I air ace, and Manfred von Richthofen—the Red Baron—Germany's World War I ace who shot down many allied fighter planes. I learned about Charles Lindbergh, the first person to fly the Atlantic, who was tabbed "The Lone Eagle." One thing that stuck in my mind was that the Red Baron had such aerial skills and such a zest for combat that he often took off on lone patrols, without his squadron and without a specific assignment, and engaged the enemy.

DPS helicopter pilots are trained to fly as a part of law enforcement teams, but in those days we were allowed to fly routine patrols without any specific assignments. This is what I did one December day when things were really slow and I was bored with report writing and routine office work. During the past few days I had assisted in a few minor missions, such as aerial photos of a murder scene, a couple of traffic surveillance flights, and one high-speed chase that was short in duration.

It was Friday, December 4, 1982, and shopping malls were already crowded with Christmas shoppers. Dolores and I planned to finish all our shopping on the next day, Saturday (usually an impossible task), in order to avoid bigger crowds later. I was dreading the shopping. What I really wanted was airborne action. Around a large metropolitan city such as Dallas, criminal minds are always active. With a little effort on my part I could always find some type of criminal activity. Such was my mindset that day. The "Red Baron" could always find the enemy.

I called an officer friend who felt as I did about boredom and action, and he also liked to fly. He was George Rice, a Mesquite city policeman. He had voluntarily served as my air observer several times when I had been called out at night from home. He had become a first-class observer and helicopter searchlight operator for me. I was in luck. I caught him off-duty, at home.

"George," I said. "Things are slow. I'm bored . . . want action. Wanta go up with me and see if we can stir up something? Maybe we can find some stolen cars in the woods around Mesquite."

George was ready.

Stolen cars I had found were usually in rural areas, in fields and woods. Some were stolen for their parts and stripped. Others were stolen for joy rides. Why bother to look for stolen cars? Because some insurance company has paid their automobile policyholders for them, and they can sometimes recoup part of their loss by selling what is left of the car.

I met George at the airport in forty-five minutes. He was a veteran city police officer who had seen it all on the streets and survived. "George, I'll bet we can find something to get into."

"We usually do," he said with a grin.

Airborne and flying slow, we were in no hurry. George was fascinated with helicopter flying. I think he would have paid for the privilege had I charged him. Like an eagle looking for prey, we searched backroads and fields in woods for abandoned cars. Our search path took us over Seagoville, a small city thirty-five miles southwest of Mesquite.

When on patrols like this one, I always monitored my police radio, listening for officers who might need help, and I was soon rewarded with a call from a DPS dispatcher: "DPS Dallas to any unit on U.S. 80 east of Mesquite."

"11-17, Dallas. Go ahead." I knew that Unit 11-17 was my good friend, Trooper Jim Bryan. As a rookie, his field training officer had nicknamed him "Cub Bear" because he was always getting into something. He was dedicated to keeping the highways safe.

"Dallas 11-17, I have a report from Terrell Police that a 1990 red Ford was stolen in Terrell and was last seen on U.S. 80 heading toward Mesquite."

"Hey, George," I said, "let's try to locate this guy."

"Go for it."

Thinking about the Red Baron, I said, "I'm not gonna let anybody know we're in the neighborhood until we jump the stolen car. We'll make 'em wonder where we came from!"

I headed Helo-101 on a course that would cross U.S. 80 about seven miles east of Mesquite, planning to do a holding pattern over the highway. U.S. 80 is a four-lane divided highway to Dallas, heavily traveled. We reached it quickly. As I crossed it at 500 feet above ground, we saw a red Ford headed toward Mesquite and Dallas, doing about 75 MPH.

"George," I said, "this one matches the description, looks like our car thief. Can't read his license up here, though."

I turned hard to the right to intercept the car, closing the distance between us and coming up beside him at a safe altitude above the highway. We were almost flying beside him.

"Gosh dang, this is fun!" said my companion.

With both Ford automobile and DPS helicopter doing 75 MPH and almost side-by-side, the Ford's driver leaned out his window and looked up. I looked him squarely in the eyes. He was a youngster, and his mouth dropped open. I would have given $100 for his thoughts at that moment. Then he accelerated and attempted to pull away from me.

"That's gotta be him," I told George. "He's running."

I called Dallas 11-17. "This is DPS Helo-101. I believe I have the stolen vehicle spotted. What is your location?"

"11-17 to Helo-101. I'm east of Mesquite about four miles. Where in the world did you come from?"

I chuckled and George snickered. "From out of the clouds!" I answered. "I'm three miles from you. I think I'm over the stolen car and I'm headin' your way. He's running from us, doing over 90 MPH . . . two people in the front seat, both looking out the windows at me. They just ran a car off the road."

"Hang in there, Helo-101. Stay with him! We need you! We're trying to get set for him."

Doing 95 MPH in a car is one thing; when flying 95 MPH in a chopper abreast and above the car, it doesn't appear you are moving that fast. We were getting close to the Mesquite city limits. I continued to give speed and position reports. Then I saw the flashing emergency lights up ahead. Two state highway patrol cars and two Mesquite police cars were moving slowly toward Mesquite on the highway shoulder. As the fleeing twosome in the red Ford neared them, they zoomed past the officers, who accelerated fast, then got in behind them and beside them. The suspects were at 100 MPH and managed to stay in front. Unit 11-17 had verified the license plate as the stolen car on our radio.

"Paul," said George, my spotter. "If I see any tall antennas coming at us, you'll be the first person I'll tell."

"Go ahead, George. I'm not proud," I said. George didn't realize how intently I always watched for antennas.

We entered Mesquite, my hometown, and I pulled up to a higher altitude while staying above the red Ford. Suddenly, the bad guys below lost control, did a dangerous spin, went off the highway, and bounced into the ditch. Police cars skidded and whirled in, attempting to surround him. I decreased Helo-101's speed and circled. I saw the suspect ram a Mesquite police car and, with wheels spinning wildly, barrel his way back onto the highway, still westbound. I was glad to be above the melee and not on the ground fighting brakes, accelerator, and steering wheel.

The car thief made a quick left turn across the grass median, bouncing as he went, completely reversing his direction. Police cars quickly adjusted and got in tight behind him. It caused panic and confusion among oncoming traffic, some leaving the road, others skidding to a stop. My flying companion gave me lots of conversation about the action, although I could see most of it. I banked and turned eastward also, to follow the new direction of the chase. Then, strangely, the Ford's speed slowed. The driver pulled over to the highway's shoulder and stopped. I decreased both altitude and speed to better observe this strange action.

City and state police cars quickly surrounded the Ford. DPS patrol car 11-17 wheeled in behind it and stopped. Trooper Bryan quickly stepped out, and knelt behind his car door, with pistol pointed at the suspect. I watched as other officers positioned their cars as shields for protection. Then, Trooper Bryan's car, with no driver, began to "crawl" forward. Bryan, apparently distracted and excited, stood up as if to jump back into the driver's seat. He evidently changed his mind and continued his crouching walk behind his moving left front door, pistol still pointed.

I hated to laugh in the middle of a dangerous moment, but George and I did. I knew what Trooper Bryan was thinking. I had once been in that situation, as a highway patrol trooper. Which would be worse—getting shot, or having to tell his sergeant that he forgot to put his gear shift in park before he got out?

Luckily, Bryan's black and white patrol car came to rest against a highway sign, very close to the red Ford with its two occupants still inside. His pistol still pointed at the car thieves, Bryan was in a good position; he had made the right decision. The other trooper had parked his patrol car on the other side of the stolen car. He ran to the stolen car and jumped up on the hood, with shotgun pointed at the driver through the windshield. I knew the two troopers were giving the two occupants stern commands.

The daredevil car thieves' options had run out.

Overwhelmed by the determined action of the troopers, the driver and his passenger got out with their hands up. The officers immediately handcuffed them. The dangerous chase was over, and the situation was under control. A Mesquite city police officer placed the twosome in a squad car.

Still slowly circling, I gave radio congratulations to the DPS troopers. "Good job, troopers, you guys did it right. But, hey, why did the guy stop?"

Trooper Bryan chuckled. "He ran out of gas. Helo-101, it was nice to have air support. We still don't know where you came from or who sent you to us!"

"Nobody knows from whence the eagle comes," I said.

Coming in at our nearby airport, George and I grinned at

each other. We had turned our dull day into action with our "Red Baron" patrol.

"Thanks for the ride," George said. "Call me again."

"*Adios,* partner," I said. "Have a nice evening. Maybe you can catch something exciting on TV."

When I arrived home, Dolores asked the usual question: "How did it go today?"

"The Red Baron struck again," I answered.

She gave me a questioning look. Then she smirked.

CHAPTER 6

Oklahoma shootout

As a policeman, I was trained to be alert, observe everything, and always know what's going on around me, whether it's real or potential danger. Officers call this being "street smart." Ordinary people, not trained in this manner, go about their daily lives unaware of dangers that may be around them.

In 1976 nine citizens from Texas, Oklahoma, and Virginia lost their lives to two vicious, cold-blooded killers. After murders occur and the killers are seen, it is not unusual for someone to say, "They didn't look like killers." I agree with that statement somewhat, but what *do* killers look like? Some look just like you and me.

Billy Denton and Nelson Latham grew up in southern Oklahoma around Tishomingo and Caddo. They knew the area well for miles around. It was heavily wooded and contained fields, pastureland, and wildlife. They had hunted and fished the area for years and were accomplished woodsmen. They knew how to live off the land and survive.

Denton and Latham started their killing spree in the area they knew so well. They carried pistols, shotguns, rifles, and hunting knives with long blades that were honed to a razor-sharp edge. Starting out as burglars and robbers, they soon began to leave no witnesses. Their various methods of killing were to strike their victims in the head with a hard object, stab them, slice their throats, shoot them, or do a combination of all. Little did I know that in 1976 I would be faced with the possibility of being involved in a real air-to-ground gunfight with these two predators. Since Denton and Latham were accused of committing crimes in Texas, the elite Texas Rangers became involved in the investigation.

The Rangers, the oldest law enforcement agency in the state, are known and respected worldwide. In 1836 Texas won its independence from Mexico. In the new Republic of Texas, the Rangers were created to keep the peace on the frontier by fighting hostile Indians and outlaws. Today the Rangers are a part of the Texas Department of Public Safety. They are charged with investigations of the most serious crimes in Texas.

Texas Ranger Jim Gant was assigned as the investigating Ranger in the Denton/Latham crimes. Gant was a model of what a Ranger often looks like, as described in old Texas history books. He was lean, tough, and tall at six feet, one inch. His cowboy boots made him look even taller. He wore western attire with a wide-brimmed cowboy hat and a western decorative gunbelt. His badge was made in the same fashion as the Ranger badges of old, with a large star cut in the center of a Mexican silver cinco peso coin. On the round outside edge of the coin were the words "TEXAS RANGER." When Ranger Jim Gant walked into a place, everyone paid attention. He meant business.

I had assisted Ranger Gant with the helicopter many times in other investigations. At Jim's request I assisted him in his investigation of Denton and Latham in Texas soon after they started their crime spree. He told me of other crimes that they had committed in southern Oklahoma. I'm sure that some of their criminal activities have never been attributed to them or even been discovered.

In early 1976 a rancher from Bonham, Texas, and his pickup truck were reported missing. Foul play was suspected. Gant began to assist the sheriff in Bonham in trying to locate the missing man. During the course of the investigation Gant had learned that a friend of the missing man had seen him in his red pickup truck, driving away from his ranch, with two men sitting in the seat beside him. The twosome matched the descriptions of Denton and Latham. I assisted Ranger Gant in a countywide aerial search for the missing truck. We never located it. To my knowledge neither the pickup nor the missing man has ever been found.

Denton and Latham, who were described as young men (about twenty-seven), were involved in other Texas crimes. They were moving cross-country on foot and came upon a farmhouse on the outskirts of Denison. They went inside with the intent to burglarize it. As they were ransacking the house, a high school teenager who lived there drove home from school and parked in front of the house. As he entered, Denton jumped him and the two of them tied him to a chair with electrical cords. After they finished burglarizing the house, they asked the teenager for his car keys. The youngster told them they were in his front pocket. They took the keys. Then, with the teenager still tied to the chair, begging and pleading for his life, they shot him. Assuming that the boy was dead, they left in his car. The seriously wounded youngster was somehow able to loosen his bonds and summon help from a neighbor.

A search was conducted for miles around. The searchers found the boy's car parked near the Red River at the Texas-Oklahoma border, several miles from Denison. After several hours of searching by officers on the ground and by me in the helicopter, we were unable to locate the two. The search was terminated. Denton and Latham had melted into the cover of the woods and escaped.

A few days later, a woman walked out of the woods onto a highway several miles east of Denison. She was naked, bruised, and cut. A car traveling on the highway stopped to help her and took her to the sheriff's office in Denison, which had received a missing person's report on her the day before and had been looking for her. The woman related her story to the sheriff, telling how two men fitting the description of Denton and Latham had broken into her house. She said, "They shot and killed my husband, robbed us, made me go with them, and tortured me."

Ranger Gant was summoned by the sheriff to help. They learned from the woman that Denton and Latham had forced her to walk several miles through the woods to the banks of the Red River on the Texas-Oklahoma border. They camped there on the bank of the Red River next to a farmer's field and kept her chained to a tree by her neck. She told of a farmer who came to the field on his tractor. As the farmer worked the field, she remembered, he kept getting closer to the campsite in the woods. Denton had said, "If that guy comes any closer to us, I'm gonna shoot him off that tractor."

At sunset, the farmer quit plowing and left to go home. During the rest of the evening and into the night Denton and Latham raped the pleading woman repeatedly. Sometime during the night the two kidnappers fell asleep. During this time the woman was able to get loose, escaping into the night.

An extensive search that day failed to locate the cruel pair. They had faded into the woods again. The search team was able to locate the campsite where the woman had been held hostage. There were no clues left behind as to their whereabouts. The Texas officers decided that the two had crossed the river into Oklahoma.

Denton and Latham were not heard from again until a few weeks later, when they surfaced in the state of Virginia. On a Sunday morning, when many people were in church, the duo burglarized the rural home of an elderly retired schoolteacher who was attending church. When she arrived home and walked into the house, Latham grabbed her from behind. While Latham held the screaming, struggling, terrified old woman, Denton hit her repeatedly in the head with a hammer, crushing her skull. He then sliced her throat with his hunting knife, and as she lay on the floor bleeding, he shot her with his pistol several times.

The murderous pair then stole her yellow Ford car. Although the investigating officers in Virginia broadcast an all-points bulletin, Denton and Latham made it all the way back to Oklahoma without being spotted.

Late in the evening of May 26, near the town of Tishomingo, an alert Oklahoma highway patrolman spotted the car and gave chase. The chase lasted for a short time until the highway patrolman lost the car near the Tishomingo Wildlife Refuge. A search was organized by the Oklahoma Highway Patrol, and a search team soon found the yellow car abandoned in the woods. Again, the predators had disappeared.

It was late in the evening and darkness soon overtook the search team. Due to the dangerous nature of Denton and Latham, the ground search team was pulled out of the woods for the night. It would be too dangerous for them to come upon Denton and Latham in darkness. The area was kept under constant surveillance by roving patrol cars all night.

Because Denton and Latham had committed crimes in both Texas and Oklahoma, Gant had made several trips into Oklahoma to obtain information on the two.

The Highway Patrol commander in Oklahoma knew Ranger Gant. He notified him of the search. Gant called his Texas Ranger captain, G. W. Burkes, for permission to go to Oklahoma and assist. Burkes knew the seriousness of this search and granted permission. He was in command of all Texas Rangers in North Texas.

I had worked with him many times when he was a Ranger private before he was appointed captain. A quiet, stocky man, less than six feet tall, he was a hard-driving leader, not afraid of anyone, and he expected nothing but the best from his Rangers. I was with him on many manhunts, and he never gave up until all efforts had been expended. Sometimes the local sheriff would call off the search, but Burkes would not dismiss his Rangers or me. Many times his persistence worked, and the criminal suspect would be captured by the captain's pure determination and tenacity. At times, when we were having difficulties locating a criminal suspect on the ground, he would say, "Let's fly low and slow and try to draw gunfire so we can pinpoint him." I was not too excited about "drawing gunfire," but I admired and respected this Ranger captain and trusted his judgment.

There is a bumper sticker on some vehicles that says "NO FEAR." Burkes truly knew no fear. When he worked in Fort Worth, Texas, as a Ranger private, he gained a reputation as a tough law enforcement officer. His reputation spread among the criminal element in Fort Worth. Rumor was that if a criminal suspect needed to be questioned about a crime or was wanted on an arrest warrant, Burkes would just pick up the phone and call the suspect and tell him to come to his office. The suspect would voluntarily come in.

Late in that same evening of May 26, Captain Burkes walked into our pilots' office at Regional DPS Headquarters at the city of Garland and talked with my partner Billy Peace and me. He told us what was transpiring in Oklahoma, and said that he had gotten permission from our director for us to go to Oklahoma and assist in any way we could. Captain Burkes would accompany us.

Billy and I packed our bags for a long stay and said good-bye to our families, the kind of good-byes that are tough. Because we were not familiar with all of the murders and crimes committed by Denton and Latham, we could not fully realize just how dangerous this mission would be. We knew that they were wanted for murder, kidnapping, robbery, and burglary, but we didn't know how many people they had killed.

Early the next morning we were in our Bell Jet Ranger helicopter, headed for a place in Oklahoma that I had never heard of—Fort Washita. It was a camping park southeast of Tishomingo. The Oklahoma Highway Patrol (OHP) had established their command post there. The park had been closed to the general public by the highway patrol. It was to be our base of operations until the search ended.

Fort Washita had been established as a U.S. Cavalry fort in the late 1800s. The duty of the cavalry was to quell Indian uprisings and to protect the new settlers who had come from the East. During the Civil War, the Confederates used it, and afterward the U.S. Cavalry again commanded the fort.

We landed at Fort Washita and were met by Texas Ranger Gant. He walked with us to the command post nearby, where we met the Oklahoma Highway Patrol commander, who gave us a cordial welcome. He expressed appreciation for our help and especially the use of the helicopter. In those days the OHP did not have any police helicopters; they had only a couple of airplanes to cover the entire state.

The OHP commander briefed us, showing us on a map where the yellow Ford from Virginia had been found. He told us how vicious Denton and Latham could be.

"When we find this pair," he said, "you can be assured that we will have one heck of a gun battle. They are mean, and I know they won't give up." He related the stories of murders that they had committed in Oklahoma. He asked, "Do you pilots have a radio with our highway patrol frequency? No? I don't have enough handheld radios to go around. Ranger Gant has one, and he will have to be your communications link with us."

He continued, "We believe that we have contained the area and feel that the suspects are still in the area where the yellow car was abandoned. We have the area surrounded by three teams, forming a circle around this entire area for twenty-five miles. The first team is the nucleus and will be on foot, on horses, and in cars. They are searching the woods where the two abandoned the yellow car. The second team has formed a circle two miles from the first team. They are a roving team in vehicles and have established roadblocks at every highway intersection. They are searching every vehicle that moves in their area. The third team has formed a circle twenty-five miles from the center of the search area. They are a roving team in cars. They will be constantly moving and checking anything that looks suspicious."

The Ranger, my partner Billy, and I listened quietly as he continued. "We don't have a specific assignment for your helicopter. Since my troopers located the car yesterday evening, no one has seen or heard anything. If something happens, we'll let you know. So stay in touch with Ranger Gant."

I said, "Commander, we need to top off with fuel soon. If it's okay with you, we'll fly around the search area to familiarize ourselves with this country, then go to Ardmore, fuel up, and come back here."

"That's probably a good idea," he said.

Captain Burkes, Billy, and I took off. Billy would be acting as pilot-in-command. The weather was calm. We flew over the area where the yellow car was abandoned. The trees were so thick we couldn't see the ground. Realizing how hopeless an air-to-ground search would be, we departed for Ardmore for fuel.

We arrived back at the command post at Fort Washita. The search teams had not spotted anything. Billy and I killed time by strolling around on a self-guided tour of the scenic Fort Washita Park. I had participated in a lot of criminal searches and spent time at many command posts, but this one was the most beautiful setting I had ever seen. It was very relaxing as we explored the old army barracks and the parade ground with a small, clear lake near it. The relaxing beauty of it replaced our thoughts of the two killers hiding only a few miles from there.

At about 11:00 A.M. we were summoned to the command post. The OHP commander briefed us. "We just got word that Denton and Latham came upon a rancher and his teenage son feeding their cows. They tied both of them to a tree and stole their pickup truck. The man and his son were able to free themselves, walk to a house, and call the sheriff. The rancher told the sheriff that he knew Denton personally and that Denton said that the only reason that they weren't going to kill them was because the rancher had let Denton hunt deer on his ranch one time. The rancher's pickup truck is a blue Ford."

He showed us the approximate ranch location on the map. It was about two miles from where the yellow car was found. He continued, "I have pulled the number-one search team out of the woods. They are now searching the area around the ranch in patrol cars, looking for the truck. I would like for you men to go up in the helicopter and help us locate that pick-up."

We were eager, and quickly took off heading for the area. Captain Burkes was in the helicopter rear seat. I looked over my shoulder at him. It was reassuring to have him with us. He looked at me with no expression, his mouth clinched tight. I knew it would be bad news for the two killers if this Texas Ranger captain caught up with them. With his "no fear" attitude, it would be bad news for anyone that got in his way.

He and I both clutched DPS issue military-type AR-15 rifles with thirty-round clips and had ammunition belts filled with extra ammunition clips hung over our shoulders. Our bulletproof vests were uncomfortable, clinging tightly to our chests. Our pistols were loaded. We were ready for anything that Dennis and Lancaster could dish out.

"Let's get this over with and go home to Texas," I said to no one in particular.

We had searched the area for about forty-five minutes when the radio crackled. It was Ranger Jim Gant. "A deputy is following a blue Ford pickup that matches the description of the one we're looking for. He's headed north on Highway 48A just north of the little town of Emet. I'm seven miles from Emet. The pickup has two white males in it. The deputy is staying about 500 yards behind. He won't stop the truck until he gets some back-up."

Smart deputy, I thought.

Gant continued, "He's not close enough to verify the license plate number. I'll try to get to him as fast as I can to back him up."

"We'll head that way, Jim. We should be there in about three minutes," I said to him.

Billy banked hard and turned north, pulling in full power on our Bell Jet Ranger. We would have no radio contact with the deputy. I hoped that Jim would soon arrive to back him up.

"I see the deputy and the blue truck up ahead, Billy," I said. "It does match the description." We followed the deputy at slow speed and kept our distance. We felt that our presence might excite the two in the pickup, and if it was Dennis and Lancaster, they might open fire on the deputy before our ground officers could get into position to help.

The deputy spotted our helicopter and thought that we were his backup. Feeling the comfort of the helicopter, he sped up, closing the distance on the blue pickup. Ranger Gant said, "Helo-101, I'm about two miles away."

"Ten-four," I said. "It looks like the deputy is about to stop the pickup." Captain Burkes was quiet in the back seat, gazing intently out the window at the pickup.

I clutched my AR-15 rifle tightly. My adrenaline was beginning to pump. Captain Burkes and I were both trained to shoot from the helicopter, but I knew if the deputy got into a close-quarter gunfight that we wouldn't be able to shoot from the air for fear of accidentally hitting the deputy. We would be a poor back-up, to say the least.

Captain Burkes said, "Get closer, Billy. If the shooting starts, we're his only back-up until Gant gets here." Burkes was thinking the same thing as me: that we would have to land and back the deputy on foot, with no cover.

Billy banked and descended. The deputy's car was close behind the truck. We watched as he stopped the pickup on the shoulder of the highway. I saw him using his car door as a shield as he pointed his pistol at the driver. Ranger Gant had not arrived yet. I hoped our helicopter circling low overhead would have a psychological effect on the men in the pickup.

I called, "Hurry up, Jim. The deputy has the truck stopped."

Ranger Gant answered, "I'm approaching him now."

I saw Gant coming fast in his unmarked car with red lights flashing in the car grill. He stopped beside the deputy's car and behind the pickup truck. With his pistol in his hand, he also used his car door as a shield. They were taking no chances.

I could imagine the tenseness in the deputy and Ranger as they ordered the two men out of the truck. Shooting could start at any time. I saw both the driver and passenger step out of the pickup and lie down on the ground. After a few tense minutes, Ranger Gant and the deputy stood up and went toward the men. "Helo-101, this is not the suspects. Wrong pickup truck. The license plate doesn't match," declared Ranger Gant.

I breathed a huge sigh of relief. We had escaped a gun battle this time, but what about next time? I could imagine the thoughts of the two men in the truck after the officers had explained to them why they had been stopped so rudely. Bewildered and scared, they were probably thinking, "This is not a good day to be driving around in a blue pickup truck."

The captain, Billy, and I relaxed as we flew away from the scene to continue our search. As my adrenaline slowed, I felt a great emotional letdown. I glanced at Captain Burkes. He didn't seem to be troubled by variations of adrenaline. Not knowing a good place to search and with no particular plan, we flew around aimlessly, searching wherever the wind took us. All we could do was wait for Ranger Gant to call and tell us that the two had been spotted somewhere.

Gant did call: "Command post said that Denton's ex-wife called the sheriff's office in Durant and said that Denton had called her and told her he was coming to Caddo and was going to kill her when he got there. She's plenty scared. Fly toward Caddo and keep searching for the blue pickup."

On our map Caddo appeared to be a small town about forty miles into Oklahoma from the Texas border. Soon Ranger Gant called again: "Helo-101, I just heard a radio transmission from a highway patrolman. He's being fired on and is screaming for help, says his partner is dead, and he can't see. He has glass in his eyes. His location is on a county road somewhere east of Nida and south of Highway 22. That's all he said, and he's not answering his radio. We're all headed that way. I'm about eight miles from that location. It's about eight miles southeast from where we stopped that other blue pickup truck."

"That has to be a trooper on Team Three working the outer perimeter," I said to Billy. He nodded agreement.

"We'll be en route," I said. As Billy banked hard toward the south, I scanned the highway map, trying to read the names of the towns that were written in very small print. I found Highway 22, and finally Nida.

"Billy, turn back toward the southeast to a heading of 120 degrees. We should be there in about five minutes," I said.

Billy said, "It's not that way. It should be further to the south, shouldn't it?"

"Negative. I'm looking at it right here on the map and this is where we are," I said, pointing to the spot on the map. "Fly 120 degrees and break the sound barrier." Billy turned to 120 degrees and flew as fast as possible. Captain Burkes still remained silent in the back seat. Not a good sign for the bad guys, I mused.

I had the feeling that when we caught up with those guys, somebody was going to die. I knew that Denton and Latham would try to shoot our helicopter down. It could be air-to-ground combat. I knew I might be killed that day. I wondered if my Texas DPS life insurance was any good if I were killed while doing combat in Oklahoma. More morbid thoughts possessed me. How would my children grow up without a dad? I remembered what my dad had taught me when I was a teenager. He said that when confronted by a problem over which you

*First shooting site. Squares mark empty shotgun shell casings
where killer approached and assassinated the trooper.*

have no control, always take it to a Higher Power of Authority.
I prayed a silent prayer to God that if I were killed that He
would be with my family and take care of their needs. I prayed
for the safety of the other officers involved. I sensed that I
would soon be surrounded by death.

I shouted and pointed, "I see a highway patrol car sitting
on that road over there in front of that house!" I was excited
and scared. Billy circled the patrol car. "There's a trooper
lying on the ground behind the patrol car," I said, horrified at
what I was viewing. Seeing a brother officer lying on the
ground in a pool of blood is the worst nightmare of any law
officer.

Captain Burkes said, "Let's land and check his condition." Billy banked hard and set up for a final approach to a
landing. There was a cow pasture beside the road, a perfect
place to land. From out of nowhere an OHP patrol car came
sliding to a screeching halt beside the downed trooper. Billy
climbed and circled, waiting for information from the trooper.

Ranger Gant called. "Helo-101, I'm about three miles
west. The trooper at the scene says that it appears that the bad

guys went east. Both troopers have been shot dead at the scene."

Silence. This was unbelievable. Two on two, and the highway patrolmen were killed.

Billy banked east following the county road at high speed. I was angry now, praying that we would be able to overtake these madmen alone on this isolated county road. We would give them a gun battle that would quench their taste for violence.

Ranger Gant called, "Helo-101, an OHP airplane has located the blue pickup. They're on Highway 22, one mile east of Kenefic, eastbound. They're doing 100 MPH."

"Can you go any faster, Billy?" asked Captain Burkes. "We need to get 'em before they reach Caddo."

"It's wide open, Cap'n," said Billy.

Oklahoma trooper's car, after slayings.

At 120 MPH our hard-working chopper was barely gaining on the pickup. Billy was flying as fast as the Jet Ranger could go, desperately wanting to overtake the pickup before it reached Caddo. Calculating the mileage to Caddo in my mind, I said, "We'll never catch 'em before they reach Caddo. We're six miles behind them."

Gant responded, "The OHP airplane says that they are entering Caddo."

There was no chance of our taking them out now. Shots from the helicopter in a city would be too dangerous to the innocent people on the ground. It would be left up to the troopers on the ground.

We were three miles from Caddo. I could see the town in the distance. Oklahoma Highway Patrol cars, driving at speeds of over 100 MPH, were strung out on Highway 22 in front of and behind us. Ranger Gant was two miles behind us.

Gant: "Shots are being fired in Caddo."

In minutes we were over Caddo and began trying to locate the gun battle. We had no idea where to look. Billy banked left and right, and circled the little town. All three of us peered intently out of our windows, looking for OHP cars or the blue pickup truck. Several patrol cars were moving fast within the city. Apparently they didn't know where to go either. To us, it was like looking for the proverbial needle in a haystack. Our eyes desperately scanned the ground. So many houses and trees obscured our vision.

I shouted on the radio, "Jim! Where's the gunfight?"

"They say it's on the south side of town on Milam Street."

I thought, *Where in the world is Milam Street?* We didn't have a street map, and Jim wasn't familiar with the town either. We desperately needed better communications with the OHP.

I spotted several Oklahoma state police cars on the street below. I said, "There it is, Billy," pointing. Some officers were milling around near a blue pickup; others were running around. We saw two people lying on the ground.

"Looks like the bad guys are down," Billy said.

The battle was already over. "Yeah, let's land," said Captain Burkes, with disappointment in his voice.

We landed in a large vacant lot one-half block from the battle scene. As we walked down the street toward the scene of the battle, I saw hundreds of bullet casings lying in the street. I saw the truck, and then two bodies lying on a lawn. It was Denton and Latham. They were covered in blood and were handcuffed, their sawed-off shotguns nearby. On their belts they wore empty hunting knife scabbards and empty pistol holsters made from an automobile rubber innertube. Nearly a dozen officers stood nearby with weapons out, not taking any chances with these two dangerous men. Latham was still alive, barely. I stood over him. He was lying on his back. As he tried to breathe, bloody foam emitted from his mouth and nose. His eyes were wide open in a horrified stare as if he were looking directly into the gates of Hell. I had no feeling at all for him. He had reaped what he had sown.

I asked a trooper nearby, "Any officers hurt?"

"One trooper is dead, and one wounded," he said. He had participated in the gun battle, and he was breathing hard. His adrenaline was still pumping rapidly.

After the shooting, which occurred at upper driveway.

The bodies of the two killers.

Mine was pumping, too. I had been a part of this. Five minutes earlier and we would have been involved in the gun battle ourselves. Counting their latest victims, Latham and Denton had killed at least nine innocent people and three highway patrolmen. It was a sad day in Oklahoma; a sad day for all law enforcement officers.

Pointing toward the blue pickup, the trooper said, "Those scumbags were parked in that private driveway and hid the pickup behind that large hedge next to the house. The first troopers that spotted them were in an unmarked car. They spotted the two killers standing beside the pickup in the drive-way. Our men stopped in the street in front of the house where the driveway meets the street, and that's when the gunfight started. The trooper in the right front seat was killed, and the other was hit in the shoulder and his thumb was shot off, but he continued to return fire. I heard the trooper say, 'We have the suspects and they're shooting at us.'"

Bullet holes in Oklahoma trooper's car where officer was killed.

Still reliving the terrible scene, he continued. "I arrived a few minutes later just as the wounded trooper was driving away down the street to where you see his patrol car parked." He pointed to it. "The trooper continued to return fire from there. I think our trooper hit Denton before he moved his patrol car, because Denton looked and acted like he was wounded when I arrived. It seemed like the battle lasted twenty minutes, but I know it couldn't have lasted more than a few minutes."

"I wish we could have overtaken them on the county road," I said.

Billy and I walked around, looking at the bullet casings lying everywhere. There was blood in the street. Parked beside the blue pickup under a carport was a boat, full of bullet holes. Miraculously, only a few bullets had hit the houses. A travel trailer in an adjoining yard had several holes in it, and the blue pickup had several holes in it. Bullet holes in the front of the pickup indicated to me that the trooper who was killed on the road had shot accurately, even though partially blinded with glass in his eyes. For some reason, his bullets failed to hit Denton or Latham.

As I looked at the mortally wounded trooper still lying across the seat in his patrol car, tears came to my eyes and anger arose within me. I did not know him, but he was my brother. I quietly prayed for his soul and his family. An empty pistol clip lay on the ground in front of the patrol car where the trooper who had been shot in the thumb had reloaded and returned fire. *Gallant soldier for public safety,* I thought. I hoped his community had appreciated him.

I looked inside the pickup. I saw a Winchester lever-action .30-30 rifle and two pistols that had belonged to the two troopers who were killed on the county road. The scumbags had not only murdered the officers but had stolen their guns as well.

After Billy and I walked around for about thirty minutes, looking at the scene and recalling what the excited trooper had told us, we realized exactly what had happened. It confirmed the trooper's report.

When the unmarked patrol car stopped, Denton and Latham had been standing in the driveway to the right side of the patrol car and started shooting at the officers with 12-gauge sawed-off shotguns loaded with slugs and buckshot. They were very accurate, and the loads were devastating. The patrol car was parked broadside to Denton and Latham, who shot into its passenger window. Several buckshot and slugs hit the side of the car. The trooper in the passenger seat tried to return fire through his window with his AR-15 rifle but was killed by a shotgun slug to the head. He dropped his rifle outside of the car and fell over against the other trooper who was behind the steering wheel. This trooper fired his pistol through the open window. A shotgun pellet shattered the thumb on his gun hand, but he continued to fire his service pistol until it was empty. He then grabbed his Winchester .30-30 rifle, jumped out of the car and stood behind it, using it for cover. Evidence on the driveway indicated that Denton and Latham had charged the trooper, who managed to wound one of them.

Weaponry found in killers' car. Includes trooper's pistols and rifle.

The officer had continued firing until his rifle was empty, then dropped it and got back into the patrol car. Because his dead partner was lying across the seat, he had to sit on the edge of the car seat, but managed to drive one hundred yards down the street to cover.

As other troopers began to swarm the scene, the wounded and courageous trooper had reloaded his pistol and continued to shoot. It must have sounded like a war zone, with hundreds of shots being fired and bullets flying everywhere.

Soon the gun battle had ended. Denton and Latham had fallen, mortally wounded.

Captain Burkes summoned me. "The OHP captain re-

Sawed-off shotgun used by Denton and Latham.

quests our help. Since the OHP was so heavily involved in this, he wants an outside police agency to do the investigation on both shooting scenes. Ranger Gant and I will handle the paper work, and I would like for you to do the police photography of the shootings."

Even though it had been a while since I had done any criminal photography work, I was confident that I could do a good job. The Texas Department of Public Safety had trained all of its officers in police photography of crime scenes.

I began by photographing the crime scene in Caddo. When I finished, Billy and I flew to the scene on the county road. Two troopers were guarding the ghastly scene. They appeared as lonely sentinels surrounded by the smell of death. Although the bodies of the two slain troopers had been removed, there were pools of blood and empty rifle and shotgun shells everywhere. I greeted the troopers and told them that their captain had assigned me to take pictures. They said little as I went about my work. It was not a time for small talk.

As I took pictures I analyzed that the two troopers who were killed had met Denton and Latham head-on on the county road. Both drivers had stopped their vehicles facing each other, forty yards apart.

Denton and Latham had stood behind the opened doors of the pickup and immediately started shooting at the two troopers. Shotgun shell casings in the road and holes in the patrol car indicated they were using slugs and buckshot. The trooper behind the steering wheel was killed instantly by a slug to the head. When the slug hit the windshield glass, particles sprayed into the eyes of the other trooper who was sitting in the front passenger seat. He grabbed his rifle and, using his car door for a shield, emptied both his rifle and pistol at Denton and Latham. He grabbed his dead partner's shotgun and ran to the back of his patrol car. From behind it he had fired two shots when his shotgun jammed. With the glass cutting his eyes, he desperately tried to clear the jam.

Denton and Latham moved the pickup closer. They saw that the trooper had a problem, and one of them rushed him on foot, firing his shotgun as he advanced. Then, standing beside the patrol car, he had fired point-blank, executing the helpless trooper. Words cannot describe what the close-range shotgun blast did to the trooper. After stealing the dead troopers' weapons, Denton and Latham left tire marks on the road as they spun out in their haste to leave.

There was a farmhouse across the road. No one had been home when the shooting took place. Nobody was there to help the endangered troopers.

I finished my photography and stood surveying the scene. The beautiful countryside was quiet and peaceful. A few hours ago this tranquil setting had been shattered by the sounds of battle. Now it was a sad and lonely place. I was glad to be finished. I asked myself why circumstances allowed me to arrive minutes after all this was over and be the post-investigative officer.

With our work finally done in Oklahoma, we took off just

before dark for our home in Texas. We had done our best to help our brother officers in Oklahoma. I only wished that we could have done more. As the engine hummed and the rotor blades played their "going home" song, hardly a word was spoken between Texas Ranger Captain Burkes, Billy Peace, and myself. I knew that Burkes had seen it all before, knew that he regretted not being able to arrive earlier and help save some lives.

Recalling this has been very emotional for me because I had to relive the experience again. Even though it happened many years ago, I still vividly see the carnage left behind by the cruel killers, Denton and Latham, and still feel the same emotions I felt that day.

My pictures were all good. We received compliments from the OHP captain for a job well done. The Texas Department of Public Safety Training Academy heard about the photos and requested that I send copies to them to be used in training new recruits. They also used the pictures for years to train veteran troopers in how to protect themselves in future confrontations with dangerous criminals.

Who knows? Maybe my pictures have saved the lives of some of our own troopers.

CHAPTER 7

Lights out at 140 MPH

In flat West Texas and on the high plains of the Texas Panhandle, ranchers, truckers, and other motorists tend to get a heavy foot on their accelerators in an effort to cover great distances a little faster. But when a fleeing car thief races long highways and narrow roads at 140 mph at night with his lights out in the more populated areas of North Texas, Texas law officers see him as a definite public safety threat, worthy of their undivided attention. Such was the nature of my flying assignment on a bitter cold night in January 1997.

Our dispatcher, Nolan, rang me at 11:30 P.M., just as I turned off the light to go to bed. "Paul, want to go flying?" he asked discreetly.

"Nolan," I said, "you know I like to fly—but not at obscene hours. Go away."

"But Paul, you'll like this one. The Hood County Sheriff's Department (SO) caught a guy burglarizing a store in Cresson, he broke away, and they're chasing him on foot. They're asking for your help."

"Cresson . . . Cresson . . . where the heck is Cresson?"

"It's about fifty miles southwest of Fort Worth on U.S. 377," Nolan said. "You can get there quick, get the job done, and be back in bed in no time."

"Yeah, sure, Nolan," I replied, somewhat melancholy.

The late phone call, of course, woke my wife Dolores, who is a state police officer with the Texas Alcoholic Beverage Commission. She had just come home after a four-day absence working on a case.

"Why don't we open up a little arts and crafts store," she murmured, "work days and come home together at night like normal people?"

I knew she didn't mean it. She was dedicated to her job, too. "Because," I answered, "some guy would walk into our store some afternoon, rob us at gunpoint, I'd call for a state police chopper pilot to chase him, and there'd be some other pilot flying it. I'd wish it were me, and be unhappy. Go to sleep, you've earned it."

She gave me a hug and a kiss at the door. "Be careful. What are you looking for?"

"A booger on the ground." As a state police officer herself, she knew that I would be searching for a dangerous criminal on the ground.

Once airborne, I flew to Cresson in forty minutes and landed in an open field as instructed.

A fine young state trooper named Roger Hull met me. He would fly with me, act as my observer. He boarded, and I briefed him on operating my "Night Sun" searchlight.

"Since the dispatcher called you," Roger said, "the subject stole a car, then wrecked it when a deputy chased him, and is on foot again in the north edge of town."

Arriving over the north outskirts of Cresson, we circled and searched, using different altitudes and the searchlight for an hour and twenty minutes. All we saw were lots of officers searching everywhere on the ground. "Roger," I said, "I have to go for fuel, and the closest airport with jet fuel is Fort Worth. Want to go with me? We'll come right back."

Roger said yes readily. He was young and eager for anything, enjoying the ride and working the searchlight. I supposed he hadn't been married long.

Airborne again after refueling, we got another update from the sheriff's dispatcher. "They jumped him while you were gone. He stole a truck, our deputy chased him. He wrecked the truck at Granbury. He's on foot again."

My A-Star helicopter would do 140 MPH. "This guy is desperate not to be caught," I said to Roger. "If we jump him again, there's no way he's going to get away from this chopper."

As we arrived over Granbury and began searching again, a deputy called on our radio: "I've spotted the suspect stealing another car from a car dealer's parking lot. It's a new red Camaro Iroc. He's headed east on Farm Road 4, and I'm in pursuit. He's doing 120 MPH with his lights out. Repeat, with his lights out."

"Stay with him, deputy," I replied. "Helo-101 is only a few minutes behind you."

As we closed on Farm Road 4 at an altitude of 400 feet above the road, the fast-moving deputy called again. "I've lost him, couldn't stay with him. That sports car can move!"

"I see your emergency lights flashing. How far ahead of you was he when you lost him?"

"About a half-mile. I lost him when he made a curve. He must have turned off."

As a former highway patrol trooper myself, I had been in the deputy's situation. I knew the stress he was under, the way his adrenaline was flowing. Even after a high-speed chase is over and the fleeing suspect is apprehended, it takes a while for the officer's adrenaline to quit pumping so fast. I had lost a highway patrol friend, killed in a high-speed chase. I was thankful that this chase was occurring in the wee hours of the morning, when traffic was light.

"Look sharp, Roger, he's running with no headlights."

We circled and watched the ground intently. I saw a flash of light. It was a streetlight reflecting off the windshield of the Camaro Iroc, which passed quickly under our helicopter as I banked sharply to keep him in sight. He was still driving at high speed with no headlights. I prayed that no rural driver would be up this early to risk sharing the two-lane road with this zooming Camaro comet.

"Roger, I see him. Shine the light on the road to your right. He still has his lights off."

My young trooper swung the powerful searchlight and found the sports car. As he did it, the suspect floored his accelerator and pulled away from Helo-101. In hot pursuit, I increased speed. He got about one-fourth mile ahead of us, with Roger's light locked on him and lighting up the area around him. I called on the radio: "This is Helo-101 to all units. I have him spotted, we are in pursuit on U.S. 377 eastbound. I'm doing 120 MPH. He still has his lights off. Come to our searchlight beam if you can see it."

"We'll throw up a roadblock," said the deputy.

We sped on at 300 feet above ground. Watching for antennas in the darkness, I glanced at my trooper handling the searchlight. He was steady. Good lad. "Hang in there, Roger," I said. "We'll get him."

I was aware that many police patrol cars were trailing us at a distance. We quickly reached the roadblock. Patrol cars were parked crossways in the road. Suddenly, the speedster below turned off the highway into an open field to evade the vehicular barricade. As he did so, still with his lights off, he had to slow down and the pursuing officers gained on him. They also turned into the field and tried to surround him with patrol cars.

I moved Helo-101 into a hover directly over the scene as Trooper Hull kept our searchlight on it. The field was muddy, and the deputies' cars—six of them—jockeyed for position to block the Camaro. It was almost like watching a pro football game played in the mud, from a high pressbox above the fifty-yard line. As the Camaro turned, reversed, and surged forward to evade, it appeared he was stuck in the mud. Spinning and slinging mud in every direction, he suddenly found traction, saw an opening, and sped back onto the highway.

The chase was on again, with the sports car zooming west on U.S. 377, the deputies hot on his tail. I knew there were lots of motors and transmissions meshing, groaning and straining, but I couldn't hear them over the sound of my whining jet turbine engine and whirring rotor blades. The fleeing suspect suddenly put his lights on, and his hot little engine helped him gain on his pursuers again. I could see the gap between them widening, and I gave Helo-101's engine all it had to keep up with the Camaro. There was practically no other traffic on the highway. *Thank God,* I thought.

Under full power, my airspeed showed 140 MPH, but I was bucking a head wind. I could stay up with the suspect but could not gain on him. He then gradually began to pull away from me.

Golly, that sleek red sports car was really moving! At 140 MPH, if he hit a cow or deer he would go end over tea kettle many times. There were cool but desperate hands on that steering wheel. The same was true of the officers in pursuit. Race car drivers get extra money for this kind of driving. Deputies and state troopers do not.

In the dawn's early light we could see the deputies' cars strung out a mile or more behind the Camaro Iroc, except for one deputy in a Ford Mustang, who was only about a quarter of a mile behind. He was holding his own with his quarry. Watching it all, my trooper/partner was excited. "He's moving away from us!" exclaimed Roger.

"I know. This ship is giving us all its got."

Suddenly, the suspect lost control and spun out, almost struck an oncoming car, hit the ditch, and swerved across the road into the opposite ditch. Throwing mud and spinning his wheels, he made it back on the road, then spun out again into the opposite ditch. Closing my distance on him, I thought, *That kid has a charmed life, or else that sports car has Batmobile features!*

During his loss of control, deputies' cars had closed the gap again and got behind him and beside him. Back on the highway again, with the deputy in the Mustang beside him at breakneck speed, the guy purposely rammed the Mustang with a side-glancing blow. He then gained on the deputy a little, but the Mustang stayed right on his tail. *Gutsy driving job, deputy,* I thought. *Hang in there!*

The Hood County sheriff, who had been notified at home of the chase, had now joined it. I heard him on my radio. "Bill, are you okay"

"Ten-four, Sheriff," came the answer. "He just bent the Mustang a little."

The sheriff replied, "That does it. Men, he tried to kill Bill. This has gone far enough. Use those new machine guns and take him out."

A deputy answered, "We will, Sheriff, if we can get close enough!"

The little Mustang was again about a quarter-mile behind the Camaro, and holding. The others were much farther behind and losing ground. We were falling behind, but when the highway curved I cut the corners and gained again. I was holding my own in this grand chase, and it was taking us into the North Texas city of Stephensville. I could see the city lights as we approached. I called the Stephensville police dispatcher and told her the situation. "The suspect in the Camaro Iroc is doing 140, is wanted for burglary and car theft," I said. "We'll be there in about eight minutes!"

"We'll have units waiting," she said.

"Roger," I said, "when we get into town, I may be able to get in front of him, turn and come straight at him pretty low. When I do, shine the searchlight right into his windshield and blind him. Maybe we can stop him that way."

"Gotcha, Sergeant."

The bizarre, high-speed caravan entered Stephensville, its aerial escort booming and popping and its powerful searchlight streaking across sleepy city streets. Fortunately, this was a country town that "rolled up its sidewalks" at night. Not many cars moving. The Camaro slowed to about 80 MPH and I gained on him quickly. Local police cars tried to stop him, but he wove in and out and turned down side streets. Then he slowed to 60 MPH. Here was my chance.

At full power I lowered Helo-101's nose to increase airspeed and flew past the Camaro Iroc. With a sharp turn, I came barreling straight at him, at 200 feet above ground, and Roger's searchlight was flashing straight into his windshield. He slowed to a crawl. I did a "quick stop," and hovered in front of the now slow-moving sports car. He stopped, opened his door, jumped out, and ran.

"Stay on him, Roger," I said. "Hold the light on him."

With our searchlight illuminating him, the determined car thief ran hard and jumped fences. Police officers on foot were running right behind him, about 100 yards back. A woman in her housecoat who had just stepped out to get her morning paper suddenly dropped to her knees in shock as runners flashed by her, and our searchlight illuminated her. The determined suspect ran into her backyard and into a storage building. We had him and the building in our light.

I radioed the pursuing officers. "He's in the storage building under our searchlight. Right in front of you."

With handguns drawn, the officers surrounded the little metal building. Suddenly, he burst out, running hard, and trying to dodge officers. One tackled him, others jumped in; a vigorous struggle ensued. They subdued him, lifted him to a standing position, searched him and handcuffed him. Still in our 200-foot above-ground hover, I glanced at my searchlight operator. My young trooper was transfixed with the scene. Glancing below again, I could tell that the lady of the house, still standing in her backyard, was also stupefied.

Relaxing and looking around, I saw the little town come to life, as house lights came on and people began standing on porches, looking at the commotion—the flashing red lights of the police cars, and of course, Helo-101 up above them making that "wake up" popping noise. I looked at my watch. It was 5:45 A.M. It had been a tense and dangerous chase of thirty miles, from Granbury to Stephensville.

Roger was ecstatic. "Man, I've been in some chases before," he said, "but never one like this."

"That's because you saw this one through the eyes of the eagle," I said, sagely.

"When my wife asks me about what I did on my midnight shift, I'll sure have something to tell her," he said.

On my radio I arranged to meet some of the deputies at the Stephensville airport. I landed there. Everybody was drained, but we all had some coffee and a nice visit. I shook every hand, including that of some Stephensville city policemen. We realized that we had chased the guy by air, by car, and on foot—and that it had been a dangerous chase.

Flying back home and watching a peaceful sunrise, I thought, *Sometimes public safety asks a lot of those who maintain it.*

CHAPTER 8

Tragedy at Waco

Law officers don't often get to view the scene of their next crisis assignment, but I unwittingly viewed it on television during a noon hour in March of 1993. The breaking news story was about an armed and militant religious cult near Waco, Texas, who had fortified themselves in a large old building and were resisting law officers' attempts to serve a search warrant for illegal firearms. The cult leader was a man named Vernon Howell, who viewed himself as Jesus Christ but had named himself David Koresh. The television announcer said the Koresh followers, known as Branch Davidians, had vowed to fight to their death rather than be arrested.

A violent shootout was occurring on camera, right before my eyes. Federal Alcohol, Tobacco and Firearms (ATF) agents were storming the compound. Bullets were flying. Several agents on a porch-like extended roof were trying to enter a second-floor window as cult bullets tore at them through the roof on which they were standing. Other federal agents took nearby cover behind walls and cars. Some were hit and others began retreating down tall ladders to the ground.

Transfixed before my television set, I wondered who these people were and what had set them off to violence. I had never heard of David Koresh or Branch Davidians. Even as I pondered, I knew that my helicopter and I would have to respond. Experience had taught me that when anything bad like this happens, the nearest DPS helicopters are always sent to the scene.

Knowing that my phone would soon ring, I hurriedly dressed, packed my bags, and watched the newscast while on the move. The scene before me was so bizarre and unreal that I fumbled with my suitcase items. But the scene was real: lots of people were involved, and it was a warlike battleground. I saw officers pinned down behind automobiles, unable to rescue fallen comrades for fear of being shot.

Then came the telephone call. My supervisor said the Texas Rangers had requested Helo-101 for assistance.

It was time to go. Dolores followed me into the garage. We both knew there was no way of knowing when I would return home. After I kissed her, she looked deep into my eyes and held my arms. "Be careful," she said.

"I'll fly very high, where the bullets can't reach me," I said with a smile.

As I left the warmth and comfort of home and drove to the airport, the cold north wind dampened my spirits. I thought of my nearest neighbor, whose warm, snug executive office was only ten minutes from his home. *Lucky guy*, I thought. *Even when he has to return to his office and work nights, he at least can tell his wife when he'll return home.*

Then I thought, *I'm really the lucky one. Flying is in my blood. I'll be fine as soon as I get airborne.* Soon I was sitting in Helo-101 with my helmet on. I was Pilot/Investigator Paul Creech again, confident and content in the job for which I had been well-trained.

The wind was coming crosswise to my flight direction at 22 MPH, but my little ship could handle it. Helo-101's rotor blades whirred, I gave it necessary throttle, and became airborne for the ninety-five air miles to Waco.

Coming in low over Waco, I radioed DPS Communications and advised them I had arrived. Then I flew over the compound. The fortified old building was very large, in the middle of some open country outside the Waco city limits. Banking at 25 degrees and observing, I saw things looked peaceful; no agents at the compound. Widening my circle, I then saw that the ATF agents had the fortress surrounded but at a safe distance. Then I saw state troopers and other officers waving at me and pointing away from the compound. My radio crackled and a voice told me to get clear of the area. "National Guard choppers received gunfire earlier from .30-cal. machine guns. They took hits, sustained damage but landed safely."

I said to myself, *Machine guns? I'm outta here!*

I gave Helo-101 full power, gained altitude and distance from the compound, then landed at a DPS command post that had been established about six miles from the Branch Davidian's fortress. Stepping out of my chopper, I was warmly greeted by several state troopers. I knew some of them. "Glad to get you back on the ground, Paul. That machine gun fire on the Guard choppers was accurate and scary. Those guys are making war on us."

My commander briefed me. He had decided that keeping helicopters airborne might aggravate the situation, so he kept them on the ground, but close and available. Negotiations were in progress, and he hoped there would be no more violence. "We have them surrounded," he told our group. "They're not going anywhere!"

I remained there on stand-by for two days, drinking lots of coffee, eating junk food, sleeping in a Waco motel, and mingling with other officers. Many who were manning barricades and possible escape routes were cold, wet and homesick, sleeping in their cars or in tents. We were on both local and national TV news.

After two days I was ordered to return to my Dallas headquarters. A helicopter from the Waco DPS district office was retained, along with FBI choppers. It was great to get home to Dolores and a hot meal, and to get out of my flight suit.

Through updates from my supervisor and newscasts I soon got a more complete picture of the standoff. There were many women and children inside the compound. The McLennan County sheriff, Jack Harwell, knew David Koresh and was negotiating with him by telephone, trying to get him to surrender. He also met with cult leaders face to face. FBI negotiators also tried, but none of the negotiations were successful.

Other reports said that Koresh had a sort of hypnotic religious control over his followers, in effect had "brain-washed" them with his religious teachings, and he had controlled several young girls as his "wives" with full marital privileges. The Davidians inside the fortress had lots of weapons and large stockpiles of food and ammunition. Reports also said that the Davidians were extremely dedicated to Koresh but that one of his "lieutenants" had deserted and fled to law officers.

Estimates held that there were approximately 128 cult members inside the compound, including women and children. The Texas Department of Public Safety rotated approximately eighty officers per week in and out, from all over Texas. ATF used slightly more, and their ranks included some female officers.

As the siege wore on, several Waco citizens brought hot food, coffee, and goodies to officers. Some of the federal agents, far from home and often homesick, were both surprised and appreciative of this Texas kindness. Kudos to the people of Waco!

More violence erupted when three cult members who had jobs in Waco attempted to walk through fields and pasture land to join cult members at the besieged compound. Four hundred yards from reaching it, a federal SWAT team confronted them at close range and ordered them to halt. One of the Branch Davidians opened fire on the officers with a semiautomatic pistol. Officers returned fire, killing one cult member. Another was captured, and a third escaped through the woods.

Through my years as a pilot/investigator I had developed an additional skill which law enforcement found useful. It had started as a hobby: metal detection. I was trained in metal detection by the master himself, Charles Garrett, owner of Garrett Electronics, Inc. From simple crime scenes to complicated ones, I had developed expertise using various types of Garrett metal detectors in reconstructing crime scenes and in locating weapons, bullets, bullet casings, knives, and other metallic items that could be used as evidence. This skill had helped solve some crimes, and my expertuise became known around Texas law enforcement circles. This brought about my next call from the Texas Rangers in Waco.

They needed me to assist them, not as a chopper pilot, but

News reporters, as first seen (before officers' barricade)
on road to compound.

with metal detection work to gather evidence from the shoot-out with the cult trio. "Paul," said my Ranger contact, "the shooting area is close to the compound. Bring your body armor and weapons."

Dolores, also a police officer, was gone on a case herself when I left home this time. It was just as well that she was, I thought, for I knew her fears for my safety would be strong when I told her I was going into harm's way on the ground. We both preferred that I be airborne when bullets fly.

This trip, I drove from Dallas to Waco. Do law officers pray when approaching a dangerous crisis? You bet they do. En route, I prayed for my safety, for the safety of all the involved officers, and also for Dolores' safety.

As I neared the siege area, I drove by several DPS state troopers who were busy stopping cars, checking them for possible escaping or entering cult members and for illegal weapons. Traffic was heavy. Some of it was curious "lookers," some were news media people. The weather was miserable: cold rain, overcast sky. Troopers and ATF agents were working shifts, manning checkpoints in a twenty-eight-square-mile

Texas Highway Patrol outpost.

encirclement area. I knew it would be a nasty, miserable, and muddy day for metal detecting.

Parking my car at the assigned forward command post one mile from the Davidians' compound, I was met and briefed by a Texas Ranger and ATF agents. The Rangers, the ATF SWAT team, and I would be transported to the shooting scene in military tanks. I put on the heavy military-style bulletproof vest and gathered my assortment of Garrett metal detectors that I had used successfully at past crime scenes. After I entered the Bradley tank, the steel door was closed and latched. I looked out of a small, four-inch bulletproof glass observation port. It was semi-dark inside the tank, and I thought, *What a strange environment for a helicopter pilot.* I yearned for my Helo-101, but we were safe from gunfire inside the tank.

Lumbering and clanking down a dirt road toward my destination—yesterday's shooting scene, which looked as if it would put me within rifle range of the opposition—I saw a weird sight through the little "peep hole." A late model car at roadside had been crushed to about four feet high. I nudged the federal officer near me and pointed.

"News reporters," he said. "They slipped into this off-limits area, left their car and took off on foot after their story. Another tank driver, with obstructed vision, didn't see the car and ran over it."

News reporters, I thought. *A gutsy bunch when they're after a story. And sometimes, they put others at risk.*

As I continued looking through the tank's little window, we passed uncomfortably close to the old compound. It looked like a multi-story fort made of sheet metal. I saw no one, but I could "feel" the machine guns and semi-automatic weapons trained on us. *God help us all,* I thought. *What motivated the warlike people inside? Why didn't they come out, let officers have the illegal weapons? Or at least let the women and children out?* I prayed for a peaceful ending to this.

My driver stopped the tank. We were at yesterday's shooting location. Time for metal detection expert Paul Creech to get out and do his work. The compound fortress loomed ominously large, about 400 yards away. I wondered if the cultists' rifles had telescopic sights. I was relieved to see that a small hill partially blocked my view of the compound, providing some protection for me. The guys showed me the shooting positions of officers and cult members involved in the shooting.

I could see it had been a fierce battle. Hundreds of empty shell casings were on the ground. I placed small red flags on wire stakes in the ground to mark where each shell casing had landed. This included many 9mm pistol casings from the cultists' position. Shell evidence picked up by my detectors near the position of the deceased cult member indicated he had fired many times at the SWAT team.

Working with my metal detectors, I found bullets embedded in the dirt. I extracted one 9mm semi-automatic pistol bullet from the dirt at the officers' position. If it matched the rifling on the cultist's pistol, it would be proof that they had fired on the officers. A Ranger placed it in a plastic bag to be analyzed later.

Working wet ground with the metal detectors, I glanced up apprehensively several times toward the compound, also toward nearby officers. In the cold, wet drizzle, it was an eerie scene. The federal SWAT team, all dressed in black, had formed a wide circle around me and the other investigating officers. They were armed to the teeth: semi-automatic rifles, heavy bulletproof vests, military-style helmets. They made me feel safe! The Rangers were busy taking pictures and making scaled diagrams of the shooting scene.

After flagging all the evidence, I paused on the small hillside looking down on yesterday's gun battle scene and tried to visualize it. With a furtive quick glance at the Branch Davidian compound, I knew that this was only one skirmish in a big war. But it had been deadly, and one Davidian had been killed. And I had survived a dangerous day while doing a needed job. The ATF SWAT team had protected me well.

Settling into the Bradley Tank again for our return to the command post, my thoughts turned to the innocent children in the compound. While feeling the protection of parents, they could not know what was causing the deafening hail of bullets flying back and forth. Probably there were moments of panic inside by them, their parents, and others. Was their total subservience to the Koresh "God-man" giving them peace and courage? What was he telling them? Why wouldn't he surrender and achieve peace and safety for his 128 people? Why wouldn't he let law officers serve their well-documented warrant for his many illegal weapons?

Back at the command post, I got a delicious hot meal. It was great to get out of my wet coat and heavy flak vest. I gathered up my detection equipment and headed home to Dallas.

After a brief rest at home I was sent on other flying assignments, glad to get back into Helo-101 and get away from the grim and miserable Waco situation. But the Branch Davidian siege at Waco went on and on, day after day. Lots of law enforcement negotiators—the FBI, ATF, the Texas Rangers, and Sheriff Harwell—tried to get Koresh and his followers to come out peacefully. They cut off electricity to the fortress, leaving its occupants in the dark, with no refrigeration, no power. Tension built. I wondered if the siege of the Alamo had been like this. Two more cultists fled and surrendered, but Koresh would not surrender.

Gunfire continued. Four agents had already been killed. Aggressive news reporters kept the coverage going. Television

*Scene of shooting outside compound, where metal detectors
were used to search for spent shells.*

brought the scenario right into living rooms across the nation.
Officers allowed some reporters into special observation towers in areas previously forbidden. After fifty-one days, with no
surrender, no concession by Koresh, federal officers rammed
the side of the old compound with a military tank.

As this operation began, the unthinkable happened.

Flames began to lick out of the southeast corner of the old
building, the direction from which a strong 30 MPH wind was
blowing. Within minutes, the wind swept the flames, and the
compound was an inferno. The nation watched it on television. To everyone's horror, nobody ran out of the building.
Waco fire engines were called, but their arrival was too late.
Everyone inside perished. Law officers watched it, aghast. I
was not there, and was glad I wasn't.

Afterwards, Texas Rangers and other officers found
charred bodies of men, women, and children. Many had been
shot at close range before they burned. It appeared to investigating officers that David Koresh or his lieutenants had shot
some of their own cult members, including women and children. Others appeared to have committed suicide. Texas
Rangers and other investigators found evidence that parts of
the interior had been soused with an inflammatory liquid.

Texas Ranger (left) and ATF/SWAT member who assisted Creech in metal detections.

Rifles, pistols, machine guns, and live hand grenades were found in the charred remains of the building.

The next, and last, time I saw this terrible place was when I was assigned to fly an aerial police photographer above the scene in my helicopter. His job: to get photographs that could be used for future court evidence. As I circled the charred mass below, hovering, then banking left and right as the photographer snapped the pictures, I pondered the event. My mind would continually hit a blank wall.

At first I thought: Madness. Then I reasoned . . . the self-proclaimed Jesus Christ, Vernon Howell, alias David Koresh, the Prophet of Doom, had apparently led his followers along a pathway of destruction.

This tragic incident was typical of many law enforcement assignments I handled, in which I carried out orders without ever personally seeing or realizing their conclusions.

Arriving home from Waco for the last time, my duties there concluded, I hugged my wife for a long time. Yeah, law officers have deep feelings, too. Sometimes they even weep, but usually no one sees them.

CHAPTER 9

Guarding presidents

Helping protect the life of a U.S. president can put stress on a person.

As a police pilot with the Texas Department of Public Safety, I was privileged to be assigned to assist the Secret Service many times with airborne security in protecting many U.S. presidents. These included Lyndon Johnson, Richard Nixon, Gerald Ford, Jimmy Carter, Ronald Reagan, and George Bush, Sr.

In 1980 Ronald Reagan was nearing the Republican nomination for president. If victorious, he would make his acceptance speech at the Republican National Convention in Dallas. The event was being held at the Dallas Convention Center. A capacity crowd was anticipated, which would include many high-profile Republican Party state and national leaders. Police and Secret Service security was tight.

The Secret Service had requested helicopters from the Texas DPS and the Dallas Police Department. Along with fellow pilot Bill Isbell, I was to work with the Secret Service as part of the security team, using the Dallas Police Department's aircraft hangar as our base. It was very close to the Convention Center; we could make a quick aerial response if needed. Bill and I would work two twelve-hour overlapping shifts. Mine was 6:00 P.M.–6:00 A.M., Bill's was 6:00 A.M.– midnight. That meant we would fly together from 6:00 P.M.

until midnight, which would be the busy time at the Convention Center.

Our helicopter was equipped with a FLIR, an infrared camera that would greatly improve night vision. Connected to it were two black-and-white TV monitors mounted inside our cabin, one in front for the copilot and one in the rear passenger compartment. The picture on the screens could show anything at which the camera was pointed, revealing the smallest details, even people's faces.

A Secret Service agent was to work with Bill and me. He

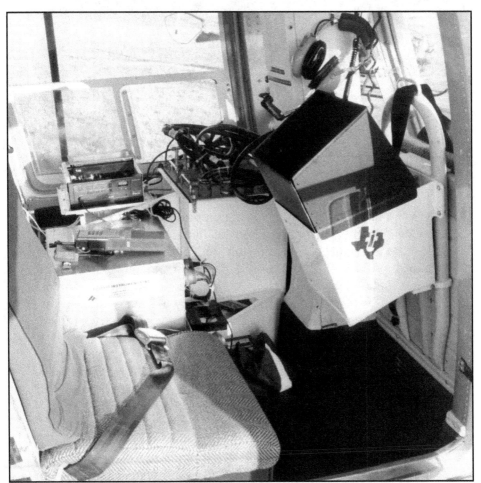

Infrared equipment. Secret Service agent sat here.

Helo-101, with infrared camera attached.

was in charge of our flying assignments. He did not stay at the police hangar, but came when he had an assignment for us. For the first three days, during which the Republicans hammered out their platform and groups from all the different states held meetings, our agent had few assignments for us. On the third night, he entered the hangar briskly and escorted us to a private area, away from some Dallas city officers. He was very secretive, even around other officers.

"Ronald Reagan has just been nominated to be the Republican presidential candidate," he said. "He will give his acceptance speech tonight at 9:00 P.M. Our intelligence has learned that a terrorist is going to make a suicide attack on Mr. Reagan by crashing a motorized ultra-light aircraft into the Convention Center between 8:00 and 10:00 P.M. His aircraft will be loaded with volatile explosive devices. He intends to kill Reagan."

He paused to let that statement sink in, and looked us in the eyes. I suddenly had dry-mouth, tried to swallow but couldn't. A motorized ultra-light aircraft is a little "build it yourself" craft that is very light and comes in a box. A real amateur job, but some flying enthusiasts like to build and fly them. The pilot is not required to have a pilot's license. It would be hard to spot at night.

"Our job tonight is to circle the Convention Center," he said, "using your FLIR to try to locate this nut in his ultra-light. My orders are to shoot him down. We'll need to remove the chopper doors so I will have a clear field of fire."

I asked, "What kind of weapon will you use?"

"A machine gun," he said, "with a night-vision scope."

"What about the people on the ground?" I asked. "A stray bullet could kill an innocent person. And what if you shoot down some dumb pilot that accidentally flies into our area?"

"My orders are to shoot down the ultra-light aircraft. When the president or a presidential candidate is in danger, we protect him first. If an unauthorized aircraft gets within a mile of the Convention Center, I will shoot him down."

I thought, *Wow. This guy is serious, and this is serious business.*

"When do you want to take off?" Bill asked the federal officer.

"Thirty minutes," was the agent's answer. "I'll get my equipment from my car and meet you at the helicopter."

As Bill and I hurriedly began removing Helo-101's doors, I realized the big picture. The man whose life we would protect might soon become the most powerful man in the world, with his hand near the red telephone that could decide war or peace, and with his judgment came the decision to use or not use nuclear weapons. If the terrorist managed to crash into the Convention Center with explosives, he might kill hundreds of other ordinary people, in addition to Ronald Reagan. Yeah, the Secret Service agent had a worthwhile mission, all right.

I said to Bill, "If this guy shoots some innocent person while spraying lead around, how will you and I stand legally and on liability?"

Bill didn't know the answer, and he was concerned, too. We decided that since we were only acting as pilots, we could not be held liable. "Well," I said, "I sure hope this guy knows what he's doing."

The agent approached the helicopter, ready to go, as Bill and I were removing the last helicopter door. He was carrying night-vision goggles and a military-looking machine gun with a night-vision scope. He climbed into the back seat. Although he was careful with his weapon, I sure hoped he wouldn't get excited and shoot us all down. I'd been around machine guns before with our DPS SWAT team, and the darn things always made me a little uneasy. Basically, I was a rifleman and a fair pistoleer. Besides, I knew many of our SWAT guys; I didn't know this officer. When going into any dangerous situation I had always felt better if I were with an officer with whom I worked closely. I wanted to know how my comrade in arms would react in a crisis. In this situation, our lives and reputations seemed to be in the hands of a stranger. I told myself to quit worrying and do my job; the stakes in this game were super-big.

As part of the Secret Service operation, we were exempt from an FAA prohibition against any aircraft flying within one

Dallas skyline, as seen by Pilot Creech, Pilot Isbell,
Secret Service agent.

mile of and 2,000 feet above the Convention Center. We took off and were soon circling the Convention Center at an altitude of 500 feet above ground a little past 7:30 P.M. Bill was the pilot in command, and I was the infrared camera operator.

As I pointed the camera into the dark skies, our agent in the rear seat studied his TV screen intently. With our doors off, we were extremely aware of the rushing wind. Below us, the city of Dallas seemed to stretch endlessly. And so did the traffic.

"All those normal people down there," I mused, "going home to their families after work. And here I sit with a machine gunner two feet behind me and looking for some fanatical lunatic in a weird little flying contraption carrying bombs. What a way to make a living!" But then I consoled myself by remembering a lot of chopper guys who had done this very thing in Vietnam a few years ago, risking their lives for Uncle Sam, day after day. And the people below were shooting at them.

The Secret Service had requested that we not fly directly over the building. I supposed they thought that if something happened to our chopper, we would fall straight down and crash into the Convention Center. The chance of this happening was remote, but possible.

Darkness came, and Dallas ("Big D," as Texans call it) was a sea of twinkling, sparkling lights below us. The three of us circled the prescribed perimeters of the Convention Center below, watchful and pretty tense. I kept the infrared camera pointed skyward, adjusting the angles as Bill turned. I wondered if our agent had his safety in the "on safe" position on that chattergun. After two and a half hours he began talking on his hand-held radio. I couldn't hear his words over the popping of the rotor blades and the wind rushing by our open doors. I hoped he wasn't getting "the call."

Finally, he leaned forward and said, "We can return to the hangar now. Mr. Reagan has made his acceptance speech, and has left the Convention Center."

I breathed a big sigh of relief and looked at Bill. He was doing the same and gave a faint smile. As he descended our little ship toward our police heliport, I had a recurring thought about the danger of our helicopter losing control and falling straight down into the Convention Center. The reason I knew it was possible was because it had happened one time.

A helicopter being flown by a friend of mine had a malfunction that caused his transmission to disintegrate in the air. Post-crash investigation revealed that a mechanic had failed to properly tighten several bolts. My friend and the wreckage did fall, straight down. There was nothing my pilot friend could do to save himself. A terrible factor in the tragedy was that the pilot and the mechanic were very good friends. It devastated the mechanic emotionally and severely damaged his reputation. Fortunately, nobody beneath the falling wreckage was hurt.

So, I had to give the Secret Service credit. They knew their business and tried to prepare for all eventualities. Upon landing, the federal agent shook hands with us, dismantled his machine gun, packed its parts in a black case, said good-bye, looked at his watch, and hurried off to an automobile. I wondered if he had another appointment.

The remainder of our duty with them in Dallas was slow. We had a few flights, but nothing unusual happened, and we were glad. Bill and I grew tired of all the night-shift work.

I wondered if Reagan would become president.

During my career I also flew "point" on all presidential motorcades that came to North Texas. My job was to fly around and in front of the motorcade, searching for anything unusual that might create a threat to the president's life. When *Air Force One* was to land at the airport, I would make a low-level sweep of the airport area and land ahead of *Air Force One*. I always had a well-armed Secret Service agent with me and took orders from him.

The Secret Service would never let me fly any closer than 2,000 feet above or 2,000 feet to the side of any motorcade. I considered myself a part of the presidential security team, but it appeared that they didn't trust me. I knew that they had done a careful background check on me. The heck of it was that the background check probably did not show that I would give my life, as they would, if necessary, to protect the president.

Wearing the blue flight suit of a Department of Public Safety pilot, with my police badge clearly visible, it was obvious to them that I was a state police officer. Also, I wore the lapel

Air Force One, *when the president came out.*

Presidential "limo" being unloaded.

pin they gave me to appropriately identify me as a member of their security team. Still, I was never allowed to get near the president. Once when I was near *Air Force One,* I asked an agent who was standing guard beside the door if I could look inside the president's plane. His reply: "No, can't let you do that."

I was always honored and proud to work with the Secret Service guys. Mostly, they were a friendly, upbeat bunch. But when guarding the president, nobody was their friend. They became very stern. Around them I could sense their nervousness and stress. They watched everything and everybody. When you recall that President John F. Kennedy was shot and killed in broad daylight on a Dallas street, you understand these agents better. I wondered if President Lincoln had any Secret Service security. Apparently not.

In the late eighties I was flying helicopter security with the Tyler, Texas, motorcade of President George Bush. I was at my usual 2,000 feet above and 2,000 feet away (that's less than a half-mile) from the procession. The Secret Service agent in charge of the motorcade called my agent in the rear seat of my helicopter on his radio and told us we were too close. He asked us to stay at least two miles away. We could fly ahead and all around the motorcade, but must keep that distance.

I asked the agent on board: "Why keep us so far away? We can barely see the cars, much less any detail that could be a threat."

Air Force One *at Tyler, Texas.*

"I don't have a clue," the agent said, shaking his head. "We've never had to stay this far away before."

I felt useless. At this distance, there was no way I could react to a threat. *Oh, well,* I thought, *ours is not to reason why, ours is but to do or die.*

Even though I helped protect him, I never really got to see President Bush. Little did he or I know that a few years later I would be one of two pilots in two helicopters flying his son, Texas Governor George W. Bush, out of Palo Duro Canyon State Park, near Amarillo, along with Bush's wife and children. The governor had been there on official business, meeting with a citizens group concerning park improvements. The canyon was deep and in total darkness. I knew the governor, his wife Laura, and their daughters trusted me, trusted my judgment to get them out of the canyon and back to Amarillo. Had I had the tiniest thought that it was unsafe, I would have refused to make the flight.

Upon landing at the Amarillo Airport, the governor thanked the other pilot and me for a great job and a smooth ride. That night as we headed for a motel, I thought, *Wouldn't it be amazing if this son of a former president were to become president someday and have my DPS chopper pilot son Mike flying security for him?*

Guarding the president of the United States is an awesome responsibility. Having a security system that permits our president to move freely about the nation is just another "plus" that makes America the greatest nation in the world. I was honored to be a part of this. I'm glad we have sharp Secret Service agents watching over him. And I'm glad we still have sharp Texas DPS pilots to strengthen the president's security when he comes to Texas.

CHAPTER 10

The swan dive

Rockwall City Police Officer Andy Bess was on afternoon routine patrol when he spotted a car parked on the shoulder of a road in a large grove of trees. Deciding to check it out, he parked behind it, got out, and approached. There was nobody in the old model Chevrolet.

Opening the driver's side door, he saw clutter. It was a balmy spring afternoon, and he guessed that a young couple had decided to spend a romantic afternoon in the woods. Just then he heard a scream from within the trees. A woman's voice. It came again.

Bess ran toward the sound, entering the woods, and quickly saw a man lying down. As the officer approached, the young man got up and walked toward him, excitedly shouting, "Help me, please help me!" His first thought that a couple had been robbed or assaulted quickly vanished when he saw blood on the man's hands. Unfastening the snap on his handgun holster, he stopped, squared off at the man, pointed and said, "On the ground please! Face down!"

The youth looked dismayed, then shrugged and proceeded to get down. Suddenly, he charged the police officer, and they scuffled. In the slugfest, Bess managed to call for help on his hand-held radio. The youth picked up a glass bottle from the ground and hammered a vicious blow to Bess' head, stunning him. Badly dazed but conscious, Bess saw his attacker run out of the woods toward an area of large, expensive homes.

Other Rockwall officers responded. They saw Bess' parked patrol car, found the injured officer, who told them of the attack and the screams. Searching the area, they found a sixteen-year-old girl lying in the grass. She was conscious, but was bruised, bleeding, and almost naked. She stammered that she had been brutally raped. "He would have killed me if the policeman hadn't come," she told them.

A search of the car by an officer turned up the name of Billy Bailey, age twenty. The battered girl verified the name, described Bailey, and told them that she used to be his girlfriend. She further said he had picked her up in Garland, a few miles away, and forced her to go with him to Rockwall. Checking Bailey's license number with the police dispatcher, officers learned that he had done jail time for burglary and was a parole violator.

A manhunt quickly formed and included all officers in the area. A DPS helicopter was requested. That was Helo-101 and me. Also, my partner Kenny Meadows. En route to Rockwall after having been briefed, I told Kenny, "This Billy Bailey is a real 'sweetheart.' Not exactly the type guy I'd want to marry my daughter."

"Yeah, Billy the Kid," murmured Kenny.

The searching officers knew that Bailey still had to be nearby. A perimeter was quickly established around the crime scene, and a command post was set up, which included a communications dispatcher. A house-to-house neighborhood search, with residential occupants being warned, had already been set up when Kenny and I arrived in Helo-101. I was acting pilot-in-command. After checking in by radio with the Rockwall police search commander, we began circling, looking for anything that might be out of place among the houses below. We circled for hours, during which we made two refueling landings at the Mesquite Airport.

Then something developed. "Command post to all units," said the voice on our radio, "a woman just went into her house and found a man hiding under her pool table. He ran out the back door."

The dispatcher then gave the address, which was near the scene of the assault. I turned toward it and spotted the house quickly as police cars and officers on foot were hurrying toward it. A real dragnet was closing in on "Billy the Kid." I circled the area around the house. Television news vans from nearby Dallas arrived, and reporters pushed forward with cameras, sensing high drama and a big story.

Time passed. Nobody spotted him. I continued circling and scanning the area. Hours passed. It seemed impossible that with all the officers having converged on the area around the house within five minutes of the report, no one had found him. This guy was elusive—or a magician.

"Command post to all units," came our radio voice. "A home owner two blocks west of the first address just ran a man out of his house. The address is 2120 Becky Lane."

I edged Helo-101 in that direction, guessed at the house number, and circled at 500 feet above the house. I learned later that Billy Bailey had been in the house eating the home-owner's food and watching the progress of the search on live television news. Salty kid; he must have been laughing his head off.

The neighborhood was in a state of alarm. Homeowners were in yards, huddling, conversing, and pointing. I watched as police urged them back into their houses. I suspected that those who owned weapons were arming themselves. Our next radio report announced that a homeowner ran to an officer and told him that he had seen a man enter a large, three-story home only a block away, on the same street. "Billy the Kid" was having a field day with a Rockwall neighborhood, scaring everyone.

We all moved to the house. An officer who had been searching the second house about 200 yards away was there in less than one minute. I saw another encirclement form quickly. I felt that we had him now. Looking down from 400 feet above, Kenny and I scanned the garage, second-floor windows, behind shrubbery. The large house—it was a three-story home—was surrounded by many tall trees, small and large. Some of the tallest trees' foliage covered part of the roof. Officers checked windows and doors, and apparently found them locked. They searched front and back, and behind shrubbery.

Then we saw movement on the roof. A man walked out

from under some tree branches that were covering part of the roof.

It was Billy Bailey. I quickly radioed this to our ground search commander.

Bailey had obviously climbed onto the roof from an upstairs bedroom window. We watched him walk over to the edge. Later I learned that he shouted to officers below, "I'm up here!" I knew the officers were shouting up to him to come down. Then, unbelievably, he waved his hand as if to say "bye-bye," spread his arms wide, and did a perfect swan dive off the roof. "Lord in Heaven," I gasped to Kenny, "it's a suicide."

The only problem was that there were trees with lots of branches near his diving "departure." As he plunged through them, branches broke his fall. Tumbling and bouncing, he hit the ground hard. I had seen many bizarre scenes from my helicopter, but this one almost topped them all. We watched as the Rockwall police officers pounced on him. I learned later that, lying there on the ground, he had begged officers to kill him.

Billy Bailey was arrested and jailed for aggravated assault. A hospital check-up revealed his injuries were only bruises and minor cuts. After terrorizing a nice neighborhood, eluding police for eleven hours, and surviving a three-story fall from a roof, this twenty-year-old "sweetheart" wasn't hurt near as badly as the sixteen-year-old girl he had brutalized and raped. I wondered what his prison sentence would be, and also what the molested young girl did with the rest of her life.

"Billy the Kid," as Kenny and I had dubbed him, had a bad day, after causing a lot of other folks to have a bad day. He even failed at suicide, although his swan dive from the tall roof looked pretty graceful in the beginning.

CHAPTER 11

Overnight delivery by air

Not all the officers with the Texas Department of Public Safety wear uniforms, badges, western hats, or blue flying suits like mine. The narcotics agents' dress style was . . . well, any attire needed to get the job done. These silent warriors, seldom seen or recognized by the public, fight a deadly and perilous war against illegal drug traffickers. The dangerous life they live is hard on their families. Undercover work, involving infiltration of drug rings, is especially dangerous. I knew several narcotics agents who were killed. The kingpin and leaders in illegal drug trafficking are a murderous bunch because the profits are astronomically high at the top.

Along with the Texas Rangers, the DPS Highway Patrol, county sheriffs and others, I was privileged to often work with many of our gutsy narcotic agents, which often involved drug busts and raids. This type work, I always believed, resulted in reduced quantities of dangerous drugs reaching our kids.

As a pilot for the DPS, I flew with a lot of good partners/pilots. I remember them better and with more pleasant thoughts than I do the interrupted sleep, missed meals, cold nights, and frightening moments. One of these was Bill Isbell, the type of pilot/partner anyone would be proud to fly with. A graduate of the U.S. Naval Academy, Bill came to the DPS out of the Marines, after two stints in Vietnam—the first as an infantry lieutenant and the second as a Navy fighter pilot. Afterwards, he was a USMC flight instructor. He had high

DPS Pilot Bill Isbell.

moral values and was very conscientious in performing his duties—the kind of guy you'd want your daughter to marry.

He was a small man. Because of this, and because he did everything well, I called him "Mighty Mouse." I just knew he could leap tall buildings without needing a helicopter. Bill was my pilot/partner when the following incident occurred.

Those who deal in narcotics often use airplanes to transport illegal drugs. A narcotics sergeant contacted Bill and me. He told us that a narcotics suspect had been arrested in Texarkana. In his efforts to stay out of jail, the suspect was cooperating with narcotics officers by naming his associates and detailing their drug trafficking activities. He had agreed to continue his association with the group and furnish the information to a DPS narcotics agent that was assigned to work with him.

The informant told our people that a large shipment of marijuana was to be transported by airplane from Mexico to DeKalb, Texas. The shipment was to arrive three nights later. The airplane would land at night on a private unlit airstrip a few miles southwest of DeKalb. The grass airstrip had been located and reconnoitered by narcotics agents.

The sergeant needed helicopter help in taking aerial photographs of the grass airstrip. The photographs would be used later to assist in planning the arrest strategy and briefing the narcotics agents that would be involved in "taking down" the airplane crew and ground loading crew when the airplane landed.

The next morning, Bill and I were flying to DeKalb in

Helo-101. We flew over the grass airstrip at an altitude of 3,000 feet while an agent in the rear passenger seat took the pictures. I thought about how dark it was going to be in these woods the next night. "Bill," I said, "we better memorize the layout of the area. It's gonna be mighty dark here tomorrow night. The only thing we're gonna be able to see is what the searchlight reveals."

The date that the drug-carrying airplane was to land arrived. It was a cool day in March. Normally, March in North Texas is rainy or has low overcast clouds. We were lucky. The weather was clear and was expected to stay that way a few days. Since the operation was to take place in the wee hours of the morning, with no moonlight to help us see the ground, we could use all the luck we could get.

Bill and I flew from our headquarters near Dallas to Texarkana, which was thirty-five miles from DeKalb. The briefing was set for 5:00 P.M. in Texarkana. We arrived at 4:45 P.M. A narcotics agent met us at the airport and drove us to the district headquarters.

The briefing room was full of narcotics agents. Everyone was anticipating the strategy meeting. A chalkboard and the blown-up aerial photographs we had taken were prominently displayed. All of the "narcs" were dressed in camouflage clothing with pistols hung low on their hips ready for action. The room was noisy with friendly banter being voiced back and forth.

"Listen up, men," said Lieutenant Montana, who was half Native American. Bill and I knew he was a good man to lead us on a night raid. The room became quiet. He began. "One of our sources says that tonight at about 11:00 P.M. a twin-engine airplane will land on an abandoned cow pasture airstrip near DeKalb. It will be loaded with 1,500 pounds of marijuana. The airstrip is on private land. Search warrants have been obtained. Three bad guys will be waiting for the plane to land. Their job is to unload the marijuana from the airplane and load it into their pickup trucks.

"All of you will be strategically hidden near the airstrip. It will be very quiet in the country at night. It is of the utmost importance to keep quiet. You know how clearly sound travels on cool, clear nights out here."

The lieutenant continued, "There will be four teams. Each team will have a team leader. Each of you will be assigned to a team."

He then named three sergeants as team leaders, and assigned each agent to a team. The fourth team was our helicopter group. Two agents familiar with helicopter operations were assigned to the helicopter with Bill and me.

Montana knew his business. "Now listen carefully," he emphasized. "We will have only one chance to capture the airplane crew and the ground loading crew. When we hit 'em, hit 'em hard and fast. The bad guys are expected to have lots of firearms, so be ready. All teams will act together and exactly at the same time. I don't want to see that airplane taking off into the night sky because one team was late getting there."

The lieutenant paused, briefly drawing the layout of the airstrip and nearby county roads on the chalkboard. He showed us on the chalkboard and with photographs where each team would be positioned.

"Teams One and Two will be the forward arrest teams. You will hike in on foot to the airstrip before dark, take cover in the brush near the strip, and wait. I will be with you. Team One will set up on the east side of the airstrip, and Team Two on the south side.

"Each of you will need a hand-held radio. When you hear my signal to go, move fast. I will also fire a parachute flare. Team One will take down the load truck. Team Two will take down the airplane, assisted by Team Four in the helicopter.

"Team Three will operate out of two vehicles and stay hidden in a concealed position off the county road. If any bad guys try to escape by vehicle, they will have to use the county road. Your team leader will show you where to park your cars where they won't be seen from the road. Your job will be to intercept and stop any bad guys that try to escape by vehicle on the county road."

Montana then looked directly at Bill and me. "Team Four, the helicopter group," he said, "will land before dark in the woods in a place of your choice. Try to land close to the airstrip, but keep in mind the noise level of the helicopter. Our source tells us that when the airplane lines up on the airstrip to land, their ground crew will light up the flares. When I hear the plane coming in, I will call you. When you are coming in, key on the airstrip flares. They may be the only lights you'll see. I'd like for your helicopter to land in front of the airplane, if possible. The two agents with you will get out and position themselves in front of the airplane. Don't let it take off. If its pilots try to take off, shoot out the two main tires. Our pilots say that if the tires are flat, he can't take off. If you have to shoot, be careful. I don't want any accidents. I'd rather the airplane escape with a load of dope than to accidentally shoot one of our own people."

Speaking now to the entire group, he said, "I'd like each of you to study the photographs here and memorize the airstrip layout. In the dark, it's gonna look different. Besides your weapons, each team member will need water canteens, flashlights, body armor, coats, raid jackets, and two pairs of handcuffs. Any questions?"

There were no questions. All of us were professionals. Each had listened carefully and knew what his job was.

The lieutenant concluded: "It's 5:20 P.M. It'll be dark about 6:30. Each team report to your team leader for any further instructions that he may have. Be at your assigned locations by dark. Good luck, and be careful."

The agents met with their team leaders, then left in a hurry to be at their assigned locations before dark.

I volunteered to fly Helo-101 as pilot-in-command. Bill and I were quickly airborne with our two agents in the rear passenger seats. Arriving near the airstrip, we selected our landing area, which looked, even in the twilight hour, identical to our pre-raid aerial photography.

The area we selected was a small fifty-acre pasture surrounded by trees. We chose this particular landing area because it was at least three miles from the airstrip. From this location we could take off and be over the airstrip in three minutes. It was 6:30 P.M. The plane was due to arrive in about four hours.

As the darkness settled in, so did the cold. We sat in the helicopter with the doors closed. Our body heat was our only source of warmth. Even with our heavy bulletproof vests and coats on, it was uncomfortably cold. I checked the thermometer. It read 35 degrees F.

As we sat and waited, the four of us talked about whatever came to mind, including embellished war stories and jokes—anything to help pass the time and take our minds off the cold. The helicopter seats are not made for pilot comfort. The longer we sat, the harder they got, and the cold made our limbs stiff. We occasionally got out to stand and stretch until the cold forced us back inside. We discussed starting the helicopter engine and turning on the heater, but realized that the noise of the jet turbine engine and whirring of the rotor blades could be heard a long way in the cold night air. We couldn't chance it.

The stars were shining, but it was dark outside. It gave me an eerie feeling. I thought, *We are going into a very dangerous situation. One or several of us could be killed tonight.* I said a silent prayer for God to protect my friends and me tonight. I knew my pilot/partner Bill Isbell had prayed also. I was especially glad that Bill was my partner in those moments.

Eight o'clock. Lieutenant Montana whispered on the radio, "Heads up, guys. The ground loading crew just arrived. There are four bad guys in two pickup trucks. Everybody hold your positions and stay quiet."

Time passed. My watch showed 11:00 P.M. "It's showtime," I said to no one in particular. My adrenaline began to pump. Eleven o'clock passed with no call from the lieutenant. We were ready for action, but were getting antsy.

Time continued to pass slowly. I could hear my watch ticking. One of the agents stifled a sneeze. Talking in whispers, we became pessimistic, deciding that the plane would not come. I thought that maybe someone had tipped them off.

At 1:40 A.M. the lieutenant whispered on the radio, "I hear the airplane. He's close, but I don't see him. He's flying with his lights out. Helo-101, get airborne and head this way. Everybody else hold your positions until I say go. I'll wait until the plane shuts down."

My adrenaline really began pumping then. I quickly started the helicopter. When the rotor blades indicated 100% RPM, I took off. We had to move fast. We climbed to 400 feet above ground. As we were closing on the airstrip, the lieutenant shouted on the radio, "Go, go, go!" As the lieutenant fired the parachute flare, we saw it explode in the sky, then drift slowly downward, casting an eerie light on the ground. The shadows on the ground danced as the flare came down.

I said to Bill, "Shades of Vietnam."

He said, "Yeah, I'm having flashbacks." Marine Bill Isbell had been in night firefights in the jungle.

I lowered the nose of the helicopter for max airspeed. Bill turned on the "Night Sun" searchlight, which lit up the area as bright as day. In its beam we saw a pickup truck bouncing across the pasture at high speed. We didn't pursue it; our job was to secure the airplane.

Flying low on short final approach, I could see the airplane sitting down on the end of the grass strip. It was a twin-engine propeller job. At fifty feet I flared Helo-101's nose up high and hard in order to stop forward motion quickly for the landing. While in the flare position, a narcotics agent ran between the airplane and our helicopter. He fell to the ground as if he had been shot. I shouted to the agents in the back seat, "We got a man down!" I leveled the chopper for landing. The skids touched the ground, and we slid fifteen feet before stopping thirty yards in front and to the side of the airplane. It looked strange and ominous, sitting there in the middle of nowhere. I kept the engine on.

As soon as we stopped, the guys in our back seat flung the rear doors open, jumped out, and ran to the airplane. As one of them stopped to check the agent on the ground, the downed agent got up, dusted himself off as if he was oblivious to the danger around him, then walked briskly to the rear of the airplane wing.

I saw a propeller start to turn. I lifted up to a twenty-foot hover and moved to within twenty feet of the airplane. As the wind from the rotor blades rocked the wings of the airplane, Bill shone the powerful searchlight straight into the windshield of the airplane, blinding the pilots. There was confusion and dismay in that cockpit.

Meanwhile, our two agents had taken up positions in front and to each side of the airplane cockpit, pointing their pistols at the two pilots, who stopped trying to start their engines. One of the narc agents said on the radio, "We have the airplane secured."

The lieutenant said, "Helo-101, try to locate the pickup that ran off across the pasture."

"Ten-four . . . how's the agent that went down?"

"He's okay," said the lieutenant, "the rotor blast knocked him down."

As I lifted off straight up and then moved forward to gain airspeed, I monitored the Torque Gauge and Turbine Outlet Temperature Gauge (TOT) on the instrument panel. I was using full power as I kept the Torque and TOT needle pointing to the top of the green line on the gauge.

Suddenly, without warning, the instrument panel lights went off. Everything was dark except for the searchlight that Bill was shining in front of the helicopter. I reduced power a little. I didn't want to over-torque the transmission or over-

After the arrests: 1,500 pounds of bagged marijuana
(under airplane).

temp the engine, which could result in a transmission or engine failure.

"Bill," I shouted, "I can't see the instruments. Get a flash-light—quick—and shine it on the instrument panel. I can't see the gauges!"

I continued to climb higher so I wouldn't have to worry about the trees or small hills. Feeling around in the darkness, Bill searched frantically for the flashlight that we kept between our seats. Leveling the helicopter, I reduced my power setting to cruise power by the sound of the engine. I had thousands of hours in the Bell Jet Ranger; my hearing told me that I had all the instruments operating within the green lines.

Bill found the flashlight and shined it on the instrument panel. I was relieved to see that all the instruments were indeed operating within the normal safe range.

I said, "Look, Bill, they're in the green (normal perimeter). Am I good, or what?"

"Yeah," Bill said, "but it was exciting for a while."

Everything was under control, but the instrument lights were still out.

Circling the field at 400 feet above ground and scanning the tree line, we began searching for the getaway pickup truck. Bill was operating the searchlight with one hand, the flashlight with the other, lighting up the instrument panel. We saw where the tires of the pickup had pressed down the dew-covered grass in the pasture and followed the tracks.

"There it is," said Bill, "in the ditch."

I called the lieutenant on the radio and said, "We found the pickup wrecked, out in a ditch. We don't see anyone in it or around it."

"I'll have a search party over there in a minute," said the lieutenant. "They're probably hiding in the bushes."

To our surprise, the instrument panel lights suddenly came back on. Bill said, "I'm sure glad. Working the flashlight and searchlight at the same time gave me a pretty heavy work-load. It's tough when you have to scratch and don't have a free hand."

In a few minutes the flashlights of the search party twinkled in the bushes and trees below. The lieutenant called us

Narcotics arrest team in front of smugglers' aircraft.
Note bags of marijuana.

and said, "At least one of the bad guys got hurt. There's a small amount of blood in the truck."

After having counted the agonizingly slow minutes waiting for "showtime," the time now seemed to pass quickly. We searched continually until dawn, and after refueling, in the morning sunshine. Unable to locate the escapees, the lieutenant terminated the search in the immediate area at noon. The drug runners had sat out the cold, predawn hours handcuffed and shivering in a narcotics service van. Through interrogation of the arrested suspects, the agents had learned the names of the two escapees. Warrants would be issued for their arrest.

Those arrested were taken to jail at Texarkana. With the search terminated by the lieutenant, I landed on the grass strip to look at the drug airplane and the huge load of marijuana.

Lieutenant Montana greeted us and said, "Men, you did good. Even though two escaped, the mission was successful. We arrested two pilots, two of the ground crew, confiscated the airplane, 1,500 pounds of marijuana, two pickup trucks, and several guns, including four pistols, one shotgun, and one AR-15 military rifle. Not a bad night's work." He continued, "You should have seen that airplane on short final approach to the airstrip. He lined up with the ground flares on the airstrip and came in with lights out. When he was about one hundred feet off the ground, he turned his landing lights on and landed immediately. He only had four flares, two at each end. I thought he was gonna crash for sure. He is one heck of a pilot."

We celebrated our victory by taking pictures of our entire team of officers standing beside the airplane, with 1,500 pounds of marijuana packaged and ready for delivery.

The two who escaped were arrested the next night at their houses. They were both cut and bruised from the truck wreck.

Bill and I felt very proud to have been a part of this dangerous and difficult mission. The warmth of success seemed to dull my memory of that dark cold night in the woods of East Texas where we had caused the air delivery to fail.

At the DPS maintenance shop the next day the mechanic told Bill and I that the problem with the instrument panel lights was due to an electrical short in the wiring. He repaired it, and Bill and I took off for home to get ready for our next adventure.

At this writing Bill heads the Texas Department of Public Safety Aircraft Section as chief pilot, supervising twenty-six pilots and several aircraft. In words from the Old West, Bill Isbell is a good man "to ride the river with."

CHAPTER 12

When seconds and inches counted

When state police helicopter pilots are "on call" but nobody is calling, they do routine catch-up chores, such as cleaning their helicopters. With the winter weather cold and dreary outside, it seemed a good thing for Kenny and me to do. It was two days after Christmas in 1996.

"It's too cold and damp to do a good wash job," Kenny ventured.

"Yes, and a good day to catch the flu," I replied.

Cleaning out nonessential items from under the seats, I reminisced about my early days as a highway patrol trooper. We had a saying then: "Weeks and weeks of boredom, punctuated by moments of sheer terror."

"Well," I mused, "we don't have quite that much boredom." Our supervisor and the emergencies kept us pretty busy. I heard the Amtrak train's whistle in the distance—the track passed near the airport fence line. It wafted my mind even further back—to my boyhood when I would lie in bed listening to a train passing in the night. Only then it was an old steam locomotive, with its lonesome whistle.

"There goes the Amtrak," said Kenny. "Sounds like it's on an important mission."

We finished our cleaning job and walked into the pilot's office. "Quiet today," I remarked.

"Guess the weather's too bad for the crooks today," replied Kenny.

Less than a half-mile away, just outside our base town of Mesquite, Texas, three high school boys were doing what rural Texas boys do when out of school for the Christmas holidays, never mind the weather. Two of them had .22 rifles, and they were walking a wooded area near the railroad tracks, "plinking" at tin cans, rocks, and tree stumps. They got on the track and decided to follow it toward town. They came to a long railroad bridge over the Trinity River. Well onto the bridge, they heard the roar of the Amtrak diesel. Too late to get off!

Leaving rifles behind, the three boys scrambled to the bridge railing. All jumped into the river sixty feet below.

The phone rang in the DPS aircraft office. "You spoke too soon, partner, about nothing happening," I said.

Kenny answered the phone. Watching his face, I saw his jaws tighten, and intensity sparked in his eyes. I understood it. Police pilots understand their partner's facial expressions.

The call was from the Kaufman County sheriff's dispatcher, explaining the dire predicament of the boys. "She said one boy swam out of the river, walked to a house and called for help. One boy is hanging onto the bridge, at water level, and the third boy is missing," said Kenny. "That's just down the road from us!"

"Let's go, it's my turn to fly," I said. We ran into the hangar and quickly moved Helo-101 out onto the helo pad. We climbed in, adjusted our flight helmets, started up and got airborne—all in about eight minutes. As soon as we were barely up we could see the tracks and the bridge; we were there in one minute. We flew over a sheriff's car on the county road about a half-mile from the scene—as close as he could get. He waved and pointed. I circled the bridge, descended to 300 feet above the rushing river, and could see the lad clinging to a support pole in the middle of the river, but under the bridge. It had been raining, and the water was high and looked mean.

Getting even lower for a closer look, I hovered. I could see the fear in the boy's face. He was well under the bridge, hanging on to the pole. He had swum to it after splashing into the river. At about three feet above the swift, swollen river, he had probably climbed as high as his cold and weakened muscles could take him. He looked helpless, with no options. There was no way Kenny could lower the rescue ring where the boy could reach it. I glanced at Kenny and shook my head. "This is not good, Kenny. Call that deputy and tell him we need a fire department rescue unit here fast! Tell them they may be able to reach him from above. Get an ambulance, too."

Kenny made the call. I gained altitude, moved out over the river to circle, and looked for the other boy. I hated to leave the kid under the bridge, as I sensed the despondency he must have felt as we pulled away. I thought about my eleven-year-old grandson Aaron, glad he was safe at home. I circled and banked so Kenny could get better viewing from his side. Then, banking on my side, I looked for a bobbing head or body, and checked the brushy riverbanks. I then repeated the maneuver.

The fire department rescue team soon arrived, followed by an ambulance. The guys scrambled for their rescue gear, throwing it on their backs and running down the tracks to the bridge. The nice thing about helicopter rescue flying is that we usually have a bird's-eye view of everything. Only, in this situation, watching it all from the air, I felt helpless and wished I could do more. The firemen tied their rope to the bridge and one began rappelling down toward the boy. I felt a sense of pride for the firemen. I knew some were probably rookies and some would be young, but they knew what they were doing.

Moving closer with my hover, I saw that they had him. I exhaled a slow breath of relief, and realized how tense I had been. They began lifting him hand over hand, up toward the bridge. One of the firemen carried a sheriff's radio and we were on the frequency. "DPS pilot, the boy is suffering from extreme hypothermia and needs immediate medical attention."

I replied, "Carry him to the south end of the bridge. We'll get him."

I could see the embankment dropped sharply about fifteen feet down from the railroad tracks there. *No go, there,* I thought. Kenny's eyes were on my face and I knew he was waiting on me for a plan.

"Partner, with God's help, we're gonna save this boy's life. We gotta get him. He'll die fast if he isn't warmed quickly. I'm gonna land one skid on the end of a railroad tie and hold the other skid in the air . . . keep the ship level so they can load the boy in the back seat."

"Go for it," said Kenny.

Good partner, I thought. *Steady as a rock.* What if he had wanted to debate the plan? There was no time for discussion. Precious seconds on the clock were ticking away. I knew he trusted me. That's the way law officer partners are. They back each other's decisions.

Carefully descending, watching my distance from the end of the bridge, I unlatched my door for better visibility. The door swung open. Leaning out and watching that one railroad tie I wanted, I closed the distance. The force of my whirring blades was whipping weeds and scattering wet dirt and railway track gravel. The uneven track embankment disturbed the air under my rotor blades. Danger! It would cause my helicopter to be unstable in the final touchdown.

"Easy," I told myself, "don't grip the cyclic control stick, just maintain light finger and wrist control! Relax—wiggle your toes." I had only one foot from the edge of the wooden tie to the steel track. The approaching feet became inches. The twelve inches looked tiny, but I knew I could do it. "Easy, easy," I repeated to myself, "keep it level. Steady on the controls." I knew that several firemen, one shivering boy, and one deputy sheriff were watching with bated breath.

Contact! I could feel the skid on the railroad tie. I was on it. "Steady, steady," I whispered to myself. "Keep it level, keep it steady." A fireman opened the back door, and with Kenny's assistance, lifted the boy in and crawled in after him. With the doors shut, we lifted off. The firemen below gave me the thumbs-up signal, and I returned it.

Relaxing just a little, I looked at Kenny and winked. Kenny looked at me, placed his hands together in a symbol of prayer, and smirked. The gesture, the smirk, said it all. Yeah, law officers do that stuff. Especially young grandfathers. This one believes in divine help.

I looked back at the boy, huddling with the fireman, wearing the fireman's coat. I knew he was soaking wet under it. His skin looked blue and he was shaking badly. He was obviously in shock.

I called the deputy on the radio: "We're landing on the road near your car. This boy needs to get warm immediately. Have the ambulance ready."

"Ten-four, DPS."

I landed, and opened the doors. The EMS technicians loaded the boy into the ambulance and quickly covered him with blankets and drove away.

After the tense ordeal, Kenny and I needed to relax for a few seconds. I cut the engine, then we got out as five Dallas County rescue firemen and Kaufman County sheriff's deputies approached.

"Super job, DPS," said one.

"Thanks—you, too," we said. "Which one of you rappelled on that rope? That was a great job!"

"Me," said one, grinning and shaking my hand.

"Well," I said, "we've gotta find the other boy." There was no time for praising each other, and we all knew it. There was still a boy missing, either in the water, or somewhere in shock.

Game warden's boat shows where drowned boy's body was found.

"We'll walk the riverbanks," they said.

Getting airborne again, we flew up and down the river, which still looked angry. Texas game warden guys arrived in two boats and began a methodical river search. Circling at low level, then a little higher, we searched for two hours. We saw no struggling third boy. With darkness approaching, we headed home. We hated to quit. As long as there is a chance, we always hate to quit.

We patrolled the river for the next three weeks. One sunny day the game wardens found his body wedged in weeds and logs against the shoreline, about one-half mile downriver from the bridge. The river had decided to give up the boy's body.

A holiday afternoon adventure by three young boys had resulted in tragedy. A father and a mother had lost a son; grandparents had lost a grandson.

But we had helped save one. I knew life was precious; I had lost someone, too, in an emergency situation. Kenny and I talked of that on other slow and dreary afternoons. The boy that we rescued recovered and is doing well today. He never wrote me a thank-you note, but that's okay. Maybe he will save someone else's life someday—or develop a cure for cancer.

CHAPTER 13

The unselfish extortionist

Mr. David Smith, a former high-profile political figure of Arlington, Texas, received a chilling phone call at his home on a warm September afternoon. "Your house is being watched," the voice said. "I know where your family is. I want $4,000 by 5:00 p.m. today. If you do not deliver, one of them will be killed. Listen carefully. Here are the instructions."

Then the voice told Mr. Smith to put the money in a paper bag and deliver it to a specific railroad crossing in his city. It struck terror in the heart of Mr. Smith because his eighteen-year-old daughter was away from home shopping, he knew not where. He called the police.

An hour later my phone rang. It was Arlington Detective Sgt. Tom Ingram, whom I knew well through having worked with him. He and his department were on top of the situation, and he briefed me.

"Paul, we're going to need the eyes of an eagle on this one. This may be a hoax, but we're taking it seriously. Mr. Smith is a high-profile man; this scumbag probably figures he's an easy touch for big money. We've sent undercover cars to the house," Tom continued, "but so far they haven't seen anything suspicious. The chief intends to follow the extortionist's instructions and drop the money. Our officers will be hiding near the drop area, watching for someone to pick it up. Mr. Smith will personally take the money bag and leave it where the railroad tracks cross 29th Street. Hopefully we'll catch this guy, but we need aerial help. Can you come?"

"You bet, Tom," I said. "It's four o'clock right now. I'll meet you at the Arlington airport as quickly as I can get there."

"I'll see you there."

It was the kind of assignment I liked. David Smith was a good man. His daughter's life was perhaps in danger. Detective Tom Ingram was one of my favorite people, a veteran officer on a small city police force with limited resources. And a low-life, kidnapper extortionist . . . well, I had deep feelings about those people. I could visualize the mental state of Mr. Smith at this time. I didn't tell Tom, but before his call I was cleaning my chopper and the hangar, writing reports, listening to the police radio, visiting with other officers who stopped by to make small talk . . . it had not been a challenging day. I was glad he called.

I drove to the airport immediately, pushed Helo-101 out of the hangar. Airborne, I flew the little ship at maximum speed. When I set down at Arlington's airport, Detective Tom Ingram was waiting for me. "Thanks for getting here quickly, Paul," Tom said.

"Did my best, Tom. We both know seconds count. Where to?"

"You're right, and not much time before the money drop. Go north two miles. My captain is on the ground near the drop location. He wants us to stay about a mile away so we won't scare the bad guy. He'll radio us soon with further instructions."

"Tom," I said. "Let's make a fly-by over the drop area at high altitude and off to the side so we can familiarize ourselves with the lay of the land and landmarks. We'll stay high enough that it won't attract attention."

"That's good, Paul, but hurry and get into position fast. That guy may have Mr. Smith's daughter somewhere, with intent to kill."

We flew over the money drop area at 3,000 feet above ground, looked down at the designated railroad crossing, then headed west into the wind and began an orbiting pattern about a mile away. That way, I calculated, when Helo-101 was needed, we could get there fast with the wind at our back. I descended to 1,500 feet above ground. There we waited, looking down on a small, isolated creek that curved through a green wooded area.

We had a few moments of appreciation for the pastoral scene below us. The weather was warm, with a clear blue sky. Suddenly, I saw something out of place.

"Look to your left, Tom," I said, as I banked a little. "Is that two bodies I see lying in the bushes?"

"Sure looks like it," said Tom. "Could be murder victims."

"Let's check it out."

I lowered our helicopter's nose, diving toward the ground, leveling off at 100 feet above where the bodies were lying on the creek bank. Suddenly, the two bodies rolled off a blanket and looked up at us, obviously startled. They were naked!

"Uh-oh, Tom," I said, "we just saw something we weren't supposed to see!"

Hovering above them, we laughed with surprise as they scurried around as if to try to decide whether to put on their clothes or cover up with their blanket.

"Love in the afternoon," chuckled Tom. "That's what you get in surveillance work. If they're having an affair, I'll bet they won't be using this rendezvous spot again."

I suddenly thought of Adam and Eve in the Garden of Eden. God hunted for them in their nakedness, called out to them, and they tried to hide. Seems like Eve tried to cover herself with a fig leaf. *Maybe there's a parallel between God's view and mine,* I thought, *which is always from above.*

Well, we had not expected that surprise. Neither had the couple. We had doubtless left them in an emotionally bewildered state of mind. "Hey," I mused, "we're just a couple of policemen trying to do our job."

As I climbed for altitude, I felt a little sneaky about the diversion, but it had been a sincere investigation, and we'd had no word on the radio from Tom's captain. We continued circling and waiting, still a mile away from the money drop area. I thought of Mr. Smith, sweating it out, sitting by his phone. I knew Tom was thinking about the family, too. And I knew the captain and his officers in stakeout positions would be tense and alert. Strange, how we become so conscious of the second hand on our watches in these situations. Once, when I was a highway patrolman on a stakeout, tense and with my handgun drawn, I heard my wristwatch ticking.

The captain's voice came over my radio. "Good news, guys, the daughter has come home, and she's okay," he said. "Hold your positions."

I began to doubt the bad guy was going to show. He was already thirty minutes late. Then, another call from the captain, this time with excitement in his voice. "There's a man walking down the tracks toward the money. Everybody get ready. Stand by . . . stand by . . . he walked past the money, he's walking away . . . he may not be our man . . ."

A pause in the radio voice. Tom and I looked at each other, with Helo-101 still circling. When fast response is needed, you can get there faster if you're already airborne. Then, "Standby! He's turned around, he's walking back to the money. Helo-101, move a little closer to us, but stay high. Don't let him see you."

The captain continued, "He's opening the bag, reaching into it. Now he's leaving the bag, walking away west, down the tracks. Couldn't see if he took the money or not. He's got to be our man. Helo-101, come in closer and watch him. See what he does next. Don't lose him, we're losing sight of him."

I often thought that Helo-101 gave me the view of an eagle. Earthbound people just don't realize how much better you can see when you are up above things. Although still at quite a distance, Tom and I could see the guy walking—just like any hitch-hiker.

"Captain, we have him in our sight," I said.

Flying even closer, we watched the "money grabber" continue walking down the railroad track, about a quarter-mile from the money drop area. Perhaps he heard us or saw us, because he suddenly walked off the tracks down into a ditch into some tall bushes and trees. Detective Ingram called his captain, gave him the location, and said, "Captain, he's now in some undergrowth but I think we're gonna see him as he emerges from it."

"Okay," said the captain, "stand by and keep watching. We're going to check the money bag."

Five minutes later the captain called us again. "Some of the money is missing. Don't know why he didn't take it all. Strange extortionist. I'm sending officers with our K-9 tracking dog into the brush area under you. Hold your position if you think he's still there. We're going to take him down."

"Old Max will get him," Tom smiled. He knew their big shepherd drug dog well.

I lowered Helo-101 to about 500 feet above ground, still believing that the extortionist was in the foliage under us. We saw the officers running along the tracks toward us. Just then they released Max, who dashed along the tracks with his nose to the ground. Almost directly under Helo-101, Max darted into the bushes. In an instant the suspect dashed out with Max hot on his heels. Then he practically ran into the approaching officers with guns drawn. He stopped and put up his hands.

"Well, we got him, Tom," I said.

"Of course," grinned Tom. "We do good work. Especially you—and Max."

Detective Sergeant Ingram told me later that the captured man was the only extortionist involved with the Smith family. And he had been bluffing. He never had the Smith daughter or anybody else. When captured, he had no weapons on him, and $2,000 in his pocket. He had indeed been an unselfish extortionist. Guess he wanted to leave the other $2,000 as a Red Cross donation.

A lot of law enforcement teamwork had helped nail the guy—a wise and experienced Arlington police captain, professional officers on the ground, Tom Ingram and me, and, oh yes, a well-trained police dog.

CHAPTER 14

Flying into a revolution

The Davis Mountains in far West Texas are rugged, with some reaching elevations of 7,000 feet. They are much closer to Mexico than most parts of Texas, and Highway 118, which winds its way through them, takes a motorist into even more rugged mountainous country—the Big Bend National Park area, historically known as the "badlands." In the midst of the Davis Mountains is the little tourist town of Fort Davis, which borders a true early Texas frontier fort used by the U.S. Cavalry in Civil War days and as a defense against Indians.

Little did I know, in the beautiful Texas spring of 1997, that some mean lawbreakers were doing things in those mountains that would draw me and my chopper pilot partner Kenny Meadows into the area, along with the Texas Rangers and scores of other law officers from all over the state. These tough and aggressive people were led by a man named Richard McLaren.

They frightened their neighbors with both verbal and legal battles. They said they were above the law and proclaimed far and wide that they wanted freedom, but denied it to people near them, practically paralyzing this mountain community. Their leader wrote bogus checks and attached illegal liens on the property of others. Calling themselves "The Republic of Texas," they said they did not have to obey existing laws, declared themselves a "new nation," and barricaded themselves in a mountain hideaway with a frightening assortment of weapons, including automatic rifles, machine guns, and bombs.

Their vocal leader, Richard McLaren, hissed at Texas government, its laws, and law officers. He proclaimed that the Lone Star State's government had become illegal when it seceded from the Union in the Civil War.

Things got worse. The self-professed "patriots," who included working people, professional people, and some convicted criminals, began terrorizing their neighbors and others in the county, often walking up and down the mountain roads and standing in neighbors' yards and displaying rifles as if to encourage a confrontation. Their neighbors were afraid to take action, with the exception of one couple, who openly criticized "The Republic of Texas" and its bullying tactics and called the Davis County Sheriff's Office several times. After several incidents, local law enforcement called in state law enforcement. That meant Texas Department of Public Safety (DPS) troopers, the Texas Rangers, the DPS SWAT team, and officers from several other agencies.

McLaren threatened them, proclaiming that DPS troopers and the Rangers were "foreign agents trespassing on enemy soil." In the news media—which he utilized—the situation seemed to have political overtones, but most of the residents of the Davis Mountains and the Fort Davis community called them "just a bunch of bullies with weapons." McLaren and his followers set up their headquarters in an old building high in the mountains, flew a flag over it, and declared the facilities and area the new government seat of "The Republic of Texas." McLaren named himself ambassador of the new "republic."

The revolutionaries evidently decided to take revenge on the couple who had reported them. They reportedly broke into their home, held them at gunpoint, roughed them up, broke the woman's arm, and left them tied. After several hours, the couple managed to free themselves and call the sheriff. They later filed charges, and arrest warrants were prepared. The sheriff knew the revolutionaries' compound was a fortress of weapons, ammunition, and possibly bombs. They even had a small black powder cannon similar to the one used at the

Battle of the Alamo. It could be fired by pouring powder and shot into the barrel and lighting a fuse. It could kill people.

Within twenty-four hours after the sheriff called DPS for help, a small army of officers arrived on the scene. They included state troopers, Texas Rangers, two helicopters, special crimes officers, communication officers, as well as game wardens, sheriffs' deputies, and agents of the Bureau of Alcohol, Tobacco, and Firearms (ATF). The battle lines of this weird revolution were drawn. It was into this volatile scenario that my pilot partner and I would soon arrive in our chopper.

In my years as a state highway patrol trooper I was always on call. As an aircraft state police pilot, it was the same. So it is with almost all law officers today. One can't plan very far ahead. I was packing my fishing and camping gear for a short outing with my son Mike when the Fort Davis call came. I was briefed, told that Kenny and I and Helo-101 were needed and should be prepared for an indefinite period of time away from home. My lieutenant also informed me that the Texas Rangers were in charge of the operation. I looked wistfully at some bass lures I had just bought, then called Kenny. Then I told my wife, and said telephone good-byes to my daughter and grandchildren. I called Mike to cancel the fishing trip. He was disappointed.

Everyone said, "Be careful out there."

Sure, I thought. *ACP, Always Careful, Paul.*

Humming along at 140 miles per hour at about 1,000 feet above the ground on the 460-mile cross-country trip from North Texas to the far western regions of the Davis Mountains —yes, Texas is big—Kenny and I discussed how little we knew about the unusual confrontation we were flying into. We set down at Fort Stockton to refuel, and ate our usual pilots' lunch of crackers and soft drinks. As we neared the mountains, we sighted the little town of Fort Davis at the twilight hour. The trip had taken four hours, twenty minutes. Our designated heliport was an empty horse corral at a ranch in the nearby "boonies."

We shook hands with the ranch owner, a lean middle-ager wearing dirty cowboy boots, faded jeans, and a western hat.

He was a former Border Patrol agent. "Glad to see you, boys," he said. "Things have been pretty tense around here."

The ranch was to be the staging point for helicopters. We reported to a DPS captain at a well-equipped communications bus. He radioed to the Rangers at another location for our instructions. We were to stow our gear at the cowboy bunkhouse, then report to a Texas Ranger lieutenant at Command Post #2 the next morning. The ranch bunkhouse was to be our sleeping quarters for the duration.

The arrival of this army of law officers had made the first day very busy. Fort Davis citizens had never seen so many armed officers since U.S. Cavalry days.

Three command posts (CPs) were established within two miles of the "Republic of Texas Compound," a small one being very near the compound. The second CP was about three-quarters of a mile from the compound and included a self-contained communications bus. The third and largest one, which also contained a communications bus, was located at "our" ranch, which was about two miles away. Commanders had assigned officers to perimeter posts with orders to stop all vehicles, check identities, and watch for any criminal activity.

Long-range photographic equipment was set up on mountaintops, higher than the revolutionaries and looking down on them. Electronic listening devices and movement sensors were also set up very near the compound. The net had already begun to tighten around the revolutionists when we arrived. McLaren's "army" knew they were being surrounded, were very defiant by telephone, but little realized the immensity and sophistication of the forces around them. They let it be known that they were willing to die for their cause and would not surrender.

Dawn in the Davis Mountains was an experience in itself: crisp, cool, and tranquil with the golden sun chinning itself over tall peaks. But there was no time for two state police pilots to dwell on the aesthetics. The Texas Rangers had plans for us. To report to our ranger lieutenant at Command Post #2 (CP2) we had to fly about a mile. Getting airborne and cruising at 800 feet above the ground, we looked down on a beau-

Law enforcement Command Post #2, Davis Mountains.

tiful grape orchard, which seemed out of place in this arid country, and also scattered houses that seemed empty.

"Probably vacation homes," surmised Kenny.

CP2 had a military look: rows of tents, a communications bus, Texas flag popping in the wind. I thought of early Texas frontier days, when ranger outposts and activities were the Texas settlers' main defense against Comanches and Kiowas who didn't take kindly to advancing homesteaders and ranchers. An improvised landing area had been cleared of brush and rocks.

"Look, Kenny," I said. "They got us lights on this 'frontier' heliport! And we even have a fuel truck."

"Great," said my partner, without enthusiasm, "but do they really think we're gonna fly in these mountains after dark?"

I circled one mountain and approached the heliport cautiously down a steep valley. Obviously, to take off we would have to climb out of the same valley. As our 4,300-pound little ship settled into the pad I pensively thought: high altitude, thin air, tricky winds. Taking off and landing was going to require our best, and there was no place to make an emergency landing.

The Texas Ranger lieutenant greeted us warmly, and quickly began briefing us. He showed us a map of the areas, with marks on it. A narrow road through a canyon climbed high to the "Republic of Texas" stronghold. It was the only ground access to the fortress. There were tall mountains on both sides of the canyon.

"Men, we need you to fly our people and their equipment to different locations around their compound. I must warn you. They have machine guns, sniper rifles, high explosives, and a cannon. They are serious, dangerous, appear ready to fight. They have bunkers scattered on the mountain side. I want you to keep a respectful distance from their compound— don't provoke or escalate anything. They have armed guards at their main entrance gate. Also, we'll need you as an aerial platform for surveillance."

Kenny said, "Did you say machine guns, Lieutenant?"

"Yes, machine guns." The Ranger continued. "We have them surrounded with SWAT team units in high places with night-vision binoculars and scopes. Our revolutionaries aren't going anywhere."

His briefing reminded me of the siege of the Alamo: complete encirclement. Kenny and I were getting pretty focused on the situation. I requested permission to make an exploratory flight just to get the "lay of the land" and locate potential danger points.

"Okay," said the Ranger, "but keep your distance from them. And by the way, there's a good supply of rattlesnakes out here."

Funny, how dangerous and stressful situations make you think of people and things you love. I thought of my wife, Dolores. I suddenly missed her terribly, and I thought of my old father on our farm in East Texas, and how he warned me about rattlesnakes when, as an eight-year-old, I took a .22 rifle across plowed fields and into the woods.

"Republic of Texas" headquarters. Note cannon in foreground.

Then it was time for takeoff: first mission into what looked like a real revolution. *Stop the nostalgia, Paul,* I told myself. *Do your job and fly.*

The day was bright with the blue skies of Texas as we got airborne. From a mile away we could see the compound. It didn't appear to be much—just a ramshackle building on a mountain. It looked peaceful enough. Then we saw the small cannon at the compound entrance, pointing toward the entry gate. Two tiny figures—guards with rifles, no doubt, were standing at the gates. I took two slow, wide circles around the dangerous mountaintop. Kenny spotted a couple of our SWAT observers high on nearby mountaintops, nudged me, and pointed. Then I headed back.

A word about DPS SWAT officers. The words "Special Weapons and Tactics" don't really convey the intense expertise of these officers. I can testify that they are heavily armed combat warriors with the latest weaponry, ready for battle. They are elite people carefully chosen from the ranks of Texas Department of Public Safety services, ranging from highway patrol, narcotics service, white-collar crime officers, and others. Like the Marines, a medic is on the team. They are called into public safety situations where lives are threatened, and where negotiations have seemingly failed. Their goal, however, is to save lives, not to kill people. They are specially trained for dangerous confrontations and hostage situations, come ready to shoot, but try not to shoot.

By now we knew they were positioned on mountaintops in two-man teams. It was our job to shuttle them on and off their posts in shifts, and also supply them with food and other needs.

Meanwhile, another DPS helicopter had arrived, flown by a fellow DPS pilot named John Brannon. He had already flown a long "supply" mission to the mountainsides. When we landed and chatted with him, we asked him if there were any landing places upon the high places. "Only one," he answered, "and it's tight." We soon learned what he meant.

Our first mission was to take food and water to a SWAT outpost. Both choppers would be used. We loaded them up with MREs (meals ready to eat) and water cans, removing our doors to lighten our loads. It was Kenny's turn as pilot in command. John Brannon took off first in his Bell Jet Ranger, leading the way to our unknown landing area. We followed in our larger Aerospatiale ASTAR. He soon called us on the radio. "See that small clearing in the trees on the edge of the mountain?" he said. "That's it. Watch out for rocks."

"Are you kidding, John?" I joked. "That looks like a fly on the backside of a longhorn steer. We'll watch and learn."

We watched as John went in, hovered, and set his chopper down gently, then unloaded. Nice job. From our altitude it looked like a tiny chip. "Looks tight, Paul," said Kenny, who was often philosophical. "But ours is not to reason why, ours is but to do or die. If it's too tight, I'll abort."

We circled until John unloaded his supplies and lifted off. Then it was our turn. Kenny flew the same approach, skimming trees, slowly raising the nose of the helicopter (flaring) to

Rugged mountaintop, typical of officers' area of operations.
Note helicopter shadow.

slow us down, and stopping in a hover at about 20-feet altitude. The rotor blades barely cleared the trees.

"Kenny," I said, leaning out and looking, "we have about ten feet clearance from the rotor blade. Watch the big rocks in front. And there are little rocks hidden in the grass in front of the skids. Stop when I tell you, and I'll watch the tail rotor area. Man, Kenny, that's close!"

It was precision flying, and dangerous. One step, one miscalculation, and we were cracked up and hurt and stranded in the mountains, perhaps for days.

The small cedar bushes near the tail rotor area worried me. I warned Kenny about them, told him to move forward two feet. He did, and landed. We were in the only landing zone. If the engine failed to start, well . . .

With the rotor blades turning, I got out and checked the tail rotor blade's clearance from the bushes. Too close! All I had to cut with was a pocketknife. I knelt and began cutting. The tail rotor blade was only thirty-six inches from me—I could feel its wind on my face. I finally cut the bush down, giving us needed takeoff clearance.

Suddenly, there were two guys standing there before me. They startled me. The two SWAT warriors looked like jungle fighters in their camouflage suits, face makeup and bandoleers of bullets over their shoulders. I was glad they were on my side. We had made our rendezvous with them safely and on time. They carried AR-15 military rifles and low-slung semi-automatic pistols on their hips, and were wearing bulletproof vests and kneepads. "Anybody on this mountain hungry?" I asked.

"You bet," said one.

"We got tasty MREs in the chopper. Help yourself."

As they unloaded, Kenny and I cut more brush and moved rocks away from the landing area.

"What's it look like up high?" Kenny asked them.

"We see the compound real good," one said. "We can see them moving around. They have rifles, for sure. We need to get this stuff down the mountain. Our other guys out here are getting hungry and thirsty. Thanks, guys. Come back and see us again."

We watched them pick their way slowly and carefully up the rugged slope, loaded down with all they could carry. Like the mountain men of old, they left behind a small cache of food they would come back for later. I knew it got cold up high in the wee hours. These guys would be shivering before dawn. Here was the wartime difference between the "grunts" on the ground and the "fly boys." Suddenly I thought fondly of our little Helo-101, and of hot food and warm beds at the ranch house tonight, never mind cold water in the showers.

Preparing to get back aboard, I paused, momentarily over-whelmed by the beauty of the mountaintop. The mountain wind was moaning through the trees, valley boulders, cacti and thorny bushes. The old rancher had told me that every-thing in the Davis Mountains either scratches you or bites you. We could see for miles, and Kenny sensed I was mesmerized;

I was a mountain man in the eighteenth century, living off the land . . .

"You ready to leave this paradise?" Kenny asked. "We got a revolution to put down."

His voice startled me out of my reverie. "Yeah," I said, "I don't want to fight that mountain lion with my pocketknife."

Looking around furtively, Kenny seemed to get aboard and start the engine rather quickly. I think he believed me about the lion. I never did tell him anything different. Later, I learned that one of our troopers in a sleeping bag on the ground at Command Post #2 roused, saw yellow eyes, and found a baby mountain lion glaring at him.

We took off from our tiny, homemade mountain helipad into a strong wind, and soared over treetops and into blue skies. Quickly we were over another mountaintop and into the valley of our descent. As we closed with the ground at CP2, we stirred up a dust storm with our rotor. We had some down time and slept some, waiting to fly a SWAT team shift relief pair of officers back up to the heights in late afternoon.

Meanwhile, big things were happening in the "revolution." The Rangers had established telephone and radio communications with McLaren, who put forth some strong demands, all the while repeating that Texas state government was illegal. Ranger leadership kept the talk steady, calm, and continuous. After considerable negotiations, McLaren allowed his wife to walk out and surrender. She did, peacefully.

Written messages were exchanged. McLaren sent his out in "diplomatic pouches" at agreed-upon drop points. SWAT team units went out in a GMC Suburban, somewhat nervous, to get the early ones, possibly under the telescopic rifle scopes of the bad guys. Later, efforts were made safer with the arrival of two armored personnel carriers ("Desert Storm" surplus) contributed by an East Texas sheriff. The news coverage on all this was worldwide. They kept DPS' public information officer busy.

A logistical public safety build-up continued, involving several support groups. These included Texas Parks and Wildlife personnel and the Forestry Service, who were concerned about bombs or gunfire setting off forest fires. Also arriving were units of the Texas National Guard, a well-equipped Baptist food van, the Red Cross, and a food kitchen on wheels from the Texas Department of Corrections. Jeff Davis County Sheriff Steve Bailey and his deputies, who had long dealt with the "Republic of Texas" situation, worked hard at helping provide food and blankets. Mobile television news vans were numerous. Some state troopers, including some female officers, slept in vehicles and on the ground, in sleeping bags. Yes, rattlesnakes were encountered.

A wide array of Texas law enforcement had come to ensure public safety and uphold its government and its laws. And three state police helicopter pilots—John Brannon, Kenny Meadows, and Paul Creech—were there to do what they were commissioned to do.

At sundown, loaded with food, water, and two "shift change" SWAT team officers, we climbed out of the valley into a crimson sunset. The valley was already covered by the shadow of a mountain. The SWAT guys were cheerful and ready to go. Crossing over several mountains, we approached our earlier mountaintop landing zone. I said, "Kenny, I thought it would look larger after all the work we did on it."

It didn't. Kenny grinned. From 800 feet it still looked like a fly on a longhorn steer's rump. I eased Helo-101 down, down onto that tiny spot, and before disembarking, one of the SWAT guys seriously rolled his eyes toward me, seemingly awestruck, and said, "Nice landing." I think he was impressed.

The guys got out and struggled off to higher ground with all their weapons and gear. The SWAT twosome being relieved was nowhere to be seen. I looked at my watch, and looked at Kenny. It was getting dark fast. We weren't thrilled about a late takeoff from this dark spot and trying to find our command post in the dark. The sun had dropped below the mountaintops and a pink and gray twilight had settled in. Then, from high above us, here they came—two tired and hungry guys, probably homesick for their wives and kids. Their camouflaged faces were smeared with sweat.

"Glad to see you," we told them.

"Man, we are glad to see you," they answered, with grins.

"Let's get out of here, guys," I said.

I started the engine, rolled in power, and we lifted off. The lift-off in our ASTAR helicopter always gave me a thrill. You got altitude fast, didn't have to get a running start into the wind on a long runway like fixed-wing aircraft. And I knew the difference; I had flown both for many years. Climbing, I thought how beautiful the mountains looked in daylight and how ominous they looked in approaching darkness. The lights of CP2's helopad looked great. As soon as I set us down, the weary SWAT officers disembarked and headed for the lieutenant to make their report.

"Tell him we're putting down for the night at CP1. No more flying for us in these dark mountains tonight!" I shouted.

Departing again for the quick trip to our command post, we settled our little chopper into our makeshift landing pad—the empty horse corral. As we secured Helo-101 for the night, I patted the little ship on the side and said, "Nice flight, baby. You did good." After all, cowboys were known to praise their horses after they brought them safely through mountains or deserts.

We got great news from a trooper. They were serving barbecue at the ranch house! We hurried to it. With all the trimmings, the real Texas barbecue was delicious. Afterwards, as we lay on our bunks with full stomachs but dead tired, I told Kenny, "It ain't home, but it'll do."

No reply. Kenny was snoring. As I dozed, I thought of the SWAT guys staying all night on mountaintops—with one sleeping and one observing the compound hundreds of feet below, with a night-vision scope. I thought of the barbecue I had enjoyed, while they had only the military MREs.

At 2:15 A.M., deep in sleep, we were awakened by a DPS highway patrol captain. "We have information that some of the 'patriots' are driving into the Fort Davis area in two armored vehicles," he said. "They're about an hour away. We need to go up and locate them on the highway. None of our perimeter people have seem them—this may be a hoax, but we need to make sure."

I inwardly groaned. No more night flying in these mountains, we had said. "Captain," I said, "it's dark as pitch out there, and we can't see the mountains in the dark. But we flew the area yesterday and saw no mountains between here and the town. We could fly as far as Fort Davis, but we shouldn't go north of it because of mountains. Kenny, what do you think?"

"Paul, it's awful dark, but as long as we can see town lights, it should be safe."

I could tell the captain was pleased with our positive assessment. We took off into the darkness, the blinking of our tiny night lights appearing rather futile in a world of darkness But we had on our ship a great piece of equipment called "Night Sunlight," which can throw a 3½ million candlepower beam hundreds of feet to the ground, lighting up a large area like sunshine. We utilized it and hummed forward above the highway. The captain sat in the rear seat. At 1,500 feet altitude above the ground and with the town lights of Fort Davis in view, Kenny and I relaxed somewhat.

Nearing the little town, we saw two sets of headlights on the highway, south of town, the direction of the Mexican border. "Maybe that's what we're looking for," I said.

"Maybe," said the captain.

Suddenly, everything went black in front of us and below us. Our powerful searchlight, which Kenny was handling, had swung completely to our rear, lighting up the ground behind us.

"Kenny, what are you doing?" I shouted.

"Nothing," said Kenny. "The light did it by itself. My directional switch is not responding."

I was really flying blind into blackness. We were bucking a strong mountain headwind and getting buffeted. Scary moment number one! Fortunately, I had an auxiliary searchlight switch on my control (cyclic) stick and used it quickly. It corrected the beam. I saw two sets of vehicle headlights up ahead, below me.

"Kenny," I said. "I'm going low over them by spiraling down. I'll try to hold the searchlight on them while you identify them. If I stay over the road we don't have to worry about smacking a mountain. Captain, hang on! I'll be in a very sharp turn."

I had my hands full, acting as both pilot and searchlight

operator. I slowed to 65 MPH, into the wind. As I went down, made my sharp turn over and in front of the cars, I tried to put our searchlight on them. As we turned downward, my airspeed suddenly decreased drastically, from 65 to 15 MPH. We were rapidly descending! The icy fingers of fear tugged at me. To heck with the cars below. Get this ship under control! I knew Kenny was looking at me, tight-lipped. I lowered the nose more to gain airspeed, gave it lots of power, and turned back into the wind. Our faithful little Helo-101 struggled and fought for airspeed and altitude. As we turned in to the wind we regained airspeed and began to climb at 500 feet per minute above the ground. I had lost 1,000 feet during my sixty-second sharp turn!

"Gentlemen," I said, "our tail wind had to be 65 MPH, and I've never flown into anything that strong. It is not safe flying. We're headin' back. Okay, Captain?"

"You won't get any arguments from me."

Kenny, the philosopher, added, "Amen, brother. The cars were probably just a couple of tourists, anyway."

I glanced at the captain. He looked about half sick.

The fierce mountain tailwind helped us back to the ranch in a hurry. Its lights were a welcome sight. It was 4:00 A.M. The wind on the ground was only 20 MPH. What a difference!

We had not accomplished our mission. Our hope was that the ground officers would intercept the incoming vehicles. Reports were that they had already stopped and checked many cars—an important function. Nobody wanted the "Republic of Texas" to get reinforcements from outside. The only result of our flight was that three officers had a hair-raising adventure. I again strengthened my resolve to not fly in the dark in strange mountain country.

Back in our bunks, trying to relax, I said, "Kenny, were you scared?"

"I was drawn up like a cutworm!"

Meantime, the "revolution" continued. Mostly a war of words, but some gunfire, too. There was sporadic rifle fire from the bad guys in scattered mountainside bunkers. Upon hearing these reports, Kenny and I realized we could have been hit by rifle fire on the ground or in the air on at least two

occasions. Making every effort to end the siege without casualties on either side, the Texas Rangers offered McLaren a surrender agreement. It would allow him to sue the state over its
"illegal" origin, and also offered his "Republic of Texas" a full
military surrender ceremony, in which its "soldiers" would lay
down their arms.

An engine oil leak which we discovered the next morning
during our own preflight maintenance inspection brought us a
definite activities change. Our chief pilot and our mechanic
advised us to fly the 400 miles to the Austin DPS Maintenance
Shop for repairs, and afterward to return to our Dallas home
station and await further orders. We made the flight there,
landing often to check the oil level. Mechanics fixed the problem, and thirty-six hours later we had an unexpected reunion
with our wives.

Suddenly, we were spectators watching the "revolution"
on television, rather than flying missions in it. Days passed. I
became anxious to go back. In an office briefing I learned that
a DPS helicopter from Lubbock which had replaced us had
been fired on and had fired back. No casualties.

After five days of uneventful home station duty, orders
came for us to return. We lifted off for the half-day flight,
arriving about sundown. Our Texas Ranger lieutenant again
briefed us: Two "patriots" had slipped out and surrendered.
Negotiations had again failed. The moment of truth was here.
The plan: The SWAT team would advance the next morning on
the compound to serve arrest warrants. Two armored vehicles
would carry them. Our assignment: Fly ahead of them, and
watch for snipers or an ambush.

At sunup the next day, preparing Helo-101 for this apparent all-out mission with a final maintenance check, Kenny
said, "Well, Paul, guess we got here at the magic moment."

"Yeah, I wonder how those 'fortress' guys will react when
they see all this coming?"

The assault force gathered. The armored vehicles warming
up their engines, thirteen SWAT warriors climbing inside,
cumbersome with weaponry and battle gear, Ranger leaders
giving final instructions, our chopper blades whirling. We were
in radio contact with our ground commander. The vehicles

moved out single file on the only road to the compound. We took off and stayed low and close. At every house along the road, the armored vehicles disgorged several SWAT officers, who checked each structure, looking for snipers. We hovered over them, looking for anything that could harm them.

At about one-quarter mile from the compound, we were able to keep a small mountain between us and the compound guns. Without the mountain, and hovering, we would have been an easy target for an expert sniper. The tanks approached the main gate. The two gate guards ran quickly to the junky-looking old "headquarters" building with its "Republic of Texas" flag flying overhead. Minutes passed as the tanks halted at the gates. We hovered. We knew that a loudspeaker voice from a tank was telling the revolutionists to surrender. More minutes passed. Then the tanks rumbled forward, smashing the gate and trees and everything else in their path.

We watched carefully. Nothing more outside. Yes, we were armed in the chopper. Rifle, pistols, shotguns—same weapons as carried by highway patrol troopers.

At the compound the two tanks separated, each moving to opposite sides, still crushing trees and other objects. Again, the order to surrender was shouted. Now the SWAT officers were outside and around the compound, rifles at the ready. McLaren walked out and surrendered, followed by some of his "revolutionaries." SWAT officers went in and got the others still inside. There was no gunfire.

Hovering, Kenny and I watched it all happen below us. Then we were told by radio to leave, in order to provide surveillance over nearby mountains. We knew there were still snipers scattered around the sides of the mountain. We helped in the ground/air search. Some ran, pursued on foot by SWAT officers and by our helicopter. Two evidently made a desperate escape effort. One was wounded by an officer; the other got away. McLaren and his followers were arrested. Later they were tried and convicted.

This "Republic of Texas" revolution failed. But the first Texas Revolution in 1836 succeeded. The Alamo fell, with all defenders killed, but another battle followed that won Texas its independence from Mexico. It formed the *first* Republic of

One of the "Republic of Texas" mountain outposts.

Texas, which lasted nine years, until Texas became a part of the United States. McLaren's revolution—if one could call it that—ended with practically no bloodshed, thanks to the professionalism of many law officers. They and other Texans did well in upholding the state laws and public safety.

Someone has said that wars are started by kings, dictators, presidents and emperors, but they are won by captains, lieutenants, sergeants, corporals, and privates. So it was in the mountains of Fort Davis, Texas. Kenny and I, two sergeant-pilots, were there. We didn't always know the "big picture," because, like many soldiers and pilots, we were busy staying alive and helping others stay alive. We did our jobs, did our best. That's what law officers do when public safety is threatened.

CHAPTER 15

Bad boy in the woods

My numerous years of flying helicopter searches for criminals included the pursuits of many who were extremely hardened, dangerous, and elusive. One of the worst and most elusive was Ralph Davis, who dealt lots of misery to both citizens and law officers.

He grew up in a heavily wooded area near the little community of Bogota, Texas, in Red River County, which is near both the Oklahoma and Louisiana borders. Trees, creeks, hillsides, ditches, secret trails—he knew them all well for many miles around his boyhood home.

A big guy and a loner, he was, according to reports, the "baddest" of the bad. He assaulted people, robbed them, and committed burglaries. He had done prison time, was paroled, then violated parole. When I got called into his pursuit in December of 1994, several felony arrest warrants had been issued for him.

Folks in the county, many of them fearful for their lives, said he was mean as a young boy, and would torture animals. One thing was certain. He was a cunning, expert woodsman and a survivalist. He knew about hidden springs, edible plants, the habits and paths of wild animals. He lived in the woods, would come out and commit crimes, then disappear into them again—all of which was plenty frustrating to the Red River County sheriff and his deputies. They followed many leads and spent many days and nights searching for

Davis. He was seen several times by country folks who knew him, but by the time the sheriff arrived, he had disappeared—into wooded areas where no patrol cars could follow.

The sheriff had contacted Davis' parents, asking for their help. They told him they had not seen their son for months and denied any knowledge of his whereabouts. The sheriff didn't believe them. Then he got a tip that Davis was camping in the woods within walking distance of his parents' home, sleeping in a blue tent. The sheriff promptly arranged a stake-out around the parents' home.

When this did not produce results, the sheriff grew increasingly frustrated, called DPS, and requested helicopter help in trying to locate the blue tent in the woods. That call soon had me airborne in Helo-101 and heading for Bogota. I mused while en route, "It's nearly Christmas, and not so many leaves on the trees. The blue tent should be easy to spot from the air by daylight." Besides, I was a specialist with blue tents. My son Mike and I were veteran campers and owned a blue tent. Maybe this bad boy was in for some bad luck.

I landed at the little Clarksville airport near Bogota on December 22 and picked up a deputy who knew the area. We began the search, making various circles at different altitudes, scanning every area the deputy knew to look. We saw nothing suspicious—no blue tent. We finally gave up. I took the deputy back to the airport and flew home.

Two days later, the bad boy from within the deep woods struck again. A homeowner had returned home, walked into his house, and discovered that his television was turned on and a warm plate of food, half-eaten, was on a table beside a recliner. Christmas presents around the tree had been opened. Someone had made himself at home, enjoyed a Christmas meal in front of the TV set, and had apparently fled out the back door when the homeowner had driven into his driveway. A dirty shirt and pants were lying on the bedroom floor. Clean clothes had been stolen from a closet—and a pistol from a closet shelf.

Ralph Davis didn't leave the owner a Christmas card, but he sure left his trademark. The sheriff had long known Davis was armed—now he had added to his arsenal. He called for my help again.

Upon arriving at the scene, I picked up my deputy/observer and began another search. We had high hopes, but it had been several hours since the break-in and the trail had grown cold. We didn't know which way the burglar had fled, so we flew ever-widening circles in an effort to cover more ground faster. I was encouraged to learn that the sheriff had requested tracking dogs from Coffield Prison at Palestine, and they were on the way. Getting low on fuel, I flew the twenty-six miles to Paris for jet fuel and returned to the search area. The dog team had arrived. I landed beside the house to meet with the dog team handler. Prison trustees were saddling horses. Tied to a horse trailer were eight bloodhounds, ready to go.

I was extremely pleased to see that the dog handler was my old friend, Sgt. Charlie Sparkman. I'd worked with him before, with about a 95% success rate. We shook hands and chatted a brief moment about the situation and the "bad boy of the woods." Sparkman was an expert horseman, dog handler, and woodsman. He had trained his dogs himself and cared for them as if they were his own children. He knew each dog's capabilities. A few years earlier an escaping convict had cut the throat of one of his dogs, killing him. Sparkman swore that this would never happen again. He had trained his dogs to fight when they caught up with their prey.

I had a growing confidence that the "bad boy" would be "treed" soon, and quietly said to my deputy/observer, "I'll bet we catch our man now, with Sparkman on his trail. He's as crafty in the woods as Davis. And if the dogs get near him, he'd best climb a tree if he values the seat of his pants."

We took off and circled above the house at 400 feet for a few moments and watched Sparkman below as he released his dogs and mounted his horse. The dogs were excited and running in small circles as Sparkman rode to the rear of the house. Near the back door, the scent hit the dogs, and the dogs hit the trail. Even though the trail was five hours old the experienced dogs had it and were running hard. To them it was a game, but to Sparkman and other officers it was a deadly busi-

Sergeant Sparkman's dog team on the trail for Davis.

ness. Death could be waiting at the end of the trail for Sparkman or his dogs.

Even though a helicopter at slow speed or in a hover is a pretty easy target for a rifleman, I always felt safer up above than if I were an officer on the ground. Maybe I was. However, my DPS helicopter had been shot at twice before on other criminal searches.

I circled at 400 feet above and one-fourth mile ahead of the dogs. I hoped to keep Davis from escaping, or at least slow him for Sparkman and the dogs.

The woods were vast and thick. I marveled at the quick way the bloodhounds threaded their way through them. I couldn't hear Sparkman shouting to them from behind, but I knew he was.

Suddenly, the dogs came to a shallow creek, stopped, and began milling around on both sides. I had seen this behavior before. They had lost the scent. Davis, the wise woodsman, had fled into the water, which eliminated his scent. It would take valuable time for the dogs to pick it up again.

Davis knew the deep woods, but so did Sparkman. He led his dogs up the creek a short distance, then reversed their direction back another short distance. The maneuver worked. The dogs hit his scent again, where he had left the water. Quickly they were strung out and running fast through the woods on a trail that was hot. Davis was close, and Sparkman knew it. I moved out into my forward position again.

Noting that we had quickly gotten too far ahead of the dogs, I turned, went back and my deputy/observer located them in the woods again. The dogs had stopped and appeared to be rubbing their heads and noses on the ground. We saw Sparkman dismount and begin checking them. He called me on his hand-held radio: "Helo-101, the scumbag gave my dogs a dose of red pepper. I can smell it. He must have poured out a whole can on the trail. My dogs won't be able to smell a thing for hours. This chase is over."

Our hearts sank with disappointment and sympathy for Sparkman and his sneezing, pawing, coughing dogs. All that effort gone for naught, because a cunning outlaw woodsman had apparently outsmarted us. The elusive bad man of the woods had escaped again.

With little chance of capturing him in the vast forest, the sheriff terminated the search. He called me on his hand-held radio. "Thanks for coming again, Sergeant Creech. We'll catch him later. Sooner or later, he'll make a mistake. I just hope we get him before he hurts somebody."

A day later, on December 23, Davis surfaced again. He threatened an attorney about twenty miles from the dog chase area, and at gunpoint took his Suburban station wagon. It was found the next evening, Christmas Eve, at the edge of the woods, only a few miles from the hijacking. Again the sheriff called me. There would be no Christmas with my family, who had already gathered. I knew I had to go. The bad guy was hurting people again, and he might bring death and sorrow to another family . . . maybe on Christmas Day.

I flew to Bogota quickly, again, and picked up my deputy. We were soon airborne, diligently searching the thick woods around the car from a low altitude. My deputy/observer and I had gotten to be real companions by now. There was no sign of life. Discouraged, I called the sheriff on Helo-101's radio and asked him to meet me on the ground. I landed, shut the engine down, and opened my chopper's door as the sheriff walked over to me. He looked discouraged, too.

"Sheriff, this is an exercise in futility," I said. "We'll never catch this guy in these deep woods. He knows what he's doing. We have a helicopter in Austin with an FLIR mounted on it. With your permission, I'd like to call and see if we can get it up here."

"What's a FLIR?" asked the sheriff.

"It's an infrared video camera that can see in the dark. If the camera sees anything warm or hot, it will show up as white on a dark TV screen inside the helicopter cabin. The hotter it is the brighter it will be on the TV screen. You'll be able to tell if it's a man or animal. Since the helicopter will be flying over the woods without a searchlight on, he won't even know we are looking at him."

"Let's do it," said the sheriff with an encouraged expression.

It was late, and it was Christmas Eve. I truly hated calling the headquarters "on-call" pilot in Austin and asking for the FLIR. I knew the pilots were enjoying their Christmas holidays. They would have to fly 300 miles just to get here, and probably wouldn't like me very much for my timing. Trusting that they would understand when I described the situation to them, I made the call on my cell phone, standing beside my chopper, with the sheriff nearby.

DPS Aircraft Safety/Training Officer Richard Nesby answered. With humility, I apologized for the Christmas timing, explained things briefly, told him about "Bad Boy" Davis and the dangers to the local folks. I gave him my GPS latitude and longitude coordinates.

Nesby: "We'll head out immediately. Should be there about 10:00 P.M."

God bless, I thought. *God bless Nesby and God bless the DPS Aircraft Section Pilots.* Not a whimper or even a sarcastic remark from Nesby. Not even a joking reminder that it was

Christmas. It was pure dedication to public safety—all our pilots had it.

Darkness was closing in. A fresh norther had just blown in and the temperature began dropping rapidly. The cold was uncomfortable for us, but ideal for FLIR operations, since it was a heat-seeking device. I was hungry, and Helo-101 was low on fuel. I flew the twenty-six miles to Paris, Texas, refueled, and got the usual pilot's meal from a vending machine— a chocolate bar and a soft drink—and returned to the rendezvous point for the incoming Austin helicopter. While I was gone, deputies and other officers from surrounding areas had kept the search going with patrol cars on the dark country roads.

After landing, the sheriff invited me to sit in his car with him and wait for the Austin helicopter. It was dark as pitch, and the ground was wet from a rain the day before. Soon I heard the whine of the jet turbine engine and the popping of the rotor blades. I asked the sheriff to turn on his overhead emergency light so the pilot could find us. I stepped out of the car, looked up and saw their lights as they circled. They turned on their Night Sun searchlight and suddenly the darkness was gone. I knew they were looking for a landing spot, and called them on my hand-held radio.

"Helo-100, this is Paul. There are no wires here, just an open pasture. Land beside Helo-101."

They landed, shut down and got out, stepping gingerly over small puddles of water. Along with Richard Nesby was DPS pilot Eric Myers. Both were veteran pilots. We had been friends a long time and had worked together often. The usual banter started. "Paul," said Richard, "what are you doing, making us fly 300 miles in the dark? You know we'll pay you back for this."

"I wanted to wish you a Merry Christmas personally," I countered. "Plus, the sheriff wanted two helicopters and the best pilots here tonight. I told him the best was already here, so he told me to send number two and three."

They moaned at that, and Eric snickered. Good guys. The kind you'd want for a wing man in aerial combat. I introduced them to the sheriff, who briefed them on the details of our search. He also expressed his own concern that Davis was dangerous and capable of hurting or killing someone. Richard and Eric opted to relax and stretch a few minutes after their long flight. Our thoughtful sheriff produced a thermos jug of coffee.

Richard was concerned about all the water puddles on the ground. "Due to the heat of the day," he pointed out, "the water on the ground stays warm longer than the ground around it. We'll be picking up a lot of heat signatures from the water, but we'll do the best we can."

It was time to try it. I climbed into Helo-100 to observe. Richard would do the flying, and Eric would operate our heat-seeking camera, the FLIR. Airborne at 400 feet above the thick woods, we searched in ever-widening circles. Evidently there were little pools and puddles of water everywhere, for "hot" targets were showing all over the dark screen, little white blotches everywhere.

"Guys, this is not gonna work," said Eric. "Too much water down there."

Richard and I agreed. Soon Richard landed Helo-100 near the sheriff's car, and we reported our bad luck. I felt sorry for the sheriff. The poor guy had pursued the bad man of the woods so often, but he was plucky. He had grown accustomed to disappointment. "Well, I guess we have lost him again. We'll get him yet. Maybe he'll show up again somewhere and we'll try again. Thank you, fellas. Go on home to your families. It's Christmas."

To me he said, "I'll call if we jump him again. Hope we're not wearing you and that helicopter out."

"I'll come back if you need me, Sheriff."

I shook hands with Richard and Eric and thanked them profusely for coming at Christmas. They took off for Austin, and I took off for home base. I was weary, and it was way past my bedtime. I hoped I didn't collide with Santa's reindeer and sleigh.

We had a late Christmas at my home, but it was a good one.

On December 27 the sheriff of Red River County called again. "Sergeant Creech, Davis was seen yesterday trying to break into a car at a home. He realized he had been spotted and ran into the woods. We're searching for him again. Can you help us?"

These fruitless chopper trips were getting old with me, but I said, "I'll be there as soon as I can, Sheriff." I was soon airborne to Bogota.

Texas Ranger Roger Lough had joined the search. A seasoned officer and friend of mine, we had flown and worked together many times on criminal cases, often with good results. He and a deputy sheriff were driving down a road through the woods when they saw an old travel-trailer at a deer hunter's camp. It sat on the edge of a cow pasture that adjoined thick woods. There were no hunters' vehicles around.

The Rangers and deputy drove up to the trailer, got out, and approached it. Ranger Lough reached out to knock on the door. Shots rang out from inside! Bullets flew through the walls of the trailer, narrowly missing Lough. He scrambled for cover toward the rear of the trailer, with the deputy right behind him.

The bad guy inside saw them running past a window and continued firing through the walls toward them. He had lots of fire power. When the ranger and the deputy reached the rear of the trailer, they fired blindly into the rear trailer wall. The shooting from inside the trailer ceased. Things became dead quiet. Not a sound came from within the trailer. The Ranger's ears were ringing from the sound of the gunfire, but he and the deputy remained poised and ready to protect themselves. They knew it had to be Davis inside.

Ranger Lough shouted for him to come out with his hands up. There was no answer.

Lough and the deputy ran back to their car parked nearby and called the sheriff on the radio, telling him what had happened and giving their location. Soon several deputy sheriff and highway patrol cars converged on the scene. The officers took protective positions, kneeling behind parked police cars. Ranger Lough shouted several more times for him to come out. The trailer remained quiet.

All this was happening as I was flying toward Bogota. I heard the Ranger's radio report to the sheriff on my radio. I called the sheriff and asked for explicit directions to the shooting site. The area was unfamiliar to me, and I wanted to reach it as soon as possible. I didn't want Davis to escape again. The sheriff gave me good directions, and I was soon circling overhead at 500 feet above the old trailer.

Ranger Lough called, on his hand-held radio: "Paul, the shooter is still inside, and we're getting no response to my shouts to surrender. Stay up there, help us watch!"

I continued to circle. So there it was. Officers and patrol cars in strategic barricade positions around a battered and shot-up trailer, a Texas Ranger and his deputy companion waiting tensely with pistol barrels hot and at the ready, no action, and deadly silence from within. A determined shooter waited inside. From above, it appeared to be a stand-off. I wondered what the guy inside thought he would prove by not coming out. There was no way he was going to get away. Surely he could realize this.

The sheriff called me and asked me to land. He needed to talk to me. I landed about 100 yards from the trailer, using a grove of trees as cover from gunfire. I thought, *Why would he want to lose his aerial observation at this time?*

"Paul, I've called for the Paris Police Department SWAT team to come and help," the sheriff explained. "They should be here in about an hour. This bad boy is not going anywhere. We have him surrounded. He may be dead, because we haven't heard any sound from inside. But I'm not taking any chances. I've also called for an ambulance."

He continued, "When the SWAT team arrives and is ready to move in, I'd like to go up with you so I will have a better view of what's happening!"

"Whatever you need, Sheriff," I said. "That's fine with me."

This was the sheriff's county. He was in charge of this operation.

I stayed on the ground and waited, close to Helo-101. Everything was quiet except for an occasional shout from the Ranger for Davis to surrender. In the humid air the acrid smell of gunpowder drifted my way. *Small wonder,* I thought. *A small war has already been fought here, lots of rounds fired.*

The SWAT team arrived in a large van and stepped out near me. They looked sharp, dressed in black helmets, black combat uniforms with the words "POLICE - SWAT" on front and back of jackets, which covered their bulletproof vests. They had gas masks strapped to their belts, low-slung pistols on their upper legs, and carried shotguns and rifles. Some carried tear gas guns. They looked like they meant business.

The SWAT commander talked briefly to the sheriff, who then walked toward me and Helo-101. "Ready to go?" he asked.

"Yes, sir."

We boarded and took off, as the SWAT team dispersed into strategic positions behind the parked cars of other officers near the trailer. The sheriff and I watched this grim scenario from about 300 feet above it. A last plea was given by megaphone for anyone inside to come out and surrender. There was no response. We saw the SWAT guys don their gas masks.

From above I saw three SWAT officers with tear gas guns fire two volleys each of tear gas projectiles at the trailer. The projectiles pierced the windows. Some missed the windows and stuck in the side of the aluminum trailer, emitting a white cloud of tear gas harmlessly into the air. I saw clouds of tear gas billowing out from the windows.

With the precision of a well-oiled machine, the SWAT team quickly moved on the trailer and, in a split second, was standing beside the outside walls. Instantly, one officer flung the trailer door open and threw in a concussion grenade, immediately followed by two more. Above them, still at 300 feet, I clearly heard the *"boom-boom-boom"* of the concussion grenades and saw smoke boiling from the opened door and windows. Without a pause three SWAT officers entered the trailer. We watched and waited anxiously, as did all other ground officers. In a few minutes they came out, and everyone took off their gas masks. A relaxed atmosphere washed over the crowd of officers. It was finally over.

The sheriff and I landed and walked over to the trailer, where all the officers had gathered. We learned that Davis was dead inside by a self-inflicted gunshot wound to the head. A few bullets had hit him when the Ranger and deputy had fired defensively and blindly through the rear trailer wall. The coroner's examination later indicated that although those bullets were lethal, Davis was already dead by his own hand by placing the pistol to his head and pulling the trigger.

It was the end of the line for the bad boy of the dark woods. The dangerous, cunning survivalist—who had evaded the sheriff often, escaped Sergeant Sparkman with his tracking dogs, was lucky on the night we had the infrared camera and had "magically" disappeared into the woods so many times—was finished. The bad boy who had played rough with everybody found out that law officers could play rough, too. He had not survived a shootout with a Texas Ranger and a deputy.

As the ambulance carried his body away, I wondered how a man grows up to be so bad. The loss of human life is always tragic, but Ralph Davis made the decision that led to his death. He was given many chances to surrender and plead his case in a court of law. Two days after Christmas, 1994, he reaped the rewards of what he had sown over many years.

And the citizens of Red River County could start the new year without fear of harm or property loss.

CHAPTER 16

Neighborhood watch

Law officers will tell you that thieves, robbers, drug pushers, and other bad folks work Sundays, holidays, and in all kinds of weather. On a cold February day when the north wind was whipping in at 25 mph—the kind of day most people would want to stay indoors near a warm fireplace—thieves were plying their trade by driving around Van Zandt County in East Texas, looking for an easy target. They felt safe in one particular area because few sheriff's deputies patrolled there.

They found what they thought was an easy "take"—a rural farmhouse with apparently nobody at home. After determining that the house was vacant, they broke in and began helping themselves to household appliances and other items. They didn't know that they would have to reckon with the neighborhood watch, where "country" neighbors watch out for each other, just as they do in the city.

At 12:30 P.M. on this cold, dreary day, a neighboring farmer, driving slowly past the house in his pickup truck, noticed "strangers" loading his neighbor's possessions into an old white van. He went home and called the sheriff.

A deputy responded and drove up on the burglars just as they were leaving the house. The bad guys gunned the old van, sprayed gravel and dirt getting back on the paved road, and fled. A hot and lengthy pursuit followed, with the deputy on his radio calling for any officer to help. There was no officer readily available as officers were few and far between in small rural counties in East Texas.

After twenty miles, the chase crossed the county line into Rains County. The burglars, determined not to be caught, turned onto a dirt road, with the deputy hot on their tail. This East Texas dirt road was very dry, and the big old van, with its driver pushing its speed to the maximum, began putting out a cloud of dust behind it. The deputy was soon "dusted" out, unable to see the road clearly, and fell behind. Finally, he lost his quarry completely. But before he lost visibility, he had gotten the van's license number. This made possible an all-points bulletin broadcast to the entire northeast Texas area with the van's license number and description.

Within the hour, Department of Public Safety Trooper Roger Maynard, a good friend of mine, heard the bulletin while on routine patrol in Hopkins County, thirty miles from the scene of the burglary. Keeping a sharp eye out for the van, he soon spotted it parked on the shoulder of State Highway 19. Stopping behind it, he saw the engine had overheated and was smoking, and there was engine oil all over the road. Roger judged that the driver had blown his engine. There was no one around the van, but the cargo area was loaded with TVs, VCRs, microwaves, and other small appliances.

Roger called for assistance. Soon other officers—sheriffs' deputies, a constable, a game warden and another trooper—arrived to help him search the area for the burglars. As they cruised the area, Roger went house to house, asking if anyone had seen the van. Although rural homes are some distance apart, word spread quickly, and Trooper Roger Maynard was a quick beneficiary of the rural "neighborhood watch." Roger talked to a man on his front porch who lived near the location of the abandoned van. The man told Roger that he had driven by the van a "little while ago" and had seen three people—a woman and two men—walking into the woods. The man didn't remember much about their description but said the woman was wearing a purple jacket.

Roger called the officers patrolling in the area and told them what he had learned. The search area was then established as a two-mile area surrounding the woods into which the threesome had reportedly walked. My trooper friend's next call was the one that got me into the situation. He made a request through the DPS dispatcher for our helicopter to assist in the search.

Since my partner Kenny Meadows was gone in the Cessna 210 on another assignment—we both flew the Aerospatiale A-Star helicopter and the Cessna airplane—I would be the only pilot on this mission. It was a short flight from my duty station near Dallas to the Hopkins County area in northeast Texas. I was soon in the area and contacted Trooper Maynard by radio, without landing. He briefed me on details of the burglary and the chase, and said that the van was full of loot. Then he directed me to the van. I was soon circling over it. With no idea as to the direction the burglars had fled, I began my search around the van with ever-widening circles. Using this method I could cover a lot of ground in a hurry.

The strong and persistent winter wind was actually an asset to me. It had stripped trees and bushes of their leaves. I could see almost anything that was out of place in the woods that bracketed the road. As I pulled away from the van, widening my search, the radio crackled. It was Roger. "A highway department truck driver just stopped me and told me that he had been talking to a man who owns a junkyard nearby. The man had told him that he had seen a man and a woman in his junkyard only a few minutes ago. Paul, the junkyard is about six miles south of you on Highway 19."

"Ten-four, Roger. I'm on my way." The word of the search was spreading fast via the neighborhood watch.

I increased speed and reached the junkyard within minutes. It was full of wrecked automobiles and old auto parts. There was nothing moving there, but suddenly I spotted two people about one-fourth mile from the yard, walking down the highway. I flew over them, decreased my speed, lowered Helo-101 to 500 feet above ground, and studied the pair. It was a man and a woman, trudging along with hands in pockets. The man wore only a T-shirt, and the woman wore only a light jacket. I thought, *Strange dress for this cold and windy day . . . the chill factor must be down around 20 degrees . . . the jacket color matches the farmer's description.*

Air-ground pursuit coordinations. Note Helo-101.

I called Roger. "I have two people spotted. I'm over them now. They may be the pair we're looking for."

"Ten-four. I'll be there in a minute."

I continued to circle above the couple as I waited on that familiar black and white patrol car with Roger at the wheel. I continued my surveillance on the pair below, and they never looked up, completely ignoring Helo-101 popping the air above them. They exhibited a sure sign of guilt that I had seen on other criminal searches.

Roger soon arrived and stopped beside the couple. I knew he was watching them carefully as he got out of his patrol car and began talking to them. Everything seemed to be under control, but I took nothing for granted.

I continued circling over Roger, watching like his guardian angel. I was his only back-up. I remembered years past when I was a highway patrolman and made a midnight stop on a lonely country road. There were no back-up officers, and the car I stopped had three people. An officer can feel pretty lonely in that situation.

Still circling, I glanced up and down the highway on the chance that the other fleeing burglar might show himself. About one-fourth mile away I saw a house, with a pickup truck in the driveway and two men standing beside the truck. I turned toward it, drew near, and descended. One man quickly jumped into the truck and sped away in the opposite direction from me at high speed. Turning toward the remaining man in the driveway, I slowly flew over him at about 400 feet. He waved vigorously and pointed toward the pickup truck speeding away. I had a quick decision to make: Should I follow the truck, or go back and safeguard Roger? I was like a hard-pressed football quarterback trying to decide which of his receivers he would throw to. Banking Helo-101 in order to glance back at Roger, I saw that a deputy sheriff had driven up to him, so I knew he was safe. I banked again and went after the truck.

I radioed Roger about what I had just seen. "I'm going after the pickup. That guy may be the second man!"

Just as I increased power for this pursuit, another DPS trooper called me on the radio and asked where the pickup was. "Just north of the junkyard," I answered, "and I'm gaining on him. But go to the first house behind me and talk to the man in the driveway. See what happened there, then call me."

I continued my pursuit. The guy in the pickup had "the pedal to the metal." As I neared him, my second trooper called again. "The man said that the pickup driver took the truck from him at knifepoint. Stay with him, Helo-101, I'm right behind you."

"I've got him in sight. He's not gonna get away," I answered.

I was closing the distance fast. *What a sorry scumbag,* I thought, *putting a knife on a poor hard-working old farmer and taking his truck away from him.* As I flew low and passed over the pickup truck, I hoped that he had heard the "scream of the eagle."

Trooper number one, my friend Roger, called again.

"These two that I have are definitely the other pair. They've confessed. They were ready to give up just to get in my car and warm up."

"Good job, Roger," I said. "I'd like to stop and buy your lunch, but right now I have the other one in sight, and he's running."

Roger replied, "Ten-four. The deputy is on his way to assist you."

"He'd better hurry," I said, "if he's going to catch up with this trooper and me."

My chase was getting close and tense. I was flying low just above and beside the pickup, in plain sight of the driver, who was doing ninety. The trooper was about 200 yards behind and gaining. Suddenly, the pickup peeled off the highway and slid to a stop on the road's shoulder. The driver flung open the door and ran into the adjacent woods. I concentrated hard upon staying with him visually. I was excited and felt the familiar adrenaline surge. I turned and banked as he darted like a deer in and out of brushy thickets and around trees.

I didn't want to take my eyes off him to look for the pursuing trooper, but I was somehow aware that the trooper was now on foot and running hard, maybe a hundred yards behind. I followed the bad guy just above the barren treetops, watching his every move. I surprisingly shouted out loud to myself, "You knife-wielding little bandit, you're not getting away from me!"

He headed toward an old, unpainted abandoned barn at the edge of the trees, running hard. When he got there, he darted into the barn. I hovered above, thinking, *You jerk. Do you really think nobody knows you're in there?*

I called the trooper on his hand-held radio. "He ran into the barn, right under me, and hasn't come out."

"Ten-four," answered the trooper, breathing hard.

As the trooper approached the barn, the burglar came out with his hands held high. From 300 feet above him I "watched over" the trooper as he handcuffed the man, then walked him out to this patrol car. Two deputies were waiting at the car. I called all the other officers and told them that the last burglar was in custody.

Roger called me and said, "Good job, Paul. Thanks for coming. You had sharp eyes to see the pickup incident. Without your help they might have all gotten away."

"It was a fine team effort," I said. "I would have been useless without you guys on the ground to catch 'em, cuff 'em, and stuff 'em. Roger, I thought it was too cold today for burglars to be working."

"Well-l-l," Roger drawled, with a chuckle. "I guess these guys gotta make a living, too."

"*Adios*, Roger," I said. "I'm headin' for the hangar and then home. Keep on being careful out there."

A livin', I thought. What a dumb way to make a living. Doing all that stealing in this miserable cold weather, risking the consequences of getting caught and punished. If burglars would just spend that much time and effort working at an honest job, they'd probably make plenty of money. Maybe they thought they had understandable reasons for their getting into a life of crime, but I didn't have time, nor did I care, to analyze it. My job was to fly police aircraft, help apprehend criminals, protect the lives and property of good citizens like the ones today, and support and protect my brother officers.

I turned toward Dallas to the "going home" popping of the whirring rotor blades. Suddenly, I felt victorious. It had been a good day with three burglars arrested—one was facing an assault with a deadly weapons charge—and recovery of all stolen goods, including the pickup truck.

In baseball, they would say we had hit a bases-loaded home run.

CHAPTER 17

Two for one

Yesterday I had flown all day, searching for stolen cars in a rural area south of Dallas. Cloudy day, short lunch break, two refueling stops, moderate success. A chopper pilot in his fifties should try to walk or exercise a little after a day like that one, but I was so tired I had just crashed on my bed about 11:00 P.M. The phone woke me from a deep sleep, and I do mean *deep,* at 1:15 A.M.

It was the DPS dispatcher. "Good morning, Paul. This is Nolan."

"Nolan," I said, "I knew it was going to be you. You have a knack for calling me between midnight and dawn. Did they train you this way?"

"Yeah, Paul, they did. Listen, the Cook County sheriff is requesting your help in locating a missing woman. She was riding her horse on a ranch yesterday but didn't show up at dark. They believe she is lost, maybe hurt."

Rubbing sleep from my eyes I responded with my usual Paul Creech reply: "Advise the sheriff my estimated time of arrival (ETA) will be about 2:45 A.M., and I'll call him when I get close."

I got a cup of instant coffee going quickly and sipped it as I struggled into my flight suit. I sipped it some more while driving to the airport. It was a calm, warm August night with lots of stars out. I knew that Cook County was about seventy-five miles away and figured that my ETA of 2:45 A.M. was about right. The streets and roads of Mesquite were deserted and so was the airport. All normal people are sleeping now, I mused. But after the hustle, bustle and clatter of yesterday, the quietness was pleasant.

I pushed Helo-101 out of the hangar and gave it a quick preflight check, then took off. Getting airborne and climbing to 900 feet above ground level, with bright stars above me and twinkling lights of little towns drifting by below me, I really felt at peace, and my weariness partially left me. My wife once said I was like the weary and tired comedian who had to drag himself up to the microphone. But when the stage lights went on and he saw the audience in front of him, he became rejuvenated and did his routine like a champion. "That's the way it is with you," Dolores had said. "When you get up there and get lined out, you're transformed."

Guess she was right. The miracle of flight had never failed to lift my spirits. Especially helicopter flight. I wasn't sure I always performed like a champion, but I was going to find that missing woman.

I was flying over three counties en route to Cook County. My 641-HP turbine engine was humming its familiar sweet song to me, and my GPS indicated I would be there in thirty minutes. Although the ground below was mostly open country with thick trees, brush, and cow pastures interspersed with small towns, I marveled at all the light on the ground. The star-lit night helped.

As I approached Cook County I called the sheriff's dispatcher, who told me to meet a Deputy Stephens at the Gainesville airport. I set Helo-101 down there, and found the terminal building dark—everything shut down. That meant nobody here to refuel me until 8:00 A.M. It was 2:35 A.M. I had missed my ETA by five minutes and had used thirty-five minutes of fuel.

Deputy Stephens got out of his car, approached, shook hands with me and climbed in the chopper. "Sergeant Creech," he said, "the lost woman, Christi Baker, is twenty-eight. She keeps her horse at a 3,000-acre ranch fifteen miles north of here, near Moss Hill Lake. Christi is not very familiar with the ranch land; she has only boarded her horse there a short time. She's definitely lost. We just hope the horse didn't throw her or hurt her."

"Sounds as if we must find her fast," I said, "so let's get going. But I'm concerned about my fuel. Due to my fuel burn coming here I'll need to refuel in two hours. Will you call the dispatcher and have her get someone here about 4:30 A.M. to refuel us?"

He called and was told it couldn't be done; the fuel truck was broken down. "We'll have to go to Sherman, then," I said. "It's only twenty minutes away, but it'll cut down our search time by about an hour and a half."

We took off. Seven minutes later we were over the ranch. At 600 feet above ground level, then at 300 feet, I could tell we were over rugged country—ravines, plateaus, areas of thick trees and lots of brush. Hovering, then moving on, hovering, then moving on, I used our powerful Night Sun searchlight diligently. In the darkness we couldn't be sure of ranch boundaries. No woman, no horse. Just a startled small herd of cows.

Stephens told me that sheriff's deputies had searched on foot for the woman all the previous day, quitting at midnight. They were now at home resting, planning to resume the search at daybreak. One deputy was still on the scene, at the ranch, in his car. I mentally saluted this deputy. He was doing his part to find the lady.

I tried to visualize the woman—crumpled, perhaps in a ravine, in agonizing pain from a broken ankle, shivering in the morning chill, her horse gone, possibly suffering from shock. I had been in similar scenarios like it before. Speed in the rescue effort was vital.

I banked Helo-101 in sharp turns, alternating my speeds—then made wider turns, moving the searchlight. My companion strained his eyes, following the light. I looked at my watch, then at my fuel gauge. Time had slipped by.

"Time to go for fuel," I told Deputy Stephens.

I called the deputy on the ground also, told him we were going for fuel. In flight to the Sherman airport I called the sheriff's dispatcher there and asked her to request 4:15 A.M. emergency refueling at their airport. Helo-101 made short work of the thirty miles to Sherman. A lineman was waiting for me when I landed. He looked rather downcast. "I have a problem with my fuel truck, can't pump fuel," he said.

My heart sank. I explained the emergency. "Look," I said. "I understand. But I gotta have fuel. I don't have enough to reach McKinney airport. Can you help me at all? The lost woman may be dying."

He scratched his head, frowning apologetically. "Well," he said, "I might be able to draw a few gallons out of the truck by gravity."

He did it: ten gallons—not much for a chopper, but it would get me to McKinney with a twenty-minute reserve before flameout (engine failure). The deputy and I took off for McKinney. Filling my thirsty little Helo-101 there at 5:25 A.M., I noticed the sky seemed to be growing a little bit light in the east. Forty minutes later, we were back over the ranch and it was daylight. I could see the ground, and deputies were walking and searching.

I got back into circling and hovering. The morning was glorious. A pink sun topped the horizon. We squinted and scanned. At least we could see ground details.

And there she was, on horseback in a slight ravine, waving cheerfully to us.

"Look," I said, "there she is."

I hovered above her. Deputy Stephens waved to her. I called the ground deputies and directed them to her. Soon they saw her and waved. Never saw so much waving. A bunch of lawmen and a pilot, waving at a pretty girl at dawn on a huge Texas ranch. At least I supposed she was pretty. I really couldn't tell at my altitude. *Wow,* I thought, *what a way to start a new day.*

She had been lost—if she truly was lost—about as far away from the ranch as she could have been.

Soon she was following the deputies on horseback as they led her back to the ranch. I spotted a bare level piece of ground and set Helo-101 down for a quick rest. As we stepped out, Deputy Stephens seriously shook my hand and said, "You did a great job."

"Thanks. I guess the lady had a nice moonlight ride. Hope she enjoyed it. Lord, what I wouldn't do for a good cup of coffee—and a couple of scrambled eggs."

"I wish I could provide it," Stephens said. "Cook County sure owes you a breakfast, and the lady ought to buy you a nice dinner."

Weariness was showing on Stephens' face. He probably hadn't had much sleep. Since I'd only had about two hours of sleep, I knew it was showing on my face, too. We said our good-bye and I took off for home base. It was 6:40 A.M. I wondered how many state and county man hours, chopper hours, and fuel gallons—and how many hours of human law officer stamina—were involved in locating one adventurous woman who wandered away from familiar trails on a civilized ranch. Nobody really counts that stuff when they measure it against public safety. It goes with the territory.

En route home I passed over the town of Collinsville, cruising at an altitude of 500 feet above ground level. I saw a vegetable garden in the middle of a thick wooded area. "Strange place for a garden," I mused. Within the last twenty years I had developed a skill for spotting marijuana from the air. The Texas Department of Public Safety had utilized the skill and used me to teach our state narcotics agents, in many classroom hours, how to locate and identify marijuana gardens from 500 feet above them.

As hungry for breakfast and tired as I was, something clicked in my mind. I slowed, circled, and checked the garden carefully. Couldn't see marijuana. I descended to 200 feet.

And there it was. Tall green stalks, pointed leaves.

I maintained my hover over it. Some scumbag was growing it fifty yards from the garden under the canopy of trees. Money in his bank, if he didn't get caught. I radioed the Cook County dispatcher and asked her to send deputies and a DPS narcotics agent. "Tell them to call me when they get close, and I'll lead them to the patch."

DPS aircraft pilots have a mandated "rest" policy. If called out to fly after midnight following an eight-hour work shift, they are only allowed to fly four hours before they must have another eight-hour rest period. Here I was, having flown three hours and forty minutes, searching for a lost woman, and I was sitting on top of enough marijuana to supply all the middle school kids in my hometown. And I was waiting to help other officers make a bust in a scenario that could put me an hour or two over my allotted flying time.

I knew my chief pilot would have a firm conversation with

me about breaking the rules. But right now, I could stop a lot of marijuana from reaching lots of kids. I thought of Aaron, my eight-year-old grandson.

I moved away from the area about 300 yards and continued to hover, watching my fuel. The minutes ticked by. Where were the deputies? There were houses in the area. Possibly, the grower was waiting for me to pull out so he could pull the marijuana. Then, the radio call. They were at a familiar highway intersection. I flew to them and they followed me back to the patch. Still hovering, I talked to them on my radio and pointed out each plant, as they walked around pulling them one by one. It took time. I kept thinking about my chief pilot's reprimand.

Finally, they finished. They got a full pickup truck load. I pulled out for home base and arrived home at 8:00 A.M.

Four days later I learned the big picture on the marijuana bust. Our DPS narcotics agent had learned the name of the owner of the property where the marijuana had been grown. The owner had not been to the property in two years, but said that his son was growing a vegetable garden there. He gave the agent his son's name and address. When the agent arrived at the son's house, the young man was busy throwing his marijuana drying bins in a dumpster behind his house. His father had alerted him. With a consent to search, the DPS agent found lots of incriminating evidence: another ten pounds of marijuana packaged ready to sell, a picture of the grower standing in his marijuana patch beside his plants, and the lad's diary describing in detail the methods he used to grow the marijuana. He arrested the young man, who signed a confession. I had led the officers to a patch with forty-seven marijuana plants with a street value of $28,500.

I wrote a long letter to my chief pilot concerning the lost woman, the marijuana patch, and why I broke the rules of pilot rest. He forgave me and complimented me on a job well done.

It had been a six-hour, two-for-one search, with complications concerning fuel. One lost person found, one criminal arrested. The State didn't give me any extra pay for the double results. But that was okay. I had done my job.

Left:
  Typical marijuana plant.
Below:
  Confiscated marijuana plant.
    Note its height.

*Officer pours
gasoline on
marijuana,
preparing to
burn it.*

CHAPTER 18

Salt Flat and the desert

Ninety miles east of El Paso and fifteen miles south of the New Mexico border is the isolated little town of Salt Flat, which shows up on the Texas map as only a small dot. Desert country prevails all the way from there to El Paso, but about twenty miles north of it are some tall and rugged mountains, which are the "foothills" of the Colorado Rockies. Only one state trooper is stationed there, and it is lonely duty, fit only for an officer who doesn't mind solitude. U.S. 67 passes through the area, but there are not many speeders for him to pursue, as traffic is sparse, and almost nonexistent after midnight.

As with most desert country, the weather is hot by day and cold by night. Strong winds stir up "dust devils"—small whirlwinds on the desert floor—and turbulent winds sweeping off the mountains are treacherous for pilots flying the area in small planes. It's a sort of "Bermuda Triangle." A Department of Public Safety major, for many years a regional commander of many troopers and hundreds of square miles there, told me that his men responded to almost as many light plane crashes in the desert as they did car-truck accidents.

To understand why and how I got sent there on assignment, one must have some understanding of the enormous flow of illegal drugs that is smuggled into Texas from South American countries through Mexico. Millions of dollars are made by the bad guys in illegal narcotics distribution. And when drugs come into the United States from another country, it is very difficult to extradite and get convictions on those responsible for manufacturing and shipping the drugs. The main problem for an illegal drug-smuggling operation is in crossing the Mexican border into Texas without its operatives being arrested or losing their valuable narcotics to the U.S. Border Patrol.

These hard-working officers and also those of the U.S. Customs Service are outmanned, often losing the battle in stopping the dangerous flow which causes so much crime and wrecks so many lives in our country. To stop all the illegal drug trafficking, federal officers would have to be positioned within sight of each other from the Texas border to the California border—hundreds of miles. This mammoth task is impossible.

The smugglers use many methods to get their products into Texas. These include trucks, cars, airplanes, commercial carriers, people on foot, and even donkeys. The North American Free Trade Agreement (NAFTA) increased the flow of eighteen-wheelers from Mexico into Texas by mind-boggling numbers, which has vastly increased opportunities for the smugglers and problems for officers. Sometimes, the drug operations use men on foot, called "mules," to carry their deadly products on their backs, slipping across the Rio Grande, or at other border crossing points into Texas. Usually under cover of darkness, they walk to a transfer point where it is loaded into vehicles or airplanes and transported all over the United States.

Drug-smuggling airplanes are known to use isolated, clandestine airstrips in Texas. The "mules" load the illegal stuff into the airplanes, which are often equipped with illegal extra fuel tanks that enable them to fly anywhere in the country. They often escape detection by U.S. Customs' radar, since they did not come out of Mexico and appear as normal U.S. air traffic.

The smugglers also use another method. Drug-laden aircraft fly fast over the border at night at low altitudes for one or two hundred miles to avoid radar detection.

Before U.S. Customs can intercept, follow, and arrest them on the ground, they land on isolated roads in the desert—and quickly offload into vehicles. Then they take off and fly back across the border into Mexico.

I know a rancher who was out in his Jeep at dawn when he heard motors, and a twin-engine Beechcraft went over him at treetop level. He knew what it was. It had happened before. Many border ranchers are fearful and often arm themselves.

Enter Texas Department of Public Safety Pilot Paul Creech into this scenario. One day the DPS Narcotics Division received reports from local citizens near the tiny town of Salt Flat that airplanes had been landing and taking off during predawn darkness on farm-to-market roads near the town. Our narcotics agents "smelled" drug traffickers. My assignment: Fly the Bell Jet Ranger helicopter to Salt Flat the next morning and land at a military temporary radar site within five miles of the town; bring my camping gear and live in the desert for at least five days; work with the U.S. Army radar operators and DPS Narcotics to help intercept any aircraft coming into Texas from Mexico. When soldiers operating the mobile radar unit spotted a suspect aircraft, I would go airborne with three narcotics agents. Radar operators would guide me.

If the airplane landed on a clandestine airstrip or farm-to-market road in our area, radar unit maximum range being 100 miles, I was to fly in fast and land in front of the parked aircraft to block his takeoff. The three "narcs" would jump out, arrest the pilot and crew, and search the airplane.

I imagined the scene. I would set my little chopper down in the dark, in front of a good-sized airplane manned by a well-armed but nervous desperado "doper" pilot who might run over me in his attempt to escape. He might have a couple of companions with UZI machine guns. Mama didn't tell me there would be nights like this! Well, I was required to report for duty, but I wasn't required to be stupid and make the supreme sacrifice. I knew a couple of tricks. I comforted myself with "Mama didn't raise no fool, either."

The night before departure, I gathered my camping gear together. I used a checklist. Camping out in the desert was not my biggest concern. Camping trips involving fishing, hunting, and hiking had always been a fun thing for my family and me.

Sleeping bag, canteen, extra water jug, hunting knife, matches, flashlight—I had all that stuff. At least, I thought I had all the items, but I had never camped in the desert before. Although I had flown over the Salt Flat area in our fixed-wing aircraft on previous assignments, I had never seen it at ground level. And there would be no sporting goods stores nearby. Along with the camping gear, I packed my police combat gear: AR-15 semiautomatic rifle, .45-caliber pistol, Remington 12-gauge pump shotgun, plenty of "ammo" for all weapons, night-vision goggles, and my bulletproof vest.

Worrisome thoughts plagued me as I packed. I wondered what the assignment had in store for me. It was to be a single pilot operation where two pilots should have been requested. I'd be doing low-level flying in a dark desert-mountainous area, hopefully with a quarter moon for light. I'd have to dodge mountains and land on a highway in the boonies. I could be killed in a firefight. Well, I concluded, any officer who puts on a badge and gun faces these possibilities. I'd had them back when I was on the highway patrol.

This time, the negative thoughts stayed with me as I said good-bye to my wife and kids early the next morning. Leaving for battle, I knew I might not return. I hugged them a little longer than usual, but kept the conversation light and normal. I had never previewed them about my coming dangers. "Boys," I told Kenneth and Mike, "you are the men of the house until I get back. Take care of Mama and your little sister. Also, mow the grass for me, and maybe I'll take you flying when I get home."

At the airport I filled the helicopter baggage area with all the gear, making sure I had plenty of water. Satisfied that I had not forgotten anything, I gave Helo-101 a thorough preflight inspection, starting at its streamlined nose, then moving down the sides. I opened the cowling doors for the engine/ transmission area. No oil leaks, all nuts and bolts okay, no cracks in any metal. The tail rotor looked good, the main rotor blades were fine. One last walk around, checking to make sure all cowling fasteners were closed and locked. It wasn't as if I were going to the Persian Gulf War. But it's something we DPS chopper pilots do.

Then I checked the weather with the FAA Flight Service Station. The forecast: "Severe clear" all the way. That's pilot talk for "a clear day." Finally satisfied, I took off from Dallas on the long, 485-mile journey west.

I would have to make two fuel stops—one in Midland, one at Pecos. Bustling, sprawling Dallas, with its teeming population, congested streets, fast-pace freeways, and green trees and grass, passed quickly beneath me, 1,000 feet below. I felt like I was headed west to the frontier like the pioneers of the Old West, except they traveled in covered wagons pulled by horses, mules and oxen, and it took them six weeks to reach where I was going. My "steed" was a modern Bell Jet Ranger helicopter that cruised at 120 MPH, powered by a jet turbine engine. In it, my assignment would be like stepping back into the time zone of the Old West.

As I watched the rolling country change into flat prairie-type terrain, I knew, as a native Texan, that, with the exception of modern highways and dots on the map called towns, the country had changed little since the Civil War and the Indian wars. Because my refueling stop would be Midland and Pecos, my navigation would be easy: just follow I-20 all the way.

As the terrain below became rather monotonous, my thoughts turned to the powerful, illegal drug traffic coming into our country, so destructive to the lives of our youth. Recalling my briefing, I remembered an earlier experience, years back. I was flying with a Texas Ranger near the Big Bend National Park and its border with Mexico. The assignment was to locate cattle that rustlers had stolen from a nearby ranch. We began our aerial search at the ranch. We saw the cattle tracks in the desert sand, headed toward Mexico, and to Big Bend National Park. The rustlers cut a large hole in a chain-link fence that surrounded the sprawling park, then drove the cattle through, across the river, and into Mexico. Our authority ended there.

At the edge of the Rio Grande, on the Mexico side, we saw a flat-bottomed boat lying on the bank. We also saw, on our side, a clear, narrow trail leading from the river across the huge park, and decided to follow it. The trail headed north to the same chain-link fence where a hole had been cut in it. "For people and donkeys carrying drugs," the Ranger had remarked.

The trail had ended at an isolated asphalt airstrip about eight miles from the park. No hangar, no "windsock." Totally remote. Just a strip on which a small aircraft could land. It was not listed on my sectional chart (aircraft map). This was a drug rendezvous point where the "mules" from Mexico met an airplane from somewhere in the U.S. It was one of my early lessons in how the drug-smuggling plan works. We had lost the cattle, but found a drug rendezvous.

I passed over Abilene, a historic Southwestern city known for its early cattle drives and rugged cowboys. It was one of Texas' first railheads for shipping Texas "beef" northward. I was soon over Midland, where I landed and refueled.

Quickly airborne again after a "pit" stop and a vending machine sandwich, I began passing over flat, sandy ground, and oil fields as far as the eye could see. I saw "dust devils," small miniature twisters composed of dust carried aloft by unstable hot air. Just for fun, I flew through a few of the smaller ones and was rewarded by being bounced around for my bravado. Have I mentioned how much fun it is to fly a modern helicopter? Well, it was fun—still is fun!

Nearing Pecos, I entered the desert country of the Southwest—sparse terrain below, hot dry sand with only cactus and a few small desert plants. Although I had enough fuel to reach Salt Flat, I wouldn't have enough to fly missions, so I followed my plan, landed at Pecos, and fueled up. It was a sun-swept, wind-blown little town with a lot of early West history. I stirred up lots of dust as I took off, and began navigating by my aircraft VOR (homing device) and dead reckoning, using geographical fixes. At 500 feet above ground I could see the Davis Mountains to my left and ahead on my flight path, the Delaware Mountains. The latter reached 5,722 feet above sea level and 1,280 feet above the desert floor. I would have to climb 1,000 feet to cross.

These small mountains are the southern end of the Colorado Rockies, extending through the rugged Big Bend National Park and reaching into Mexico. A few miles west of the Delawares was Salt Flat. The name didn't sound very hospitable. But it, too, had its history. Near the town of Salt Flat is a large body of shallow salt water. Early settlers extracted the salt from the water and sold it. Then a small community sprang up on the shoreline.

I crossed the Delaware range at low altitude. I was awed by the stark and rugged peaks, very rocky. From my altitude I saw desert ahead of me and behind me, and the rugged mountains below me—not a good place to have engine failure. No airplane pilot going cross-country at much higher altitude could see and appreciate the breathtaking beauty I beheld. A few miles to my right I saw the Guadalupe Mountains, and El Capitan Peak (Spanish for "The Captain"), the tallest mountain in Texas at 8,750 feet above sea level and 4,440 above the desert floor.

Looking at the majestic El Capitan, I felt drawn to it like a moth to a candle flame. I was ahead of my trip timetable, so I nudged Helo-101 toward it. The drug smugglers could wait; my curiosity had to be fed. From an altitude of 1,000 feet above the desert, I climbed at 500 feet per minute and cleared El Capitan's mighty crest. An awesome feat for a helicopter, and an awesome sight for a helicopter pilot! I felt halfway to Heaven.

Circling over El Capitan, I suddenly could not believe what I was seeing. In its valleys were lots of green trees, and among rocks and boulders was natural running water, a crystal-clear flowing creek. I had heard that elk and mule deer flourished here. Now I believed it. It was a true oasis high above the desert. And I was seeing it from above as few had ever seen it.

I hated to leave it, but duty called. There were drug smugglers to be dealt with, and I needed to save my fuel.

With a final salute to this rugged, beautiful mountain, I flew full speed just above the treetops over the mountain's rim, like a young eagle celebrating his first successful flight. In an instant, the earth below me changed from a few feet above El Capitan's crest to 4,440 feet above the desert floor. What a thrill! I lowered my helicopter nose, banked to the west, and began a fifteen-mile descent to the desert and my destination.

I saw the town of Salt Flat in the distance. Soon I was

Creech's flight over Delaware Mountains.
El Capitan mountain is at upper right.

El Capitan, the high part, as seen by Pilot Creech.

Federal/state radar site in the desert. Lots of camouflage!

passing over it—truly a small place, just a couple of service stations, a water tower, a few businesses, and a scattering of houses with no surrounding trees or greenery. Didn't see any covered wagons, but I would have bet some of the residents' ancestors had traveled here in them. And probably a helicopter overflight was a unique event here. I headed for the radar post, calculated to be about five miles north.

Arriving over the location, what I saw at first was . . . nothing. Just a sea of desert sand sprinkled with green creosote plants with a few small mountains. Finally, after three circles I saw three cars among the creosote plants. Descending, I saw the installation: two olive-drab army trucks, a large electric generator, a large tent, and the radar unit—all covered with camouflage netting. Believe me, the camouflage stuff works. Shades of the Persian Gulf War. From a short distance away I had not been able to spot it.

Gratefully, I saw a makeshift but large square heliport, with lights on each corner. Very important, those lights—they would be my beacons when I approached out of the dark desert sky. Good guys, those GIs. They had cleared a section of creosote plants to create it, a functional heliport in the middle of nowhere. It's the kind of teamwork that wins wars. I landed, shut down, got out, and was immediately surrounded by half a dozen soldiers and four DPS narcotics agents. It was great to stand and stretch; it had been a long trip. I shook hands all around.

I knew three of the narcs from having worked with them before. The usual light-hearted banter soon broke out. It nearly always happens when Texas DPS officers get together. DPS people truly are a tight family.

"John," I asked one who had done a hitch in the Marines and was bearded, "Why is it you look so scroungy, when all these soldiers look so sharp? You'd never pass inspection."

"Ain't nobody gonna inspect us out here, Paul, except drug smugglers," he answered with a grin. "Besides, this is the frontier—or hadn't you noticed?"

The soldiers soon picked up on the jokes, too. They were good people, pretty sharp. Their sergeant, a woman named Scott from Pittsburgh, Pennsylvania, appeared efficient and cooperative. I could tell that teamwork would prevail. The radar unit was not working, I was told, but the GIs would have it working soon. I unloaded my gear and stacked it in the tent, which held several army cots, with a spare for me.

The rest of the day was spent discussing our battle plan. Three of the narcs would be my helicopter team, the other would stay on the ground in his car and try to back us up during an airplane takedown or arrest. I requested a volunteer to sit in the copilot seat, wear the night-vision goggles, and keep us from flying into a mountain. I couldn't get the nearby mountains off my mind—they were small but ominous at night. I needed a way to mark them on paper so I would know exactly where they were in the dark. Guesswork would not do.

It suddenly dawned on me. I had an R-NAV in my chopper, as a part of my VOR homing system. With R-NAV, meaning radial navigation, I could accurately mark on paper the distance by radials from the Salt Flat VOR and determine where each mountain was in an instant. With the R-NAV and the night-vision goggles, I felt much safer. I planned to stay a safe distance from the mountains. I had already seen El Capitan up close. It stayed in my mind.

I told my narc volunteer/spotter of my concerns and asked him to make a flight with me in order for me to chart the mountains and log the R-NAV radials. The day was waning, but I calculated we could overfly a twenty-mile radius before dark. I had to watch my fuel consumption. He agreed, and we lifted off. I flew over each mountain and marked its location. Satisfied that I had done all that I could do, we landed. My narc said, "There's sure a lot of desert out there."

"You got that right," I replied, "and in the dark it will look a lot bigger."

At camp, sitting on stools and folding charis, we all watched a magnificent desert sunset as we ate our MREs (meals ready to eat). Somebody had made coffee. Twilight: it was what the old cowboys called "the magic time." I thought, *I cant believe the State of Texas pays me to do this!* As it always does in the desert, darkness came quickly, and the stars popped out, millions of them. During a lull in the conversation, the silence was almost overwhelming. A quarter moon began to chin itself over a distant mountain. It was comforting. With bright stars and that quarter moon, I would be able to see the small mountains without help from the night-vision goggles.

We asked Sergeant Scott if the radar was repaired. "Not yet," she said, disgustedly, "we're still working on it. There's nothing we can do until we get new parts. My people will have them here tomorrow. There's a little motel in Salt Flat. We're going to go there to sleep. I'll leave one man here. Be back at 0800."

The narcs decided for the motel, too, and asked me to go. I declined. I didn't feel comfortable leaving my chopper sitting in the middle of the desert in the dark. Besides, here I was, an experienced camper with all my outdoor gear, in the middle of one of God's great nature scenes. No traffic noises, no sirens, no smog, no television or telephones. I had to stay.

Soldiers and narcs pulled out. My one soldier/guard climbed into a big army truck and curled up in the front seat.

Where Pilot Creech slept under his helicopter.

I began to believe the soldiers didn't like army cots. Deciding that it was too beautiful outside to sleep in a tent, I set up my military cot outside under the rotor blades of Helo-101. It seemed a fitting place. I tucked my pistol under the sleeping bag, in case a vicious coyote or other unknown dangerous desert varmint might attack me. I crawled into the bag, carefully tucking in all strings or anything that might touch the ground. I didn't want any scorpions for sleeping companions!

Lying on the cot and staring straight up, I saw millions of stars, brightest I had ever seen. They seemed to move and even descend toward me. They mesmerized me.

I rolled over, covered my head with the sleeping bag flap, and was soon into the sleep of the weary.

"Flap! Flap! Flap! Flap!" A sudden, fast-syncopated noise awakened me. Startled, I reached for my pistol and took off the safety. Was a rattlesnake striking at my sleeping bag? Then I realized the desert night wind had increased and was blowing a loose corner of my sleeping bag, rapidly striking against my cot frame. I tucked the loose corner under and tried to sleep again. But rattlesnakes stayed in my thoughts.

The noise of the returning vehicles awakened me soon after daylight. The world was bathed in sunlight, and my companions had returned.

The day was like the first day. The radar repair part was not delivered. The narcs and I stood around telling war stories. All of us were veteran officers, so there were plenty of them. With the rising desert heat and no action, boredom set in on us. John, the former Marine, had a suggestion: "Let's go visit the highway patrol trooper who works this desert. He's the only trooper within sixty miles of here, and he's probably lonesome. If nothing else, we can visit the Guadalupe Mountains."

We all agreed and loaded into one car. After a short drive we arrived at the home of Trooper Gaylord Scott, who lived ten miles from Salt Flat. Like the lonesome pioneers of old, he greeted us with enthusiasm. "Honored to have so many DPS guys visit me," was his greeting. What followed was a guided tour by Gaylord through Guadalupe Mountains State Park. It was a beautiful but lonely place, with few tourists. At the park entrance we stopped at a little general store/cafe, and I ate a delicious hamburger—the first hot meal I'd had since leaving home.

Over lunch, with the gigantic El Capitan Mountain looming outside the window, we quizzed our trooper host about his daily life. His answers fascinated us. "Do you have many traffic violations?" we asked.

"Nope," he chuckled. "The fact is, we have few cars on our highway. When I do write a ticket, it's usually for speeding. I'm not sure I remember how to write one for other traffic violations," he said, jokingly. "We don't have stop signs or 'no passing zones' out here."

We then asked, "When you have a physical confrontation with a really bad guy, do you have a deputy or some other officer who you can call for back-up help?"

"Not really. No deputy is stationed here. Even if we had one, it would take him too long to reach me. I have to handle things myself."

I empathized. I, too, had been a lonely highway patrol trooper without nearby officer back-up help, but the life style had been different: more people! I knew the Mounties in Canada had guys in lonely outposts, but their environment was completely different. Scott's patrol area here was unique.

Trooper Scott's sergeant was 100 miles away in El Paso—

a totally different management situation than the city trooper, whose sergeant is just down the hall from him in a modern DPS district office. The only time Scott saw his sergeant, he said, was when he drove to El Paso to deliver reports and pick up supplies. "No supervision," I remarked. "Sounds great to me."

"Well," he said, "I've been here fifteen years and my sergeant knows that I take care of business. They don't want me to leave because no other troopers—or their wives—would transfer out here. They can't send a rookie fresh out of the Training Academy. There'd be nobody to be his break-in (training) partner.

"This desert can get lonesome. The nearest entertainment is in El Paso. It's hard on wives," he continued. "But I'm lucky. My wife loves it here, and so do I. We both enjoy hunting for Indian arrowheads and pottery, and have quite a collection. Before you leave, I'll show it to you."

"Wow," said one of our narcs, a big-city guy. That seemed to say it all, for all of us. No shopping malls, no rock concerts, no major sporting events, no schools or churches.

Another narc: "But what else do you do for fun around here?"

Trooper Scott: "I enjoy riding my motorcycle in the mountains, and also wind-sailing in the desert. I've built a vehicle that looks like a sailboat, except it has wheels. It's broken right now. The wind was too strong one day, and I turned it over at 45 MPH. I thought I had hurt myself pretty bad, but got no broken bones."

Stopping by his home, we met his wife and saw their collection of arrowheads, beads, and other artifacts. It was a fabulous collection, to be envied by any museum curator.

Returning to the radar station in late afternoon, we found the soldiers working on the radar. The repair part had arrived. They hoped to have the radar working that night. I might be flying soon against the smugglers. I decided to take a short walk among the creosote plants, before the action started. Their foliage is oily and when crushed smells just like creosote.

One hundred yards from camp I heard a dreaded sound— the staccato sound of the whirring rattle of a rattlesnake. I froze. Cautiously I moved only my eyeballs. It was twilight.

There he was, coiled up under a creosote bush, about ten
or twelve feet away. I began easing my .45 pistol out of its
holster. Seeing some large rocks three feet away, I picked up
one of the larger ones. My first toss nailed him pretty good.
With an adrenaline high and nervous relief, I pelted him with
more rocks, making sure he was dead. I relaxed and recom-
posed myself. The Texas diamondback rattlesnake can
absolutely unnerve you.

Then, smirking to myself, I decided to have some fun. I
picked up the dead snake—he was a "grandpa"—and quietly
walked back into the campsite where the narcs were all standing together looking at another beautiful sunset. Easing up
behind them, I dropped the rattlesnake behind them, then
stepped abreast of them. We talked a moment. Suddenly I
yelled "Snake!" and jumped away, pointing. If you're a bird
hunter and have seen a covey of quail burst out of ground
cover, you have this picture. Some stumbled, others bumped
into each other trying to get away. As they stopped, looked
back, and saw me standing nearby and grinning, they realized
the snake was dead, and that they had been *had*.

To a man, they fixed fierce stares on me. One playfully
reached for his pistol. I cowered in mock humility, and apologized. Somebody chuckled, and then they all laughed. I knew
the payback would be hell, but how could I have resisted such
an opportunity? Would it be sand in my fuel tank? Anyway, it
broke the boredom.

That night dark clouds moved in. Two hours after sundown it was pitch black, the moon and stars covered by heavy,
overcast clouds. I didn't feel comfortable about flying a helicopter under those conditions. One has to understand about
older pilots. They have an inner small voice that sometimes
whispers warnings to them. The graveyards are full of pilots
who don't listen to their still small voice. Mine said, "Too
dark. Don't fly."

I knew what I had to do. I called the narcs aside and said,
"Guys, it's pitch black up there. My chopper is not FAA
Certified for flying under only instrument conditions. If I fly in
this stuff, I'll be violating FAA rules. I would also be stupid.
You've seen the mountains. If the soldiers' radar spots an air-

craft, don't call on me to fly. I'm not ready to die yet, and don't think any of you are either."

They were experienced narcs, most of whom had flown in helicopters before. They all agreed with me.

It was quite a speech for me, but I continued. "It's nearly midnight. As thick as those clouds are, I don't believe they are going to go away. If they do, however, and the moon comes out, we can fly. If not tonight, we can try it tomorrow night."

That was it. They were good guys who understood, but I didn't want anybody to second-guess my decision.

The next morning I learned that our army guys had used the radar all night without picking up a single aircraft. I supposed that the doper pilots didn't want to fly and try to land in the dark overcast, either. The next night was also no good for flying. Radar had again failed to pick up an "invader" aircraft.

The following day broke bright and sunny. We had two more nights to go. We had been here three nights, but because of radar malfunction and bad weather, we hadn't accomplished anything. Were we going to strike out on the entire mission?

The next night, a Friday and our fourth night, was a clear and beautiful evening, but nothing happened. The army's radar functioned perfectly, but did not spot any aircraft.

The next, and final, evening presented us with a glorious red sunset. After dark, a 15 MPH wind got up and the temperature dropped. We all donned jackets. Soon, another "Comanche moon" peeked over the horizon and began to bathe the desert with a soft glow. It would be a good night to fly. As the soldiers worked the radar, the narcs and I sat in the tent and talked. A soldier ran in. "We got a target! Looks as if he may have come straight out of Mexico. He's flying at 2,000 feet above ground and headed north."

I said, "He's either a doper or a fool flying cross-country in the dark at that altitude. The Guadalupe Mountains are 2,500 feet taller than his flight, and they're only fifteen miles from here. Well, let's go."

The narcs and I ran for the chopper. Faithful little Helo-

101's engine started instantly, and we took off. In the moon-light we could clearly see the desert floor below us and scat-tered small mountains around us. At 1,000 feet above ground I was able to see about forty miles. I could see little towns in the distance, even though they were small and their lights appeared as clusters.

The soldiers working the radar talked to us by radio, giv-ing me headings for intercepting the oncoming aircraft. Soon I saw the airplane's position lights coming in my direction. I needed altitude, climbed, and gave chase. He was really mov-ing it. We couldn't catch him. All I could do was watch him as he put distance between us and disappeared into New Mexico. "Too bad," I murmured.

"Yeah," said one of my narc companions. "He may have been the one we wanted, with a lot of drugs."

There was nothing to do but return to the campsite. I was thirty miles out from it, but soon saw the heliport's landing lights clearly.

The narcotics agents were naturally disappointed. After days and nights of waiting, they had been ready to make a bust. Said one, "Well, we win some, lose some—can't win 'em all."

He was right. I had not always been able to achieve re-sults on missions. I was just a soldier in a war, obeying orders and doing my job. The five-day joint federal/state anti-drug project had been given a fair trial. This assignment was over. The radar and our helicopter were needed elsewhere.

The next morning the Army tent came down, heliport lights were taken in, and everyone packed their gear. I thanked the soldiers for their work and complimented them, then shook hands with the narcs. I took off for the long journey home, and over Salt Flat I did a little circle just so I wouldn't forget what the town looked like.

Humming along toward North Texas, I felt a little sheep-ish. An assignment that I had started with worry and dread had given me much unexpected enjoyment, peace, and some special thrills: the awe-inspiring view of the surprising green world at the top of El Capitan Mountain that few people and few pilots are privileged to see; the mystical beauty of desert sunsets and the silent mysterious nights with millions of stars, which spoke to me of Someone greater than man; and the great companionship I had enjoyed with the narcotics officers. What a paid vacation! Someday I will go back to El Capitan and the desert and take my grandchildren, that I may share their mysteries and beauty.

Five hours later, coming in over Dallas, I viewed the city below with new appreciation for its ample greenery and many trees. *And when I get home,* I thought, *if Mike or Kenneth have not mowed the grass, I'll mow it myself, in appreciation for seeing its greenery again. After I get a shower and hot meal, of course.*

One thing bothered me. Some morning I may walk out to get the morning paper and discover a dead rattlesnake on my driveway. Some of those narcs have long memories!

CHAPTER 19

Hidden danger

Wire strike! Two dreaded words that all helicopter pilots fear. Many chopper pilots have hit power lines or other wires and antennas and have crashed. Participating in low-level searches, pursuits, and off-airport landings required me to fly low and slow, often encountering this danger. Although I always stayed alert for wires, there were times when I failed to see them.

If you fly into a high tension wire that hits your skids or the cross tubes on which the skids are mounted, it can flip your helicopter upside down—and you're dead. Even a nylon kite string, when entangled in the mast on which the rotor blades rotate, can cause a crash. Also, your helicopter tail rotor getting entangled with a loose piece of wire from a rancher's haystack can result in a disaster.

One of my most dangerous near misses of a wire strike occurred when I was called to help in a manhunt of a guy who had shot and killed two people in a robbery in Tyler, Texas, then kidnapped a woman and stole her car. The woman was one of our very own DPS radio communications operators. The county sheriff and his deputies, several state troopers, and officers from adjoining counties all joined forces for the manhunt. Late in the afternoon of that same day, a DPS trooper spotted the killer/kidnapper's car, and gave chase. On the outskirts of Longview, an adjoining city, the bad guy spun into a ditch, left the car, and ran into the woods.

The kidnapped woman was found in the car, unharmed.

Bell Jet Ranger without wire cutters.

Officers, helped by tracking dogs, surrounded a large area of Longview, where the killer/kidnapper was last seen. The area highway patrol captain called for the DPS SWAT team, and also a helicopter. That moved me onto the scene, with my partner/pilot Carl Mullins. A command post was set up next to a lighted football field. When we landed in Longview, nothing had been seen of the suspect, so we had no place to begin an aerial search. The captain asked us to make the short flight to the airport and pick up the two pilots who had flown in the SWAT team, and bring them to the command post.

Carl and I made the short "hop" and landed. We knew the two pilots well and had flown with them before. They had flown the twelve-member SWAT team, bristling with helmets, body armor, and sophisticated weaponry in a DPS twin-engine airplane. We had a quick visit while we refueled, then all four of us crowded into Helo-101 and took off, with me as pilot-in-command. Normally, you don't get "back-seat driving" in this situation, but we were enjoying the rare togetherness with some light-hearted banter.

Soon we were over the lighted football field, and I circled

for a low reconnoiter, looking for any type power lines or wires. I asked, "Anybody see any wires crossing the field?"

"Nope," came two replies. The field was bracketed by electrical high wires for the lights and with bright lights flooding the field, I didn't see any wires either.

"Guys," I said, "I'm not so sure about landing on the field. It looks small, we have a full load of fuel, and we're at maximum gross weight with four of us. You guys from Austin need to lose some pounds."

One said, "Aw, man, even I could land on that big ole field with all these bright lights."

Another chimed in, "Paul, you got plenty of room!"

I knew that the chopper was too heavy to make the usual steep descent over the high wire at the end of the stadium, stop, and come to a hover without overtorqueing the transmission or "overtemping" (overheating) the engine. But I was young, proud, highly motivated, and well-trained. I decided I could make a shallow, gradual approach, slow the chopper, and slide onto the ground with a high density altitude type landing. Anyway, I reasoned, if it didn't look right, I could abort before I descended below the high wires.

"I'll try it," I said, not wishing to be intimidated by my peers.

Leveling out at 65 MPH, I began the gradual descent, crossing over the goal posts at ninety feet above the green turf. Then, the forty-yard line, and everything looked good. I slowed even more, and descended to forty feet above ground. Going for a "touchdown," and still descending, I crossed the fifty-yard line. The one-yard marker lines were flashing by under me rapidly.

Then I saw the wire!

It was a single electrical line stretching from pole to pole over the thirty-yard line across the field! It was too late to abort. I was flying too low and slow, and was too heavy to climb and miss the high wires over the end of the stadium. We were in trouble. There was no football coach to call the next play for me, no referee to flip a coin for me!

Approaching the wire almost too quickly to react, I tried to make the fastest "quick-stop" I had ever made. At thirty-five feet above the ground, I asked my helicopter to do the impossible. I hauled back on the cyclic (control) stick, which raised the chopper's nose up to a 45-degree angle—a desperate effort to stop. She almost stopped, but I knew we were going to hit that wire. I banked hard right and simultaneously kicked the right tail rotor pedal, then added more power. As we sank, I quickly leveled out straight ahead and slid smoothly onto the ground parallel to the wire, which was above me and only about ten feet from my left rotor blade.

I sat for a few seconds and exhaled slowly. It had all happened in about twenty-five seconds.

"What were you doing?" asked Carl, emphatically.

"Yeah, Paul," came a back seat voice, "were you showing off?"

Slowly, I pointed to the wire. "Didn't you guys see that wire stretched across the field?"

My companions looked and were awestruck. None of them had seen it. Thank God that I had. "Paul," said one, "I believe I owe you a lunch for that landing. That was one for the books."

"I was lucky," I said.

We all got out and walked across the field to the command post. None of us said anything about the scare we'd had.

We soon learned that ground officers had located and arrested the murderer/kidnapper, with the help of the tracking dogs. The two other pilots soon flew the SWAT team officers back to Austin, and we flew home to North Texas. I was always glad to be part of a successful manhunt, but for three other DPS pilots and myself, the big moment on that mission was that near wire strike and the scary landing on a Longview high school football field. DPS nearly lost four pilots and a helicopter that night.

* * * * *

Flying a helicopter at night, looking for a criminal suspect in thick wooded areas with no moonlight, is like looking for a black cat in a dark alley at midnight. It was on such a night that I was ordered to search for a criminal suspect in the woods of the Trinity River bottoms near Corsicana, Texas. A state trooper was assigned to fly with me, acting as my observer and searchlight operator.

Upon arriving in the area, we made radio contact and he directed me to land in an open area by an oil well pump station. It was dark on the ground. I turned on my landing lights and Night Sun searchlight, brightly illuminating my landing area. I landed safely. He boarded and sat in the right rear seat, which is where my observer always rode, to enable us both to look out of the same side. We quickly got acquainted, and I learned that he had never operated our Night Sun searchlight. With no time to waste, I gave him quick instructions on operating it.

As I took off and made a climbing turn into the dark sky, I talked with him further about the searchlight, demonstrating how its beam could be directed with a toggle switch on the control box. I handed the box over my shoulder to him and said, "Here, try it."

As he took the control box, he pointed the light beam straight down below our chopper. In that powerful beam of light, I saw a microwave tower pass quickly about twenty-five feet below us!

Close!

Who would have thought that a microwave tower would be way out here in the dark and deserted boonies, in the middle of the Trinity River bottoms, miles from anywhere? But there it was, and we had almost struck the top of it with our skids! A microwave tower is normally no more than sixty feet high. This one had to have been at least a hundred feet above the ground. What had caused me to gain just enough altitude fast enough to clear the tower? It got me to thinking about Divine Guidance again.

* * * * *

DPS Pilot Billy Peace and I had been providing aerial help on a criminal search in Kaufman County, and the suspect had been caught. We were ready to head homeward when Billy, acting as pilot-in-command, decided to land at the sheriff's office to talk with a deputy. In those days the sheriff's office was located in a large cleared area outside of Kaufman. Billy had landed there numerous times, several months earlier.

There was a 200-yard-long driveway that led from a county highway to the sheriff's building. Billy made a low approach down the driveway, intending to land near the building. As he neared "touchdown" we both looked for power lines and telephone poles. Neither of us saw anything. We were about twenty-five feet above ground when I saw it.

"Wire!" I shouted.

About forty feet in front of us at our altitude was a single, thin telephone line. I thought we had "bought the farm." Billy had seen it simultaneously with me and immediately started a "quick-stop" procedure: raising the nose and decreasing power. I tensed. We were going to hit it! He raised the nose even higher, pulling up on the collective stick (power control), which increased the pitch angle of the rotor blades. He was desperately trying to stop and back up at the same time. We climbed a couple of feet, stopped, then hovered.

It was close. The telephone line was about ten feet in front of the helicopter's nose and about five feet below the whirring main rotor blade. Billy gently raised us above the wire, crossed over it and landed on the grassy lawn. "Nice flying, partner," I said.

"That was close!" Billy sighed. "That wire was hard to see."

Why couldn't we spot the telephone line? Because we never saw the poles to which it was attached. They were hidden in the trees on either side of the open lawn.

* * * * *

In the vast pine forests of East Texas, lots of lawbreakers grow marijuana. They grow gardens in the thick woods and brush areas. Some do it on a small basis to supplement their income; others do it big-time. With wholesale prices of marijuana at $500 per pound, I knew the profits were good.

One beautiful spring day I was copilot with DPS Pilot Terry Lee out of Corpus Christi, and we were on a marijuana search, flying the Bell Jet Ranger. Early spring was the beginning of the planting season, so we knew the plants would probably be small. We usually cruised at 500 feet above ground, and on this day, for better visibility, we had taken the helicopter's doors off. We spotted an area where all the pine trees had been cut. This is called clearcutting: the brush left behind by the loggers had been burned in anticipation of replanting new pine seedlings. The nitrogen left in the soil from the burned woods, we knew, made this type area a prime place to grow marijuana.

We first circled to look for tall marijuana plants. At 500 feet above ground one's eyes can scan lots of ground and spot the big stalks. There were none. Terry then descended very low and "hover-taxied" twenty-five feet above the ground, to help us better see little six-inch plants. I was studying the ground intensely as Terry cruised back and forth over the cleared area.

Suddenly, Terry shouted, "Wire!"

He only had enough time to quickly raise the helicopter about one foot. I had no time to look up before I saw the wire pass about one foot beneath our skids.

"Where did that come from?" I asked, looking out the door opening at the wire behind us, as Terry turned and circled.

"I never saw a utility pole," said Terry.

The reason: They were located in the edge of the trees on each side of the clearing. "Man, we missed that one by inches. Who would have thought that we would have to worry about wire strikes in the middle of these boonies? There are no houses within a mile of here!"

The frightening "near miss" dampened our zest for finding the little marijuana seedlings for a short time thereafter. Our helicopter was then equipped with the new wire cutters, mounted on its nose. We decided later we were glad we hadn't needed to test them.

*   *   *   *   *

For protection against dangerous high-tension power lines and other wires, all DPS helicopters now have "wire strike" kits installed. The kit consists of a set of long cutters resembling knife blades mounted up front. One is mounted on top above the windshield; the other, on the bottom front of the fuselage under the pilot's cabin. They can slice through an electrical or any other wire like a knife through butter. They only work, however, if the wire strikes somewhere between the tips of both top and bottom cutters when the helicopter has enough forward momentum.

There is a vulnerable spot on each cutter blade. If a wire barely misses the cutter on top, it will hit the chopper's shaft that supports the main rotor blade. If it barely misses the bottom cutter blade, it will hit the landing gear tubes that support the skids. Either "near miss" can be disastrous. The cutters have helped many helicopter pilots avert crashes, and perhaps have saved several pilots' lives. This valuable technology was not developed until late in my state police flying career.

In spite of the "wire strike" kits, hard-to-see utility and other type lines at low level remain a threat to helicopter pilots, who still fear them and are ever watchful for them. Fog, dust storms, darkness, and trees that conceal wire and supporting poles will always be hazards to helicopter flying.

CHAPTER 20

A pair of aces

In these fast-paced technological years of the new millennium, some say that the old tradition of a son wanting to follow in his father's footsteps is hard to find. Perhaps so. But I am extremely proud to have a son who, from boyhood, seems to have been dedicated to it. It is apparent today. How could I be so honored? I was just a flying policeman.

Today my son, Mike Creech, is a Texas Department of Public Safety pilot stationed in Corpus Christi. As I did, he flies the Bell helicopter and the Cessna 210 airplane. He got hooked on flying at a very early age. I caused it.

In 1968 I was a Texas highway patrolman stationed in the piney woods country at Kirbyville. I had a private pilot license. I gave Mike his first airplane ride when he was seven years old. It was in a little 1946 J-3 Piper Cub with no doors. It could fly a blazing 60 MPH on its little 65-HP engine. Mike was a little nervous about the open doors, but as I banked and turned and showed him a beautiful big new world, he became exhilarated. Little did I know how strongly I had sparked the interest of a future "eagle with a badge."

I should have realized the depth of my young son's enthrallment, because, during World War II, I lived two years near a military airfield and watched with awe as our fighter planes flew overhead. I had gotten hooked on flying, too.

In 1969 I realized one of my flying dreams. I was promoted from highway patrolman to a state police pilot and ulti-

Mike Creech, Paul's son.

mately was assigned to fly the early model helicopters. Then, Mike truly grew up as the son of a pilot. Many times, he watched as I circled our house in an airplane or helicopter. He was aware of the many late night call-outs by police dispatchers. Often I would give him a hug at his bedside and a quick good-bye as I changed from pajamas to flying suit.

He was aware when I sometimes battled low overcast clouds, storms, and fog in order to help save a life or catch criminals. At our kitchen table, he heard my stories of the dangerous missions, criminal searches, and pursuits as I risked my life to protect others. The stories and casual conversations, in which he asked me lots of questions, evidently became locked into his permanent memory.

When Mike was sixteen, he wanted to take flying lessons. I could tell he wanted them badly. Due to my low pay scale then, I was not able to finance the lessons. He started working odd jobs in the neighborhood and around town to save his money. When he turned seventeen, he had saved $100 and asked me if he could buy a hang glider. He had figured a way to launch himself off a hill behind our house. I said, "No way. No hang glider. Too dangerous."

Shortly afterwards, his mother and I left town on a long trip, to be gone several days. In our motel room, we got a phone call. It was Mike. "Dad," he said, "you're not gonna like this. You told me I couldn't, but I bought a hang glider, using my own money. But I landed sort of hard and, uh, broke my ankle. Our neighbor Ted took me to the hospital. I'm okay. And, oh yeah, they put a metal rod in my ankle. Don't worry; I'm staying with Ted's family until you get home."

We were stunned, worried, and angry. Our future "eagle" had worked his plan.

By getting a running start on the hillside slope behind our house, he learned to glide down the hill. Then he advanced to our home roof, from which he launched out into the blue horizon, stalled the hang-glider, and fell to the ground.

"Son," I said, "you're such a big man now, you just stay with Ted and take care of yourself until we get home. We're too far away and having too much fun to leave now. We'll be home soon. Let me talk to Ted."

Ted laughingly said, "He's okay. He just needs to stay in bed and rest. We'll take care of him till you get home."

I thought, *Maybe that will teach him a lesson.* It didn't. In his senior year in high school, at age eighteen, he had flying lessons behind him and finally earned his pilot's license. Twice I caught him skipping school with a friend, renting an airplane and flying. Coming home for lunch one day, I saw him "buzzing" the pasture behind our house. I drove to the airport and met him. We had a father-son talk.

The little eaglet kept trying to fly big-time, and like most fathers, it worried me. At nineteen, to my further consternation, and against my wishes, he took up sport parachute jumping. I never encouraged it nor ever went to see him jump. He made 160 jumps—that's a lot of jumps—before he finally quit. I often asked him why he would want to jump out of a perfectly good airplane.

Mike's next adventure was with a motorized gyrocoptor.

Similar to a helicopter, this gyrocopter had a flimsy rotor blade with an open-air seat suspended beneath it. It was powered by a small, lawn-mower size engine and a propeller behind the seat that moved the creation along at about 25 MPH. The pilot was totally exposed. Just looking at it made me nervous.

One day, one of Mike's friends was flying the gyrocopter, crashed into a tree, and was killed. Mike was not there when it happened, but he never flew a gyrocopter again.

A year later Mike's flying progressed to getting a commercial pilot's license with an instrument rating. He had decided to pursue a career in agricultural flying. Translation: crop dusting. It seemed exciting to him, but it gave me chills just thinking about what he did when he reported for work. If your engine sputters or quits at 100 feet above the cotton field, you have no glide time to look around for a place to set down. The spraying of the crops is done with the airplane wheels about five feet off the ground.

Early in his cropdusting career, on his first actual spray run on a field in West Texas, his engine quit as he was leveling out for the run. There was a high-tension wire about sixty feet high across the center of the field. He dumped his load and made a perfect "dead stick" landing, rolling on the ground, under the wire.

But he had one big problem. He was rapidly closing the distance on a terrace. Almost stopped, the wheels of his Pawnee airplane hit the terrace and the aircraft flipped over. With God's help and the expensive flight helmet I had bought him, he walked away from the risky landing with no injuries. Again, we had a father-son talk. But when sons get to be twenty-one, the influence of fathers wanes. Or so it seemed to me at the time.

Through all his early flying adventures, Mike harbored thoughts of a law enforcement career. When I was reminded of this occasionally, it gave me a good feeling. Maybe he had been listening to me. Maybe my work had made an impact on him.

At age twenty-one, he got a job as a jailer for Jefferson County. Soon he moved laterally to the Port Arthur Police Department, where he worked four years as a city patrolman.

By then I was in my seventeenth year as a state police pilot. With both flying and law enforcement in his blood, my grown son talked with me several times about following in my footsteps by starting a career with the Texas Department of Public Safety. In 1988, at the age of twenty-eight, he applied. He was not accepted. The competition was rigid.

He applied again, and in 1989 he was accepted. He underwent the same long hard weeks of recruit training that I had endured. On a bright October day in Austin that same year, Mike Creech received his commission and his badge as a Texas state trooper. And I was there to savor it all. The DPS director called the names of father-son officer combinations. I might have shed a tear. The skies seemed extra blue that day.

Mike's first assignment as a state trooper was to Garland, with the Driver License Service. It was another magic moment because— guess who else was stationed at Garland? Me— Sgt./Pilot Investigator Paul Creech, helicopter pilot with the DPS Aircraft Section. From Garland I had been flying lots of rescue and other type missions.

Father and son, both wearing the law officer's badge of the State of Texas, both stationed together. It was unique.

We were happy with this situation. But Mike was not content with office duty and issuing driver licenses. His mind was with it, but his heart was up in the sky. He wanted wings. In 1994 he began applying for the DPS Aircraft Section. He was not accepted. In the months that followed, he applied three more times. On his fourth application, he was accepted and promoted. The fact that he already had his commercial pilot's license with an instrument rating helped him. I was elated. I knew then that Mike would have the best aviation training and best equipment to fly. DPS then had a second Creech in the DPS Aircraft Service.

My misgivings were that he was stationed in McAllen, nearly 500 miles away from me. It was a sad day for me when the moving van pulled away with Mike's family. I would not be able to take my two grandchildren to the ice cream parlor every week anymore.

No helicopter was assigned to McAllen; he would be flying the Cessna 210 airplane. Two years later he transferred to

Corpus Christi, 377 miles from me. A helicopter was stationed there. Now he had the better of two worlds—flying a Bell helicopter and a Cessna 210 airplane.

Mike and I seldom saw each other during duty hours, but once, during a peculiar radio skip, I heard Mike from 200 miles away. We said hello to each other from aircraft to aircraft. Twice we flew together in an official capacity, when we were assigned to work together in the Marijuana Eradication Program. It involved search and destroy raids against those who grew and distributed the illegal marijuana.

These were special times for the Creech father-son team. The father-son bond was stronger than ever. Sometimes it even seemed like more, because of our mutual love for flying. The memories of those action flights together are forever engraved in my mind. It was a time of mixed emotions for both of us the day I retired.

In 1997 my greatest fear happened. A crazy man shot at Mike's helicopter. The helicopter took four hits, but fortu-

Paul and Mike Creech.

nately, Mike was not hit. With the skill of a true professional, he made a safe landing.

Even if I were not a DPS pilot, I would have been proud of Mike's pilot career. While flying the state police helicopter, he has saved many lives of people who, without him, would have drowned or met other deaths. His rescues and other exploits have been shown on television nationally and in Europe as some of the world's most dramatic rescues. In one Central Texas incident, a family was trapped by raging flood waters and had climbed into treetops. Mike and his partner, Ed Burris, with precision low-level flying and using the "rescue ring," airlifted the desperate people to safety. He has been awarded the DPS Director's Citation with Medal for his conscientious effort.

In 1999, Mike and Ed won honorable mention by *Rotor and Wing* magazine for having made the world's most dramatic helicopter rescues. Am I jealous of my pilot son who often seems to outperform me? Heck, no. I'm so proud of him I feel like jumping out of my flight suit!

It may sound a little "salty," but we call ourselves a "pair of aces." A big feeling I receive from Mike is one of honor. He honors me. Isn't that what the Good Book says that children should do for their parents?

CHAPTER 21

Summer Fun
on the river

There's a saying in the Lone Star State: "If you don't like the weather in Texas, wait a few minutes. It'll change."

On a certain hot August night in North Texas, in 1997, it did change. Unusual for August. After a blistering hot day, Mother Nature unleashed a hard and steady rain, the kind that makes farmers and ranchers smile and often makes the rivers rise. I had noticed tall, puffy clouds building during the afternoon.

About eighty miles away from me three teenage girls had set out on a grand summertime adventure: floating several miles down the Brazos River on innertubes. They evidently gave little thought to puffy rain clouds or television weather forecasts that morning.

Texans know that the Brazos is a full-blown river, starting in the Panhandle, winding through little towns of the northern, central and southeastern parts of the state, and emptying into the Gulf of Mexico. Not a river to take lightly. On that hot morning the girls launched on the tubes, but never came out at the pick-up point where parents were waiting for them.

Over the years I received a lot of calls for help in the dead of night. This call about the missing girls was no exception. It came at 3:00 A.M. The DPS dispatcher gave me the details. The sheriff of Somervell County needed my assistance with the helicopter to help search for the girls. I said, "Tell the sheriff it's raining hard right now and that I'll come as soon as it stops. It may be a while before I get there. I'll call them when I get close."

Awake now, I gulped down the usual cup of instant coffee, "jumpstarting" my system. I called partner Kenny Meadows, gave him the details, and asked him to meet me at the airport. Kenny went silent on the phone for a few seconds. I knew he was thinking about the heavy rain coming down. We both knew that, regardless, we had to get airborne as soon as possible. He and I had a theory that fate often conspired against us to torment us with rainstorms in the dark of night.

Trying to forget that the 3:00 A.M. hour was for sleeping, I hurriedly put on my fire-retardant Nomex flight suit. Sleep really left me when I visualized three teenage girls lost on the Brazos River, miserably wet and scared, or at worst, drowned. Seeing a plate of Dolores' chocolate chip cookies on the kitchen table, I grabbed four, headed into the garage, and started my car. Rain was pelting my windshield hard as I drove to the airport. *No need to hurry,* I thought. *We're not flying anywhere in this dark, wet sky.*

At the airport Kenny and I did our preflight check on Helo-101, nose to tail. We were both thinking about the welfare of those teenage girls on that dark river in a rainstorm. Our thoughts were also on the danger of flying the chopper in the rain in the dark. If we did, someone would have to come looking for us!

In the hangar's small office we looked through a window and could see and hear the intensity of the rain on the metal roof. I paced the floor in the office, walked out into the hangar where Helo-101 sat waiting, then walked back to the window. The rain was not furious, just a steady downpour. Kenny and I locked eyes several times, then glanced at our watches. Were they all three still afloat? Had a sharp stick punctured a couple of their innertubes? Had one of them been bitten by a water moccasin?

At 6:00 A.M., with the first streaks of dawn showing, the rain quit and we hurried to the chopper. Acting as pilot-in-command, I took off for Glen Rose, seventy-five miles away. We cruised along at 140 MPH in the heavy, moisture-laden air at 500 feet above ground. As daylight arrived fully, I was hoping for a bright morning sunrise. There was none. "Kenny," I said, "this air is so thick with water you can either breathe it or drink it."

Kenny grinned and nodded. Ten miles into the flight and near the little town of Lancaster, a few miles south of Dallas, we ran into dense fog. Descending and slowing, I stayed under it. Kenny punched in Lancaster Airport on the GPS (positioning device), and I turned to the indicated compass heading that directed me there. In five more minutes we landed at the airport.

Pacing back and forth and grumbling about the weather, we sat in the Lancaster hangar. "In pea soup like this," said Kenny, "even the ducks don't fly."

Finally at 9:00 A.M. the fog lifted enough for us to take off. From our initial call at 3:00 A.M. until we lifted off at Lancaster, we had traveled only ten miles, in six hours. The weather truly seemed to be working against us. I breathed a silent prayer for the girls. Cruising at 140 MPH, we were soon over Somervell County and nearing the sheriff's office in the city of Glen Rose. I called his office and told them we would land in five minutes. They directed us to a large lawn adjacent to the sheriff's office.

After landing, a deputy met us and filled us in on the details. "Fellas," he said, "at 8:00 A.M. yesterday morning, three teenage girls decided to float the Brazos on innertubes. Their ages were about sixteen and seventeen. They put in at the Highway 67 bridge here at Glen Rose. The mother of one of them was to pick them up at their 'take-out' point at the Highway 174 bridge about five o'clock. That's about a twenty-two-mile float trip. The girls never showed up. Darkness hit about 8:00 P.M., still no girls, and the parents got frantic."

"Wow, twenty-two miles!" I said. "That's a long float for even a well-conditioned athlete." I had floated the Brazos years ago in a rubber innertube. After six miles I was exhausted, blistered, and ready to get out of the water. I swore I would never do that again.

The deputy agreed. "It's a long pull. We're hoping they're okay and just had a rough night in the rain. The river has a lot of shallow places, so we can't use a motor boat for searching.

That was kind of hard to explain to one of the mothers. I guess it would be best for you to start at our Highway 67 bridge—it's a half-mile north of us—and follow the river all the way to the Highway 174 bridge. And guys, we're glad to see you."

I added: "If they haven't tried to walk out and are still on the river, we should find them pretty quick. Stay on your radio in case we need help."

We took off, following the twisting and turning river. I circled at 400 feet over the Highway 67 bridge and saw what appeared to be searchers on the river's banks. They weren't covering much area due to thick bushes and trees. A couple of them waved to us. "Probably family," I said to Kenny.

At low speed and low altitude, and with Kenny scanning the muddy Brazos intently, I moved on downriver. I thought to myself, *What kind of mothers and fathers would let these young girls attempt twenty-two miles on this river with only innertubes—not even a small canoe?* I hadn't told the deputy, but I knew this river. It was muddy brown after the rain, wide at points, deep at some points and shallow at others, sometimes swift, with obstructions such as floating logs and debris.

Nine miles down the river Kenny spotted an innertube lying on the bank near some trees. I circled it and descended to 200 feet above it. Then the three girls walked out from under the trees, waving their arms vigorously. "We found them, Kenny," I said.

"I know some parents that are gonna be happy."

Kenny radioed our deputy, gave him the good news, and told them we would try to land and bring them out.

I circled tight, looking for a place to land, then descended a few feet and banked slightly to my side to get a better look at the terrain. Trees covered the riverbanks on both sides; the riverbanks were not an option. Looking forward, I spotted a medium-sized rock-strewn sandbar jutting out into the river about 600 feet upriver from the girls. That would be my landing pad.

"Kenny," I said, pointing ahead, "I'm gonna put it down on that sandbar. I see lots of rocks on it. When we land, watch outside and don't let me set down on a rock that might damage a skid."

"You got it, partner."

I made the approach. The landing site was a good choice. The river was pretty wide here, with little danger of rotor blades hitting trees, and around the sandbar the water looked shallow. I hovered, then descended slowly, carefully. At five feet above it, I saw plenty of rocks, but the sandbar looked fairly level. Kenny had his door open and was leaning well out, carefully looking at the rocks and the sand.

"Easy . . . easy . . . looks good," said Kenny.

This is where pilot and copilot really trust each other. Kenny trusted me at the controls; I trusted his assessment of the landing zone. We touched down, spraying sand and making a pretty good racket within the walls of the riverbanks. I cut the engine and Kenny got out.

The girls had already started wading toward us in waist-deep water. They were a dilapidated but happy trio, grinning from ear to ear. A dog was with them. A good-sized mixed-breed mutt, paddling along beside them. "Great Scott," I said, "a dog." Nobody had said anything to us about rescuing a dog.

Jubilant, lost girls approach their rescuers.

Kenny saw my consternation and laughed. "Paul," he said, "that dog needs saving, too. He's probably a family member."

"Yeah," I said, "but which innertube did he float in?"

Stepping out of the water, wearing bathing suits and dripping, soggy t-shirts, they looked plenty tired. Their hair was hanging in a matted mess. Kenny held Helo-101's door open for them like he was a Waldorf-Astoria Hotel doorman.

"Girls," I said, "we're gonna take you out of here, but first tell us what happened."

They all tried to talk at once. Finally, they chose a spokesperson. "We didn't make it down the river as fast as we thought we would," said one. "When it got dark, we decided to stay put and camp out till morning. Then the rain came and we were miserable, wet, and cold all night."

"Well, climb in," I said. "We'll take you to your parents."

As they began climbing in, one said, "What about Sam?"

"Who is Sam?" Kenny asked.

"He's my dog. He guarded us all night."

"Okay," I said, "if you can get him in."

They all got into Helo-101's rear seat area, with Kenny helping them. Sam scrambled in also. We closed the doors and windows. Just as I started the engine, Sam did what all dogs do when they're wet. He shook—vigorously. He spattered everybody. The girls giggled. Kenny rolled his eyes at me. One of the girls said, "I'm glad you found us. I won't try that again."

Airborne now, I called the deputy and told him the girls were okay and that we would land near the sheriff's office in five minutes. Coming in for the landing, I saw the girls' families waiting on the grassy lawn. We landed. I shut off the engine, Kenny opened the door, and a happy reunion took place as fathers, mothers, brothers, uncles, and aunts took turns hugging the girls. Each mother and father shook our hands and thanked us. One mother, with tears in her eyes, hugged Kenny. A father, as he shook my hand, shook his head as if to say, "Never again will I let her do anything like this."

The deputy said, "Thanks, guys. You sure saved us a long walk down that river."

We took off and headed homeward with a feeling of fulfillment that only comes after a successful emergency life-saving mission.

Cruising along with Helo-101 singing its song, I felt like singing. Since I sing in my church choir, I thought I would give Kenny a treat. "Ol' Man River," I began, "he just keeps rollin', he don't say nuthin', he just keeps rollin' along."

Kenny cut his eyes at me and gave a little smirk. "Partner," he said, "don't give up your day job. You ain't ready for a Broadway musical yet."

CHAPTER 22

Cockfighting and carnage

If someone had told me, on the day that I reported for duty to fly helicopters and airplanes as a state police pilot, that I would someday help make arrests at a cockfight, I would have laughed. But later, when I did it, I didn't find much to laugh about. The reason: Cockfighting—and also dog-fighting—is a bloody, inhumane nonsport on which people gamble on the winner, and it is illegal in Texas because of its brutality. It is still done in Texas because there are some who like violence and fighting, it seems, and they like to gamble. Cockfighting and dog-fighting promoters capitalize on both of these factors. Large sums of money are won and lost, the victories depending upon the strength and fighting skill of roosters and dogs.

My flying assignment into this unique lawbreaker scenario started on a beautiful Sunday morning when Dolores and I were dressing for church. My telephone assignment directed me to fly to the Hill County Sheriff's Department to help them locate and raid a cockfight.

"Well, kiddo," I told my wife, "the lawbreakers work Sundays and don't care whether Paul and Dolores Creech get to go to church or not."

I knew she was disappointed, but she gamely said, "Don't sing the blues. It goes with the territory. Off with the sport coat and into the flying suit!"

Down deep, Dolores understood. She was also a state police officer, an agent for the Texas Alcoholic Beverage Commission (TABC). Before that, she had been a deputy sheriff and had helped several officers break up a large cockfight. She was the first officer to enter the enclosure where the cockfight was taking place, and saw the carnage firsthand. She understood about quick assignments that interrupted personal plans. Because we both had unpredictable law enforcement work schedules, we cherished personal off-duty times together. So Dolores went to church alone, and I headed for the airport.

Although I mostly flew helicopters, I was also trained for flying the Cessna 210 airplane, and I again admired that sleek aircraft as I rolled it out of the hangar. It was my DPS aircraft for the day, assigned to me because quiet, long-range aerial surveillance was needed. Helicopters are loud. This Cessna was one of the best nonmilitary, propeller-driven aircrafts. It carried six people, had good range, and an airspeed of 180 MPH. Its 300-HP engine keeps it cruising smoothly through most upper-level weather.

After my preflight check I was quickly airborne in a beautiful cloudless blue sky. The distance was only sixty-five miles, and I soon landed at Hillsboro Airport. Although I was early, my assigned sheriff's deputy/observer was there waiting for me. I said, "Had your coffee this morning?"

"Yep."

"That's good," I said, "'cause it may be a long day."

"In this business," he grinned, "it often is."

My initial briefing had informed me that the county officers did not know where the cockfight would be, but had reliable information through an informant that today was the day. I was to intercept and follow a vehicle to the cockfight in a rural area without that vehicle knowing that I was following from above. The deputy added his information: "We've been hearing about cockfighting in the northwest part of the county but haven't been able to locate the arena. We have a guy that we arrested who has agreed to be our snitch and help us. He doesn't know the exact location, but through him we've narrowed it down to about a five-mile area in the northwest. He has a 'friend' who will take him to the cockfight."

Five-mile radius, I thought. *I'll have to slow the Cessna pretty good, or else I'll cut too many circles too fast.* I was getting the picture. The deputy continued: "Our 'snitch" friend is supposed to pick him up this morning and take him to the cockfight. They'll be in a red Chevy pickup truck. We'll have a deputy in an unmarked car hiding at the intersection of Farm Roads 933 and 934. He'll tell us when the pickup passes, then you and I will get on the pickup, and follow it to the arena. When we locate it, we'll wait till the cockfighting starts, then call in the raid team. They'll catch 'em in the midst of the excitement. And we have the name of one of the key players: Sam Alford. He drives a white Ford pickup."

"Sounds like a good plan. I'm ready. Climb aboard."

In the Cessna I had gyro binoculars. They were like any other binoculars except they were battery-powered with a small gyro inside. The gyro spins, keeps the optics stabilized, and prevents vibrations. Before we took off, I showed them to my deputy and told him, "You may want to use these. The magnification is such that when you look at somebody a half-mile away, you can tell what he is wearing. And what you look at is rock steady."

"Wow," he said, "never saw any like this before. I'll sure use 'em."

"It's nearly ten o'clock," I noted. "Let's get airborne."

We climbed to 4,500 feet. On this clear day with great visibility, I knew we would be able to see and follow a red pickup, and at this altitude we would not be obvious to people on the ground. We soon arrived over the suspected area. While waiting for the red pickup to arrive, we slowly cruised back and forth several times—looking, looking, looking, for anything that might resemble a cockfighting location. We saw several "possibles."

There was no traffic on the unpaved county roads below, except for a single white pickup truck that appeared to be moving around aimlessly. My deputy/observer watched him carefully. Finally, the truck pulled to the side of the road and parked near our specified crossroads 933. "I'll betcha this is the promoter, Sam Alford," said my deputy.

On our radio he reported the truck's behavior to the sheriff on the ground, giving him the location. "I'll send a man to check him out," said the sheriff.

Still at 4,500 feet, and cruising back and forth, we saw another car approach and pass the white pickup truck. We heard a ground deputy call his dispatcher and request a license plate check. Then we heard the dispatcher's reply, reporting that the owner of the pickup truck was a Mr. Sam Alford. "Well," said my deputy, "Alford is our man. He's a promoter, probably a 'lookout' for the cockfight group."

Experience had taught me that with any illegal gambling activities, a "lookout" will park or station themselves discreetly near the activity and watch anyone passing him to determine if they may be police officers. If anyone passing him arouses his suspicions, he will warn his buddies. The gamblers "split," and the officers have a difficult time making a criminal arrest that will stand up in court.

Glued to his long-range binoculars, my observer got a little excited. "Paul, they're coming in for the show now. Cars and pickup trucks are passing Alford's pickup in big numbers, and he's still sitting in his pickup at roadside. Must be a big cockfight today!"

Then our snitch appeared. A deputy called us: "The red Chevy pickup just passed me heading north on 933."

This was the guy who, with his "friend," would lead us to the cockfight. I adjusted my airspeed slightly and we began to follow him, giving radio position reports to the sheriff on the ground. The red pickup stopped beside the white one and our binoculars revealed that they were talking to each other. Had they looked up, they could hardly have seen us. We were only a small moving object high in the sky about a mile away and at a great altitude. Little did they know that the eye of the eagle—with a special big eye—was upon them.

The red pickup drove away, down the dirt road, hopefully with our snitch aboard. Maintaining my same altitude, we followed.

The driver went about a half-mile and turned through an open gate, where another lookout was standing. He stopped briefly, then proceeded across a pasture, then through a small patch of woods, and stopped at a small metal barn at the edge of the woods.

"We found it, Sheriff," said my deputy. "Just go east past the white truck about a half-mile. There's a gate on your right with a lookout standing beside it. Go through it and follow the tire tracks about a hundred yards through the woods to a small metal barn close to the trees."

"Ten-four. Can you see anything?"

"Yes, sir, there are people standing around outside and a bunch of cars and pickup trucks, maybe fifteen vehicles. Also, I see small wire cages in the beds of the trucks parked near the barn."

"Good work, fellas," said the sheriff. "That's what we need."

My deputy/observer said to me, "Paul, these binoculars are outstanding!"

I banked the Cessna a little to continue my observer's view with the gyro binoculars. He saw the crowd outside the barn begin to move inside, and he relayed this to the sheriff. "Okay, men," said the sheriff to all his ground officers, "let's move in. The first deputy to the white pickup arrests Alford. The next deputy to the gate arrests that lookout. We don't know if they are armed or not. Be careful. When we get through the gate and into the barn, take 'em down fast. Don't let anyone escape."

We watched as the line of deputies' patrol cars sped down the road, leaving a cloud of dust behind them. I descended lower and flew closer to the scene. We saw them arrest the two lookouts, saw the line of officers' cars enter the gate and surround the barn, with deputies hurrying inside. Men came running out of the barn, trying to get away.

What happened on the ground next was told to me the following day by a deputy friend by telephone. Even circling in the Cessna at 1,500 feet above ground, I had somewhat visualized the action.

There had been a mad scramble by several men trying to escape, with surviving roosters flying and squawking in confusion. In the special fighting arena, so constructed so that no fighting rooster could escape as he fought to the death, there was blood, carnage, dead roosters, and the walking victors. Their owners had outfitted their combatants with sharp weapons attached to their spurs and heads for slicing or stabbing, things like sharpened spikes or razor blades. Some were wearing protective armor. Their armor and weapons resembled those worn in medieval times by warriors. Some of the roosters still alive were cut, bleeding, and crippled. They would later be killed to end their suffering. Also, a crippled rooster was a liability to a gambling owner.

The sheriff and his deputies arrested lots of people that day for illegal gambling. Those arrested included young men, older men, just plain working folks. The "bust" had not taken long; officers had done a good job.

In a few minutes the sheriff called me on the radio. "Thanks for the eye in the sky. You made our job much easier. We arrested twenty people."

"Congratulations to you and your guys, Sheriff. Good job. I'm gonna deliver your deputy back to the airport and head home. Call us anytime."

As I turned the Cessna toward the Hillsboro Airport, the deputy said, "How much would you take for these binoculars, Paul?"

"Not for sale," I grinned. "Special property of the State of Texas, issued only to special pilots who are classified as eagles."

After delivering the deputy and getting airborne again toward home, I passed over a small country church with a pretty white steeple. I thought, *Maybe I will still be able to make the evening church service with Dolores . . .*

CHAPTER 23

Justice from above

A college basketball player I once knew often said, "When you're hot, you're hot; when you're not, you're not." I thought about this on that blistering hot June day when my partner Kenny Meadows and I were flying back to our home base airport. But it wasn't the weather I was thinking about—we were actually quite comfortable cruising along in Helo-101 at 120 mph, 800 feet above ground. I was thinking about our recent "hot" success record in our work, and so was Kenny. Yeah, we were hot!

We had just helped our DPS Motor Vehicle Theft (MVT) agents break a large car theft ring in the Dallas area. One of our agents had infiltrated the ring and one of the bad guys, in an effort to stay out of jail, had given information about the location of several stolen cars. With the information, MVT agents were able to get a search warrant for the large property named by the informant. Armed with the warrants, our MVT guys requested our aerial help to search for the stolen cars.

We had responded and located several, stashed in heavily wooded areas where agents would have never found them on foot. Several people were arrested. It was a successful operation, and MVT agents gave us a lot of credit for the success.

So Kenny and I were jubilant as we neared our airport. We were even feeling sort of cocky. Teasing banter between us that had often kept our spirits up during tough and dangerous missions was extremely high. "Our batting average is tops," Kenny said. "They can't do without us!"

I was preparing to land when the radio interrupted our mutual admiration cheering session. It was our dispatcher. "DPS Dallas to Helo-101."

"Uh-oh," I said, "maybe somebody else can't do without us."

Kenny: "Helo-101, Dallas, go ahead."

Dispatcher: "Dallas to 101, two prisoners have escaped from Kaufman County Jail; sheriff is requesting the helicopter to help locate them."

Kenny: "Ten-four, Dallas. We'll get en route to Kaufman immediately. We'll contact them direct."

Kenny then switched to the county sheriff's radio channel and got more details. The two prisoners had slipped away from a county jail work party that morning, were last seen in their orange prison suits, three miles northwest of the town of Kaufman on U.S. Highway 175. We were requested to contact a sheriff's deputy, Patrol Unit 125, in the search area. I dismissed my enjoyable thought of getting home at a decent hour, and turned Helo-101 toward Kaufman.

As I banked away from the Mesquite airport, with Helo-101's rotor blades popping the air, I noticed a couple of guys below near 101's hangar, looking up at us. We had been coming in for a landing when suddenly I increased power and pulled away. Guess they thought I was practicing landings.

We were soon over nearby Kaufman and the search area. Kenny radioed Patrol Unit 125 and asked him to watch for us and direct us to the search scene. He soon spotted us and guided us to an open field, where we landed. Before Kenny got out to meet with the deputy, I said, "Hey, partner, come down off jubilation cloud twenty-nine and act like a professional. This is a brand new ballgame, and we haven't scored any touchdowns in it yet."

Kenny gave me a mock salute, grinned, and stepped down and shook hands with the deputy, who appeared to be eyeballing Helo-101 with awe. I kept the engine running as they talked. After a few minutes of hand-waving, pointing, and loud talking over Helo-101's noise, Kenny got back in and gestured eastward, away from Kaufman toward the boonies. Kenny said, "He says the bad guys ran into those woods. They broke into a house over there and shed their orange jail suits. There were no guns in the house so they're probably not armed. But one of them may be dangerous; he's in jail for assault. The deputy doesn't know what color clothes they are wearing now, because clothes are missing from the house."

"Earlier today this eagle's eyes saw hidden cars," I said. "Now let's see if he can spot hidden people."

I lifted off and we began our search over the wooded area. As always, I checked my watch. We had enough fuel to fly one hour and twenty minutes, and the Mesquite Airport was twenty minutes away. I climbed to 500 feet above ground and began circling. My banking gave Kenny the best view. The foliage below was lush and green with occasional open spots.

Suddenly, a deputy called on the radio, excitement in his voice. "Helo-101, I just saw a man run into the woods in front of me. Turn right 30 degrees and come straight at me—my car is about a half-mile east of you on a gravel road close to an old barn."

In a few seconds the deputy called again. "You are right over me. I'm pointing into the woods where he went."

"I see the deputy," Kenny said. "Turn left about ten degrees, Paul."

I lowered the nose of the chopper to pick up airspeed and flew over more woods, leveling off at 100 feet above the ground. "This ought to keep him pinned down," I said to Kenny.

"No, it didn't," said Kenny, pointing. "There he goes! He's running through the woods."

I turned and homed in on the area to which Kenny was pointing. I could see the guy clearly as he ran. I turned again slightly so he would be on my side, allowing me to keep him in sight as he ran. *Golly,* I thought, *he's running through the woods like a deer.* I slowed, keeping Helo-101 directly above the escapee. The eyes of the eagle were on him. I knew he was not going to escape. Just then I thought of our loudspeaker, which also had a siren. "Kenny, this guy's not gonna stop. Let's have some fun."

Kenny looked at me quizzically. I flipped on the loudspeaker switch, turned up the volume to near maximum, and said, "Stop. We are state police. You are under arrest."

He kept running, so I spoke again. It must have been

frightening to the guy: all that noise from Helo-101 and my voice magnified about 100 times.

Kenny said, "You just made him run faster."

"Yeah, I know, but isn't this fun?"

A boyhood memory popped into my mind. With my dad driving across a field in our old pickup truck, I was standing in the cargo bed looking down on our old dog, Bear, chasing a small rabbit. Bear finally got him cornered in a cluster of vines, caught him in his big jaws, and came prancing proudly back to me with his catch. This fleeting memory tweaked my conscience for a few seconds as I thought of all the technology I was using to run down the desperate fugitive running below me. I had him like Bear had the rabbit.

Then the law officer part of me quickly replaced the rabbit scene. The guy below me was in jail for a reason—probably for robbing or assaulting someone. The charge against him was probably pretty serious, or he wouldn't have made the jail break. My job was to help catch him, and get him back into jail so that the courts or the law could deal with him.

I flipped on the siren switch. It was much louder than the clacking of our rotor blades, blaring and shattering the silence of the woods and fields below with its high/low siren sound. Immediately the fugitive stopped, raised his hands, and looked up at the helicopter hovering 100 feet above him. Again I spoke into the loudspeaker: "You are under arrest. Walk in front of the helicopter. Cross the open field to your right. A deputy is waiting for you on the other side."

He began walking across the field. He stumbled once. I reckoned that he was tired and probably hungry. He reached the deputy, who quickly handcuffed him and got him into his patrol car.

"Now, wasn't that fun, Kenny?" I asked.

Kenny laughed and signaled his agreement with a thumbs-up gesture. "One more to go," he said.

I climbed to 400 feet above ground and resumed our search for the second fugitive by circling the area again. I checked my fuel gauge and my watch.

"Time flies when you're having fun," I said. "We gotta go for fuel, Kenny."

Officers have the prisoners, taking them to patrol cars.

Kenny called our ground deputy in Patrol Unit 125. "We're low on fuel, gotta leave you and refuel. We'll be back in about forty-five minutes."

"You guys done good catching that one," the deputy responded. "It was neat to watch from the ground. But you sure are loud!"

We landed at the Mesquite Airport within twenty minutes, refueled quickly, and were soon airborne back to the search area. Our radio crackled again: "Kaufman S.O. to DPS Helo-101, the deputies just caught the second escapee. You may disregard."

"Ten-four," answered Kenny, looking at me and shrugging.

We were nearing the same search area. I wanted to see where the deputies had caught the second guy. Seeing deputies at the edge of the field, I approached and hovered. They were standing around their prisoner, and had him handcuffed. Patrol Car 125 was nearby with a deputy inside. Keying the radio button, I asked, "It's Helo-101 again, with a question: How did you catch him?"

The deputy replied, "You guys are effective even when you're miles away. When you left for fuel, he thought the

My partner, Kenny: "They can't do without us!"

search was over and started moving out, and we saw him. We chased him and he gave up. He was only about 200 yards from where you guys caught the other one."

"Yeah, well," I said, "once we wave our magic wand over a search area, good things happen. Ten-four, guys, we're outta here!"

The deputy was still on the radio when I banked and headed west toward home. "You guys did great." He added, "Thanks for your help. We couldn't have done it without you."

"Hear that, Kenny?" I said. "He says they can't do it without us."

"I know, I know," said Kenny. "Probably the governor of Texas will give us a pay raise soon."

As I listened to Helo-101's rotor blades slapping their happy homeward sound, pleased with the day's work, I again thought, *Yeah, when you're hot, you're hot; when you're not, you're not!* We'd had other searches when we weren't this hot. But it was nice to personally score two touchdowns on the same day.

CHAPTER 24

Prey for the eagle

Texas is home to the red-tailed hawk. Often he patrols at dawn 500 feet above a field or valley, with radar-like vision. Little field mice or lizards below who ignore him pay a tough price and become his breakfast as he swoops on them at high speed. Texas also has American bald eagles in the Highland Lakes area and Mexican eagles near the border. They survive using similar skills as the hawk, only they're larger, have far better vision, fly higher, and capture bigger prey, such as rabbits, baby deer, or baby calves.

Often I have passed hawks, and a few eagles, in midair, and always banked away from them, for obvious reasons. But the similarity between their work and mine frequently crept into my thoughts. The speed, maneuverability, and visual assets of the helicopter, I decided, caused me to make the comparisons.

This comparison was again brought home to me one summer day when my partner Kenny Meadows and I were on a routine patrol in Rockwall County east of Dallas. We were flying the Aerospatiale A-Star. Our DPS dispatcher's voice broadcast a bulletin on the radio: "DPS Dallas to all units, be on the lookout for a stolen red Ninja-type motorcycle ridden by a white male. Terrell Police Department was in pursuit of the motorcycle in Terrell and lost contact with it. The motorcycle was last seen on the north side of Terrell."

As I turned Helo-101 toward Terrell, about six miles away, I said, "Let's go, Kenny, maybe we can find him."

One of our highway patrol troopers stationed in Terrell called: "11-18 Dallas. I'm in pursuit of the motorcycle two miles north of Terrell. We're headed north on State Highway 205 toward Rockwall. Contact the Rockwall units and advise them to head this way. The motorcycle is running 140 MPH."

"Well, how about that, Paul?" said Kenny. "We do get variety. Now we got a motorcycle thief."

We were only five miles away. I increased power and turned toward the chase. Helo-101 responded quickly to the power surge as if she were excited about pursuing a little two-wheel missile on the highway. I inwardly smiled. It didn't make any difference to that splendid little aircraft whether its quarry was an eighteen-wheeler, a late model Cadillac, or a two-wheeled machine. All it required was good maintenance service, plenty of jet fuel, and skilled pilots who did not abuse her capabilities. And, really, it didn't matter a lot to us. It was all in our job specifications. One constant incentive was the joy of flying a good helicopter and succeeding in our mission.

The guy on the stolen motorcycle probably got a joy out of his little machine, too. Probably enjoyed cutting the wind at 140 MPH. That was moving it pretty good, for a two-wheeler. He was "flying" on the ground!

Flying that same speed, 140 MPH, we quickly closed on Highway 205, listening to our ground trooper give more radio reports on the motorcyclist's locations. Two other troopers had now joined the chase. The highway came into view. Looking to my right as I approached it, I saw the bright red Ninja motorcycle coming fast. Descending slightly to 400 feet above ground, I could see that the rider was lying prone with his legs stretched out behind him and his knees gripping the rear part of the saddle. A real daredevil! It made the motorcycle look like a missile. The area was farm country with only a few cars on the highway, but when he passed one, it looked like the car was standing still. I felt a quiet anger that he would jeopardize public safety with such a performance.

Getting closer to the entire scene, I lowered the nose of my chopper, descending and increasing my airspeed. I thought about the red-tailed hawk, or the bald eagle, swooping down on its prey. The troopers' patrol cars were about one-fourth

mile behind the motorcycle. My plan was to let the motorcycle rider get a good look at us. I crossed the highway in front
of him at 150 MPH.

At a safe altitude above ground, I then turned parallel to
the highway and came up beside him. He sat up, looked at me
with shock in his expression, and applied his brakes hard. His
sudden action caused his cycle to fishtail back and forth. He
drove onto the dirt shoulder and stopped, sending up a cloud
of dust. Making a sharp turn to stay close, and climbing some
for safety, I saw three trooper cars in hot pursuit now closing
on him fast.

"Kenny, they're going too fast—they're gonna run over him!"

But they didn't. Their pursuit-driver training at the State
Police Academy saved everybody, and their actions made me
proud. Two cars came to a screeching stop within a few feet
of the motorcycle, raising their own cloud of dust. The third
trooper car came to a stop precisely at the left front of the
motorcycle, blocking its escape path.

Kenny said on the radio, "Good job, guys. We're
impressed."

The motorcycle driver, a slender young man with lots of
hair, gave up without resistance. I gained altitude, circled
again, banked slightly and waved to the troopers below, who
waved back. Just then one of them called on the radio.

"Good job, Helo-101. This guy said he would still be running if you hadn't showed up. He knew he couldn't get away
from you. Would you believe he doesn't even have a motorcycle license?"

Saying our radio good-bye to the hard-working troopers
below, I said to Kenny, "License or no license, that wild man
could drive a motorcycle."

"Yeah," said Kenny, "and most of it while lying down on
the saddle seat."

"When we swooped down and came across that field low
and close to that motorcycle," I said, "I felt like an eagle
swooping down on its prey."

"Yeah," said Kenny, "and he was just a fast little rabbit.
He didn't have a chance."

CHAPTER 25

Rescuing the perishing

Law officers spend lots of time searching for missing people. Children are lost in crowded places or in the wilderness. Women and children get kidnapped. Despondent people do irrational things that get them lost. Elderly people and sick people, some without all their mental faculties, disappear from familiar areas. Teenagers run away. Some missing people are victims of bad circumstances, and some are missing or get lost in dense forests, tall mountains, deserts, on water, in open fields—and sometimes very near their own homes or jobs. Finding them keeps law officers busy on the ground and in the air. The searching can involve city police, county sheriffs and their deputies, state police, citizens, firemen, Boy Scout troops, game wardens—and police helicopter pilots.

Over the years I have been involved in many searches and rescues. It was sometimes hard for me to understand why so many people turn up missing or lost. But it has not been hard for me to understand why we work so hard at searches and rescues. It is because, thank God, in our society, human life is still precious. It comes down to this: law officers care. They really care.

I have seen troopers, sheriffs' deputies, and my fellow pilots get tears in their eyes when, after hours or days of searching for a missing child or elderly person, they are told they must abandon the search because a blizzard is too fierce, or they're out of fuel or daylight. Neither I nor any of my fel-

low pilots has ever wanted to quit a search or give up on a rescue. And a rescue effort that fails—well, that's a cruncher for
us. That's why we roll out, gear up, and crank up at any hour,
in all kinds of weather, without any serious grumbling.

A lot of people seemed to get lost in Texas in the mid-
1970s. One Sunday afternoon in October, the Gandy family,
who lived near Paris, Texas, decided to take a family outing to
a popular flea market known as the Battle Trading Post. The
family, comprising parents, children, and a seventy-nine-year-
old grandfather, enjoyed looking at the bargains and the
antiques. It was a large flea market, and crowded on that
sunny afternoon. With everyone busy at the shopping booths
and tables, the grandfather, Mr. Gus Gandy, became separated from his daughter, her husband, and their children. They
searched the market area for several hours, became very anxious, and called the Paris Police Department for help.

That city's police department was small, but it turned out
all its officers to make the search. They spread out quickly
throughout the market area and beyond. Then the Paris police
called the sheriff's office for assistance. They came and
widened the search, with no success. The sheriff then called
our Texas Highway Patrol, requesting state police manpower.
The search expanded into the countryside and continued
through the next day, a Monday.

By then, the family, including the grandkids, had become
tearful and frantic.

On the next day the search became countywide. Citizens
were contacted. Someone reported they had seen Mr. Gandy
on Sunday evening walking away from the Trading Post along
the Old Bonham Road. Law officers and family derived from
this that Mr. Gandy had become disoriented and was walking
aimlessly around.

In those days, my pilot partner was Billy Peace. He was a
solid individual: calm and unflappable. I kidded him about
"always being at peace." Billy got the call from our northeast
Texas Highway Patrol sergeant requesting our services. Billy
briefed me, reminding me that it was a one-hour flight to
Paris. "It will get dark fast by six o'clock. Let's hustle."

He didn't have to say "hustle" to me, but I took no

offense. I knew what he meant. October nights in northeast Texas cool off fast, and the missing man was elderly. We did our preflight check on the chopper, rolled it out of the hangar, and were soon speeding toward Paris, with Billy as pilot.

"Billy," I said, "the old fellow has been missing three days. If he doesn't have shelter, we'll be lucky if we find him alive."

"We have a good success record, Paul," said unflappable Billy. "Let's think 'success' again."

He was right. We had found and rescued many, and it was always a great feeling. But occasionally we failed, and that hurt us. One of the reasons for not being able to make a rescue was that local police agencies—some with inadequate manpower and budgets—sometimes wait until they have exhausted all other search methods before calling in a DPS helicopter. This is regrettable because all officers agree that response time is critical. But I have high praise for the officers on the ground. I was always grateful to have a police ground unit near me to assist. They would tell me the physical condition of the missing person, the last area in which they were seen, facts about the terrain. Air/ground teamwork is important. I respect the men and women officers who drive, walk, ride horses, and man motorboats.

Landing at the Paris airport, we were met by a deputy sheriff who briefed us in great detail. "Several people saw the old gentleman walking the Old Bonham Road, several miles from Paris. Some knew him, didn't know he was lost, didn't pay much attention to him. It'll be cold tonight . . . his folks say he's wearing only a light jacket. His health is bad, he's feeble. We think he's down somewhere now. If you don't mind, I'll ride with you and show you the search areas."

"Glad to have you. Let's go."

Ten minutes later we were over the Old Bonham Road, hovering above the command post the chief deputy had established. There were lots of patrol cars below us, and about fifty officers were searching as far out as 200 yards on both sides of the road. Several of them waved; several were our guys, state troopers. There were ditches and tall weeds in some areas.

"This is the last place he was seen," the deputy said, pointing.

Billy hovered then moved, circled, hovered again, changing altitudes. All three of us scanned the ground. The light was good. I saw a dark object in a low place, signaled Billy, and pointed. Billy descended so low that our rotor blades whipped weeds back and forth. A flock of ducks sprang upward from a small pond to our right.

Faulty lead. It was a log.

The minutes ticked off. We saw no missing man, no clue of his existence. After two hours and fifteen minutes of this, Billy said, "We have to go for fuel."

I called the command post and informed them, and Billy turned toward the Paris airport. En route I suggested to Billy that he maintain a low altitude so that I could continue scanning the ground. As we got farther and farther from the search area, I knew it would be a long shot if we found him this far out. We passed over an open field with a single briar patch in the middle, oval-shaped. I saw something.

"Billy," I said, "get lower, and slower. I see something. Turn right about 30 degrees and hover."

Billy did. It was a man. It had to be Mr. Gandy. He was lying face down in the center of the oval area, in the middle of the briar patch, and he looked lifeless. "It's him, Billy, it's him!" I exclaimed.

I called the command post. "Helo-101. We've located Mr. Gandy!" I gave them our location and told them to send an ambulance quickly. Billy sat our chopper down beside the briar patch and shut off the motor. We struggled through the perimeter of the hip-high briars, which scratched and entangled our legs. It was tough going. I wished for a machete. We finally broke through them, arms and legs bleeding, and reached the old man. His clothing was torn, one shoe was missing, he had scratches on his legs and arms, and his complexion was pale. Kneeling, I checked his pulse and breathing. "He's alive, Billy, but barely."

We heard sirens. An army of police and other cars and an ambulance were bouncing toward us across the field in a cloud of dust. The ambulance guys quickly unloaded a stretcher and used it as a battering ram to get through the wall of briars. They were gutsy young men—they didn't let the pain-inflicting briars slow them down. Two EMS technicians checked vital signs. "He'll live if we get him to the hospital fast," one said. Gently, they loaded the old-timer on the stretcher, wound their way through the thorny briars again, and placed him into the ambulance, which departed quickly in another cloud of dust.

Watching it fade into the distance, and feeling my adrenaline subside, I said a silent prayer for the old man and added a prayer of thanks that we had been able to find him. Yeah, I talk to the Man Upstairs. He's been one of my regular copilots for a long time.

Deputies crowded around us, congratulating us with back slaps and handshakes. "We've been looking for him for three days," the chief deputy said. "It only took you two and a half hours to find him."

"Well, you never know," I replied. "If we had not needed to go for fuel, we wouldn't have ever flown over this field and this briar patch."

"Speaking of fuel," said Billy, "we'd better get it now and head for Dallas. It's getting dark fast."

The deputy sheriff, who had been our steady airborne search companion, needed a ride back to the Paris Airport to get his car, so he again boarded Helo-101.

Before we boarded, Billy and I paused and looked at each other, shook our heads, and grinned, a very bedraggled pair of state police pilots. The pants legs of Billy's flying suit were really tattered, as were mine. The briar patch had devastated our flight suits. We both needed to break out our first-aid kit to doctor our cuts and scratches.

Starting Helo-101's engine, Billy took off, turned, and flew back over the group of deputies. They waved, I waved, and Billy rocked our helicopter back and forth as a victory gesture. We were soon refueling at the Paris airport.

In the air again, I pleasantly visualized the joyful phone conversations as a deputy reported the good news to the Gandy family, and the family's joy as they walked into the old grandfather's hospital room. I was sure they would take the grandmother and grandkids. Probably, one of the deputies would show up later at the hospital and share in the family's joy. No doubt he would tell them that a couple of state police chopper pilots found the grandfather.

*   *   *   *   *

Some off-the-road motorcyclist found Mrs. Louise Smith's abandoned car in a wooden area near a small lake in East Texas. It was a few miles from the town of Sulphur Springs. She had been missing five days, during which Sheriff Paul Jones and his deputies had conducted a countywide search— on foot, by horseback, and by boat. Mrs. Smith's husband and children were frantic.

There had been no clues as to her disappearance. There was nothing in or about the abandoned car for clues. The sheriff suspected foul play. She had left her rural home to drive to Sulphur Springs one morning. Nobody recalled seeing her in town, and she never returned home.

On the sixth day of her disappearance, the sheriff called the Department of Public Safety and requested assistance. Billy Peace and Paul Creech were on the way. Arriving over Paris on a late spring day, we were given directions to the abandoned car. We soon saw it, and I set Helo-101 down near it. The sheriff gave us a quick briefing.

"Glad to see you fellas," he said. "We've combed the entire county and are about worn out. I'm really worried. It may be a kidnapping. The lady is only forty-four and apparently healthy."

We took off, quickly. And here's where, I have to say, sometimes we get lucky. Fifteen minutes into the air we were circling and hovering, and Billy said, "I see her. Go right 20 degrees."

I did, and descended to fifty feet. "She's lying in those tall weeds right there," Billy said, pointing.

She was not moving and appeared to be dead.

From fifty feet above, with the force of our rotor blades whipping the weeds back and forth, I studied the landing possibilities. I estimated the weeds ranged from knee-high to waist-high. If there was a swampy surface under them, my runners might sink. If there was a big rock or tree stump hidden among them, it could tilt Helo-101 and throw her rotor blades into the ground. But there was no way an ambulance could get near this one—and the clock might be ticking away on Mrs. Louise Smith, if it hadn't already quit. It was decision time.

"Billy," I said, "those weeds worry me. They may be waist high. I think I can land near her."

"You're the doctor."

I had spotted a very small opening among the weeds. Carefully and gently, keeping the tail rotor clear of the tall weeds, I lowered faithful little Helo-101 into this area. At ten feet above, Billy said, "You're looking good."

It was our lucky day again. In the tight little landing area I had selected, the weeds were scattered and short. Touchdown! "Billy, we'll have to take her to the hospital ourselves, if she's still alive," I said.

Billy called the sheriff on our radio, told him the good news and the location, and told him our plan. Billy said he could almost hear the sheriff's sigh of relief. We got out and approached the woman. Helo-101 was sitting in an opening, but the lady was lying in waist-high weeds. It was no wonder why ground searchers had been unable to see her. On the ground, we were unable to see her until we stood within three feet of her. She was a mess to look at—disheveled hair, torn dress, abrasions on one knee. I took her pulse, weak but something there. An eyelid flickered and a finger moved as I touched her. She was badly dehydrated, breathing was shallow.

"Strong woman," observed Billy. "After six days out here she's still alive."

"No time to waste, Billy," I said.

She must have weighed 150 pounds, but we successfully carried her through the weeds and lifted her into the helicopter. As I climbed into the pilot's seat, Billy sat by her in the back seat and wrapped her in a blanket. He also tried to give her a sip of water, but she was in a coma. I lifted Helo-101 straight up out of the tall weeds and quickly gained forward airspeed, heading for the Sulphur Springs hospital, thirteen miles away.

I called Sheriff Jones on the radio, reporting our success. "No time to waste, Sheriff. She's suffering from dehydration and possible shock. Please call the hospital, advise them of the situation, and ask them to be waiting for us at the hospital heliport. We'll land there in ten minutes. If the hospital doesn't have a heliport, call me back with landing instructions."

"Good work, boys," he answered. "We have a hospital heliport. Ten-four."

The Sulphur Springs hospital medics were waiting, ready, and quite professional. We later heard that she recovered and went home to the love and care of her family, who published a notice in their newspaper later, thanking us and the Sheriff's Department. Sheriff Jones wrote a nice letter to DPS Director Col. Wilson E. Speir, praising us and emphasizing the vital speed with which we did our job.

Sometimes it doesn't take long to locate a missing person. It helps if you are lucky, and we had lots of luck this time. We never did learn why the forty-four-year-old woman became disoriented and could not find her way home.

*   *   *   *   *

Experts on the aged can cite several reasons why elderly people run away and get lost. Emotional problems, mental ineptness, senility, Alzheimer's disease, anger, loneliness, and frustration with their physical limitations are high on the list. Where do the old ones go when they run away? Some are trying to go back home from their nursing home. Some who normally drive a car suddenly lose their ability to think clearly and don't know where they are. To make matters worse, they often keep on driving instead of stopping and asking for help.

I have never been able to second-guess the old ones when they are lost. Probably this is because they usually have no plan for themselves.

Eighty-one-year-old Bill Kirkpatrick was a widower with two daughters and several grandchildren. He lived with one of his married daughters and her husband in Mesquite. He was functional physically but mentally impaired. One night—nobody knows why—he raised the window in his bedroom, slipped out, and took a walk. It was the month of May, but nights were abnormally cold following a cold, lingering winter.

Our involvement—my partner Billy Peace and I—began with a phone call from Mesquite City Detective Jim Smith. We knew Jim, a no-nonsense and considerate lawman. "He's been missing for two days," Jim said. "We've searched everywhere. The Dallas police helicopter searched the first day, with no luck. Will you help us?"

"Sure, Jim," I replied. "Meet us at the airport in thirty minutes. Then you can fly with us and help look."

I briefed Billy, commenting that even an old man can walk a long way in two or three days. "Yeah," said the normally optimistic Billy Peace, "and with the rain and cold nights he could be dead from exposure by now."

Arriving at the airport, our detective friend climbed into Helo-101's back seat. We took off, heading for the east side of Mesquite and the sparsely populated subdivision in which Mr. Kirkpatrick resided. With Jim's help we located the house, circled at 400 feet, and studied the area, which had only a few homes. The house in which the man lived was surrounded by lots of open land and tall weeds. I pulled away from the house, banking sharply over an adjacent field.

I exclaimed, "Billy, I believe I see a body in the weeds down there. Look to your left, and into that low spot."

I hovered and descended over the area. "Sure looks like a body to me," said Billy.

Closing on a short final approach for landing, I looked carefully "It is him," I said, "and look how close to home he is."

"He looks like he may be dead," added Billy, as I touched down.

Asking Billy to take the controls, I got out. Detective Smith also got out. Smith and I both carried hand-held radios. "I'll call Mesquite P.D. and request an ambulance," said Billy.

Nearing the body, Smith and I saw a strange sight. The old-timer's foot was entangled up high in one of the top wires of a fence. He had evidently tried to step over the fence, caught his foot in the top wire, and fallen to the ground, face first. He looked upside-down. He had struggled to get free.

The ground showed signs of his having struggled with his arms and shoulders.

I thought he was dead. In my early farm days and later in deer hunting days, I had seen the same thing with deer. The deer had tried to jump a fence, failed to clear it with its back legs, got hung, and starved to death.

Smith checked the gentleman's pulse. I saw a thumb move. "He's alive!" I shouted to Billy on my hand radio. I held the old man's hand and brushed his white hair back off his forehead. Billy's voice came through on my radio. "Ambulance will be here in a minute."

The Mesquite Fire Department ambulance came in minutes, siren wailing. Due to brush and weeds, it couldn't get into the field, and parked about 200 yards away. EMS technicians ran toward us with a stretcher. With wire cutters they cut away the twisted wire around Mr. Kirkpatrick's foot. He remained unconscious, barely breathing. They freed him, put him on the stretcher, and began carrying him to the ambulance. On Detective Smith's radio, a Mesquite traffic officer's message reported that the freeway between us and the hospital was closed due to a multi-car accident.

Bad news for the ambulance. Bad news for Mr. Kirkpatrick. An EMS technician turned to me and said, "Can you guys fly him to Presbyterian Hospital? He needs medical treatment quickly. It may be the only way he will live."

"You got it," I said, "bring him to the chopper."

Billy and I got out the stretcher we carried in our baggage compartment. The EMS fellows transferred him to it and helped us get him into Helo-101. There was no room for Detective Smith this trip. We got airborne fast. Billy called our DPS dispatcher, who told the hospital emergency room that we were approaching with a patient suffering from dehydration and shock. We were descending on the hospital helipad within sixteen minutes after getting Mr. Kirkpatrick. Seconds later, nurses had him in the emergency room.

With great care from the doctors and nurses at Mesquite's Presbyterian Hospital, the man survived and went home to his daughter's house several days later. Sometimes we don't get a thank you, but this time we got a lot of praise. Detective Smith called later and said that Mr. Kirkpatrick would not have been found alive had we not found him by helicopter that day. He followed that up with a long letter of praise for us to one of our "big" DPS bosses.

The best "thank you" of all came in a letter from Mr. Kirkpatrick's two daughters and their families, addressed to Billy and me. It read as follows:

> Dear Sir: We have always believed in paying our debts, but there will always be one debt of gratitude that can never be sufficiently acknowledged. We were told by Detective Smith of the Mesquite Police Department that we owe the finding of our father/grandfather, to your time, efforts and energy. One doesn't send a mere thank you card for an act such as yours.
>
> Detective Smith said without your help in the helicopter, due to his being in a field of high grass, he might never have been found unless someone stumbled over his whereabouts. I'm sure to some, it seems like wasted time and efforts to look for a missing "John Doe," but he's no "John Doe" in this family. He's a very loved and wanted man who deeply touched the life of this daughter and granddaughter.
>
> There aren't words or phrases that could ever express our thanks and appreciation. All we can try to do is say a sincere "Thank You" from a very grateful family.

If I had ever doubted that rescuing senior citizens was just as important as rescuing anyone else, if there had ever been any doubt that I had chosen the right profession, that letter removed it all. And I still have the letter, years later.

* * * * *

People who have traveled "deep" East Texas near the Louisiana border, known fondly by Texans as the "piney woods country," know that it gets very dark there at night. From the highways and country roads you can't see the stars and moon because of the tall pines and dense thickets. From the air you can't see the ground, for the same reason. Concealed in the dense woods are bayous and occasional lakes. The bayous and Lake Caddo are known to contain alligators.

Much of this formidable habitat was some 1,000 feet beneath me one cold February night as I cruised along at 120 MPH heading into Marion County to help in another missing man search. I thought about the assignment, of course, but my thoughts were also on the terrain below me.

"Little engine," I mused, "don't fail me now. There's no place to land down there, just tall trees and swamps." Thankful for the bright stars above me, I climbed for the comfort of more altitude. And I remembered a verse in the Good Book that said, "I am with you always."

I liked my job, but it was sure hard to roll out of that warm bed at 12:30 A.M. and hear about a "lost man in the woods" whom I was supposed to find in the darkness of East Texas. It was 37 degrees, with a cutting north wind blowing. The sheriff of Marion County, which borders Louisiana, had called DPS requesting help by helicopter. I had grabbed a cup of instant coffee, kissed my sleeping wife on the forehead, donned flight suit, and headed out. I radioed the Marion County Sheriff's Office that I was under way, with estimated time of arrival to be 2:30 A.M., and that I would call them again when I got closer.

Flying over Marion County I could see the twinkling lights of the little town of Jefferson, population 3,000. Ah, Jefferson. That little town and surrounding area dripped with Civil War history. Out from town a couple of miles along Big Cypress Bayou, the Confederates had built munitions plants—powder factories—and had shipped the powder downriver to the Mississippi to supply the rebel army at New Orleans. Jefferson had also supplied the Confederacy with meat, hides, iron, lumber, and leather goods. It had been a bastion of Southern support. Someday I would walk this historic area and bring my grandson Aaron.

Quit dreaming, Paul, I told myself, *and focus on the missing man.* His name was Nathan Edwards. He was eighty-three and a native of this area, but got lost somewhere in the woods. The temperature was very cold, and he could be freezing. Ground searchers in the thick brush and trees couldn't see more than twenty yards in daylight.

In minutes I could see several flashing red lights on the

ground about three miles ahead. "Helo-101, we see you," said a deputy on the radio. "Keep coming straight ahead. We are in a large cow pasture. Land here."

"Ten-four. Any telephone or electrical wires?"

"Negative," the deputy replied.

With due respect to the deputy, I decided to check for myself. I was told "negative" once before and nearly hit a wire. The graveyards hold a lot of pilots who have hit wires, tall antennas, or water towers. Shining my Night Sun search-light on the ground, I circled the landing spot, keeping the flashing lights in view. I saw no wires, descended slow and easy, and set Helo-101 down on soft but firm earth.

I got back on the radio. "I'll need a deputy who knows the area well. Tell him to approach the helicopter from the front, enter the open door, and watch for the rotor blades. Tell him not to go near the rear." I knew about an accident in which a man walked into a whirring tail rotor and was killed.

I kept the engine running at full speed. If the officer start-ed walking toward my tail rotor blades, I could lift off fast to prevent an accident.

After the deputy boarded, I gave him a quick lesson on how to operate our searchlight. Then he told me to head south for one mile to a more specific search location, which was the house where the missing man lived. Soon he had our powerful searchlight beaming down on the house as I circled the area around it. He did fine with the searchlight, adjusting as we banked and turned. I widened my circles, keying on the house. The powerful light beam was like a glowing knife cutting earthward through the heavy East Texas humid air.

"Lots of trees and bushes down there," remarked my deputy.

"Yeah, dark and spooky, too."

I expanded our circling to about one mile from the house, maintaining an altitude of about 300 feet above the ground.

Suddenly, he shouted, "What's that?"

"What's what?" I pressed. "What do you see?"

"Something white near the trunk of that big oak tree."

I slowed my speed and peered at the tree. The beam of light was on it. "Don't know . . . let's check it out," I said. I descended and hovered at a safe altitude. The white object moved, from a sort of curled-up ball, and stood up.

It was the missing man.

"That's him," said my deputy. "I recognize him."

With the powerful light still on him, he walked out into the opening, held his arm in front of his forehead, and peered up at us. I called the other deputies. "We have the missing man spotted, positive identification. I am close above him. He is standing up and looking at us. Can you see my lights?"

"Ten-four," came the reply.

"I'll maintain position so you can continue seeing me. There's no road here, and it's pretty thick. You'll have to walk in. Bring your hand-held radio so I can talk to you."

As the deputy continued to shine the searchlight on Mr. Edwards, he suddenly turned and began walking away across a small open area. For an eighty-three-year-old, his stride was pretty healthy. I knew if he reached the heavily wooded area not far away, we might lose him. I called the deputies: "Hurry, guys, he's trying to get away."

I knew it must be a startling and perhaps frightening scenario for the old gentleman—a dark night near heavy woods, flashing lights and a loud clatter above him, a beam of light from above that almost blinded him, and the wind from the rotor blades pushing at him. A quick idea formed in my head: strengthen this weird scenario.

I flipped on my external loudspeaker and spoke. "Stop where you are, Nathan Edwards."

That seemed to shock him, and he stopped, turned, and looked up at us again, blinking and shielding his eyes. Then he turned and walked away again. "We have his attention," I said, "maybe he thinks it's God who has come for him."

The deputy chuckled. "Keep trying, Sergeant. I can see the flashlights of my guys across the field. They're coming. If you can hold him another four minutes we have him!"

I used the loudspeaker again. "Nathan Edwards, stop where you are!"

He paused a moment. We could tell he was puzzled by the searchlight and the loud voice. Then he started walking again, faster. The deputies were close, running. I called on their hand-held radios again. "Hurry, guys. He's running from the chopper and heading for the woods. I'll lose him sure if he gets into them."

I moved the chopper forward with the fleeing man, the deputy still keeping the searchlight on him. It was going to be close. Would they get him before he plunged into the thick woods? The deputies were closing on him, flashlights bobbing, everybody nearing the thicket-like forest of pine and oak trees.

Watching it all from 100 feet above, I felt a pang of sympathy for the elderly man. He was disoriented and frightened. He didn't know why a whirling aerial monster and a group of husky grown men were chasing him.

Soon, a deputy caught him, got a hand on his shoulder. The old man stopped, turned to the deputy, and pointed up to our helicopter. Again, my heart was touched. If that had been my old father I would have hugged him. Who knows what caused the old gentleman's flight? It might have been something pretty darn serious. Maybe someday when I get to be his age, I, too, will run from something I cannot understand.

"I was right, deputy," I said. "Our weird psychology stopped him. He thought his time had come."

I flew the deputy back to his original area. We shook hands, then I took off and headed for home. Dawn was breaking. Maybe I could have breakfast with Dolores.

A deputy called me later and told me Mr. Edwards was back home and safe. The Marion County sheriff sent me a nice thank-you letter and sent a copy to my boss.

I thought back to the many times God had protected me in tough spots, and I hoped He didn't mind my playing His role for a few minutes.

CHAPTER 26

Victory in the dark

Paris is a small town in North Texas, located about twenty miles south of the Oklahoma border. On a hot night in August 1996 at a convenience store on the outskirts of town, a clerk was getting ready to close for the night. It was 10:30 p.m.; few customers came into his store after that time, and he could soon go home. Like most small Texas towns, the good working people of Paris had already gone to bed. Not much was moving outside the store.

But there was someone—a man who entered quietly, walked straight to the clerk, pulled a pistol from his belt, and shoved it at the clerk's face. "Gimme all the money," he said.

The clerk was terrified. Sums of over $100 were kept in the safe, and the clerk was not able to unlock it. He stammered this fact to the robber, who became furious and more threatening. The clerk gave the robber all the cash register money, about $90. The intruder cursed the clerk, stormed to the door, and fired at him, but the shot missed. He ran to his car, jumped in, and sped away.

Although the clerk was shaken, he managed to get the car's license number and description, then called the police.

In small towns like Paris, police departments never seem to have enough budget for hiring additional officers to protect their citizens. However, when their city officers, sheriffs' officers, game wardens, highway patrolmen and constables all work together as one, a rather large police force can form quickly, to the surprise of lots of crooks.

The Paris police dispatcher broadcast the robbery and description of the suspect and car. Within minutes a constable spotted the car. He turned on his overhead lights, called the dispatcher for back-up, and caught up with the robber, who, surprisingly, stopped. As the constable stepped out of his car, the robber leaned out of his car window and fired a shot at the constable, missed, then sped away at high speed, leaving Paris.

Several Paris city police officers responded quickly to the constable's call for help and raced toward the scene, ignoring the city limits sign; they were coming to help a brother officer. The constable was close behind the pistol-wielding robber, when, at high speed, the robber lost control on a sharp curve, rolled his car, and landed right side up. The constable was out of his car in seconds, pointing his pistol at the slightly dazed man, ready for further action.

Before the confrontation could develop further, the city officers arrived. They got the bandit out of his battered car, searched him, then "cuffed and stuffed" him into a police car. He was slightly injured, with only cuts and bruises. Knowing that they had an armed robber who had already fired at two people, they searched his car thoroughly, but found no pistol. The officers were puzzled and disappointed. Had he tossed the weapon out a window at high speed? Had it been ejected from the car when it rolled?

They knew, as all law officers know, that to get a good conviction of aggravated robbery or attempted murder, they had to find the weapon. They questioned their prisoner about the handgun, but he refused to answer. Using flashlights and patrol car headlights, they searched the highway's grassy shoulders, without success.

At this point, Paris police called DPS and requested help—helicopter help—knowing that its powerful Night Sun searchlight could light up the area and perhaps spot the important handgun.

I was in deep sleep when I got the call at 11:30 P.M. My battle-weary "eagle" eyes were already tired from a day of flying, and I was scheduled to help DPS Motor Vehicle Theft officers look for a stolen truck the next morning.

"Sleep," I muttered silently to myself, "I need sleep." But, as with all law officers all over this great country, when the call comes, you go. And it's always been so with me.

By midnight I was airborne for Paris (Paris, Texas, that is!) 100 miles away. The big sky around me was dark, the ground 1,000 feet below me was dark. Yet I could see for miles. Day or night, the scene from above was always part of the joy of flying for me. Weary or strong, I was always invigorated when I got airborne. Is it this way with all pilots? Of course, I thought. And all this just to find a missing pistol? I knew the answer to that, too.

The average citizen might question why our society of laws saw fit to put a salaried police pilot in the air at midnight, flying a million-dollar helicopter, burning expensive jet fuel, to meet a host of other police officers 100 miles away, on the side of a highway—all for the purpose of searching for a four-pound semi-automatic handgun.

The answer: Without the weapon, the district attorney probably could not get a conviction in court for aggravated robbery or attempt to kill a police officer. The bad guy might go free. Soon, a dangerous robber with a mentality to kill would be free to drive the communities again, and perhaps take other lives. So it all boiled down to public safety. I seldom had to rationalize all this for myself, but on this night, with the cyclic stick between my knees, Helo-101's engine whining steadily, and the ground and little towns rolling away beneath me, the thought was on me.

I slid the window open and stuck my hand out. The rushing air was uncomfortably warm. It was midsummer, and I was thankful my cabin was air-conditioned.

Within forty minutes I was over the search area, a few miles south of Paris. I had seen the flashing overhead emergency lights of the police cars from twenty miles away. As I descended from 1,000 to 400 feet above ground I was pleased to see little traffic moving on the highway search area below. To be safe I requested that the officers block the highway. I circled while they did it, then landed on the highway near the wrecked car, as several officers stood nearby. After a few words of greeting and introduction, it was agreed that a deputy would board and go back up with me as observer. In looking for a pistol in the tall grass, two sets of eyes would be better than one.

The deputy boarded, and I gave him the usual quick lesson in searchlight operation. I lifted up to thirty feet and hovered there as the deputy shined the powerful light on the ground. The blast of wind from the rotor blades parted the tall grass around the damaged car, making the area look like waves on the ocean. One ground officer's hat blew off. We saw beer cans and all the usual litter that collect on a highway shoulder. The searchlight's illumination was so brilliant that we could see the officer's badges glistening. No doubt the local officers, as they looked up at us, were thinking, "That's DPS aerial technology at its best."

"There it is," my deputy/observer suddenly shouted.

He pointed. I saw it clearly in the waving grass, keyed the radio, and told the ground officers where to walk to retrieve it. As my deputy/searchlight operator held the light on it, one deputy leaned over, inserted a ballpoint pen into the pistol barrel to preserve fingerprints, and placed the pistol in a plastic bag. He stood up and gave us thumbs-up. The big grin on his face brought back a memory of another deputy who had once given me the same wide grin.

That deputy had been on an assignment pulling marijuana plants in a farmer's field in Red River County when his pistol fell out of its holster and was lost in the grass and weeds. It was a catastrophe because budgets and salaries were small in his county, and deputies had to buy their own pistols. I helped him find it from above, as in tonight's search. He was elated, and couldn't thank me enough. When he held it up for me to see from above, his grin was as big as Texas. Two lost pistols found, two officers, two grins!

The shoulder on the highway was plenty wide and level, so I landed there. I stepped out of the helicopter for a moment and several officers congratulated me. And the constable who had done the main pursuit was elated just like the Red River County deputy. I relaxed, visited with the Paris officers, and

looked at the getaway car. Then it was time to leave. I had
another flight to do the next morning. I looked at my watch
and saw that it was already the next morning.

Airborne again, I was doubly weary, but pleased that we
had locked the jailhouse door tight on the robber. We had
strengthened the case against him by finding his weapon. He
wouldn't be thrusting it in some young clerk's face again.

As I neared Dallas, its lights and those smaller surrounding towns set the sky aglow. I marveled at the beauty of it.

From my radio came a call: "Dallas, Helo-101 . . ."

"Oh, no," I groaned inwardly. "Go ahead, Dallas," I said.

"Helo-101, the Cook County sheriff is requesting your
help in locating an elderly woman who is lost in the woods.
ETA to Cook County?"

"Stand by, Dallas," I said, and dialed in the airport iden-
tifier on my GPS for the location of the Gainesville Airport,
Gainesville being the county seat of Cook County. Weary or
not, there would be little sleep for Pilot Paul Creech this night.
The GPS indicated 115 miles from my location straight to the
airport. I would need to refuel at Addison Airport north of
Dallas—all airports north of there would be closed at this
hour, which was 1:25 A.M.

I called my dispatcher: "Dallas, advise the sheriff that I
will need to fuel up at Addison and that my ETA will be about
2:50 A.M. Also, Dallas, call my supervisor, Lt. Steve Powell, at
6:30 A.M. and advise him of my assignments tonight and that
I will need another pilot to cover my assignment with Motor
Vehicle Theft agents at 10:30 A.M. He is familiar with the
assignment."

"Ten-four, Helo-101. A deputy will meet you at the
Gainesville Airport."

Full of fuel, I took off from Addison Airport and headed
for the Gainesville Airport. In my fast A-Star helicopter I soon
saw the lights of Gainesville in the distance. Upon landing, the
county deputy met me and boarded as my spotter. As often
happens with the deputy sheriffs who fly with me, this one
also had never flown in a helicopter and knew nothing about
operating a chopper searchlight. I briefed him on its operation.

Did I get tired of meeting new deputy observers and

instructing them on the Night Sun searchlight? Never. They were always top-quality people, dedicated to the assignment. And I needed them.

"I think I got it," he said. "Man, does that air conditioning feel good."

He briefed me on the lost woman. "Just before dark last night she went walking in the woods behind her house and never returned. We've been searching all night on foot and on horseback, and so far we haven't found any sign of her. It was hot work and most of us are pretty beat."

We took off and headed a few miles north to the search area, which centered on the missing woman's home. The deputy seemed entranced with our rapid movement, the dark "world" below, and the searchlight. He experimented with it as the trees and fields came under its brilliance. I could tell he grew encouraged as he lit up a deputy patrol car; he was getting pretty good with it.

I descended to a low but safe altitude in order to better see the missing woman. I told my newly trained observer, "If you see anything that looks strange or out of place, tell me quickly. You may only get a quick glimpse of her in those thick woods."

I called a deputy on the ground and asked him to park his car in front of the woman's house with his flashing overhead emergency lights on. He quickly did, and by keying on them we found the house and began searching the woods behind it. The dark woods were vast and thick, but interspersed by small logging roads and cow pastures.

After about thirty minutes of circling with the searchlight sweeping many areas, I told my deputy/observer, "It's gonna be a long night. We're not going to be able to see her in these thick trees. I'm going to fly slowly. Shine the light on the small roads and the edges of the pastures. If she's near them, maybe we can give her enough light to help her walk out into a clearing."

The deputy did it, sweeping the big light up and down, back and forth. "There she is!" he suddenly exclaimed.

I slowed Helo-101, looked where his searchlight was centered, and saw her. Surrounded by the bright light, she was standing at the edge of a section of pasture where a logging road came out of the woods. She was looking up at us and waving her arms over her head. Her white blouse seemed to glow in the beam of our light. She didn't appear too disoriented, for she was smiling!

Hovering above her, I called the ground officer and relayed the location to him. Soon we saw a county deputy's patrol car bouncing through the pasture as he "homed in" on our searchlight beam. My deputy was feeling jubilant and had really enjoyed his first helicopter ride. "This is the only way to search," he said. "And you have great air-conditioning in this cabin!"

I reminded myself that these county deputies had been searching on foot and by horseback in the over 100-degree August heat. I was grateful for the air conditioning, too. The A-Star's air-conditioning is not a luxury but a necessity, designed to prevent dehydration resulting in fatigue and an unsafe pilot.

"You did a great job with the searchlight," I said.

We watched as a deputy drove up to the woman, got out and helped her into his car. We could also visualize the smile of relief with which she must have greeted the deputy. We smiled, too, as we watched the happy scene. I called the deputy on the ground. "Is she okay?"

"She's fine," he said, "just tired, very thirsty, and relieved."

I landed at the airport and the deputy got out. Shaking hands with me, he said, "If you're ever up this way again and need a searchlight operator, call me."

"I will," I promised him, and meant it, because he had learned fast, done well, and spotted the missing woman.

It was 4:00 A.M. I took off for home, thinking of bed— and breakfast. In my weariness, I had a nice thought that made me smile in the dark of Helo-101's cabin: DPS aircraft pilots specialize in making the bad guys frown while making good citizens and deputies smile.

CHAPTER 27

Bloopers

One might think that state police pilots have enough disciplined precision training to keep them from making any bloopers. But bloopers happen. Sometimes they are caused by mistakes or minor errors in judgment. Usually they are just freak incidents that pilots laugh about later. The following are some that happened to me.

THE "GOVERNOR'S PILOT"

In 1970 I was a new state police pilot with only one year of experience with the DPS Aircraft Section. I was assigned to relieve the regular pilot in Houston while he was on vacation. I had never flown that big city. At that time the DPS helicopter fleet consisted of two Bell Jet Rangers, two Bell 47G-5s, and three Bell 47G-4As. The Bell 47 models are so obsolete today that they would be called dinosaurs. A few are still in use, but I only know of one, and I never see it flying.

The helicopter I was to fly in Houston was a Bell 47G-4A. With its Plexiglas bubble covering the cabin, it looks like a dragonfly in flight—or a Beaumont mosquito which had just had a good meal. It is powered by a gasoline aircraft engine and is plenty noisy. Its single bench-type seat for three includes the pilot, and makes for real togetherness in flight.

On my first day in Houston I got my first assignment one hour before dark: to meet Governor Preston Smith at Hobby

Airport and fly him to a downtown hotel. It sounded simple, but it would be a night flight, and night flights are seldom simple. This young country pilot was totally unfamiliar with Houston, and there was no time for a trial run. It would be different from flying over North Texas woods and small towns.

The regional highway patrol commander who gave me the assignment said, "Don't worry, Paul, the governor has stayed there many times; just get him in the area and he'll point out the hotel."

Using a Houston city map, I located the hotel address. At least I knew which direction to fly from Hobby Airport. With a few minutes to kill I mentally sorted out my assignment. *Wow,* I thought. *I'm a new pilot, I'll have the top man in Texas on board, I don't know the city by day, much less by night, and I hope the governor is a good guy and will help me find our destination. Ain't it a great life?*

I landed at Hobby Airport. Soon the governor and his aide approached the helicopter. We shook hands. I tried to be my professional best. The governor was friendly and in a good mood, and admired the new helicopter. We set down on the bench seat like "three peas in a pod" and took off in the general direction of the hotel. Then I made my confession.

"Governor," I said, "I'm just assigned here temporarily while our regular pilot is on vacation. I'm not sure I know where the hotel is, but I was told you could direct me to it."

"No problem. I've stayed there often. I'll know it when I see it."

We made small talk as we flew. The governor had the easygoing manner of Panhandle Texans, and even though we had just met, I felt that we were bonding well. Also, I felt more comfortable with the situation now. Heck, I'd really have something special to tell my pilot friends about! The governor's young aide seemed a little tense, but fascinated with the sea of lights below us that was mighty Houston.

A few minutes later, the governor said, "There it is," and pointed to a tall building with the hotel name on the side. I was internally jubilant. In moments, I would complete this VIP assignment and relax. The governor added, "I believe there is a grassy area near the front."

Good navigator, that Governor Smith.

I saw the grass, clearly lit by streetlights. I circled at 400 feet above it, checking for electrical or any other kind of wires. I didn't see any.

Feeling a little smug as the "governor's pilot," I began to imagine that the white uniformed Ross Volunteers from Texas A&M University might come marching out from the hotel lobby when we landed. Or maybe a color guard from the Texas National Guard.

I touched down softly on the lawn near the front door of the lobby, being careful not to mar the grass. I shut down the engine and looked around. There was no marching band, no color guard. The governor looked at me, shook hands again, and said, "Good landing."

His aide reached for his door handle and pulled it.

Blam! The door fell off and hit the ground.

Governor Preston Smith looked at me a long time without saying a word, an expression of puzzled disorientation on his face. I felt as if he were looking into my soul. "It's okay, Governor," I said. "He just pulled the emergency release on the door."

His aide, halfway off the bench seat, stared hypnotically out the opening at the chopper's door lying on the ground. Without another word and without any change of expression, they both stepped down from the old Bell 47G-4A and walked toward the hotel entrance.

I never saw Governor Smith again, and I don't think he ever flew in another DPS helicopter!

Oops!

As with automobiles, helicopters are susceptible to mechanical malfunctions. If a helicopter malfunctions at low altitude, the pilot doesn't have the option of stopping on the shoulder of the road, slowly analyzing the problem, and then taking action. A pilot must quickly analyze the problem and immediately take the necessary action.

Such was the case one hot summer day in July with DPS Pilot Eric Myers and me. We were assigned to search for marijuana gardens in the tall pine forests of East Texas. Although

DPS Pilots Paul Creech (left) and Eric Myers.

Eric was a good airplane pilot, he had only recently started flying helicopters. The chief pilot had asked me to "polish up Eric's flying skills." Although Eric would be doing the actual flying, I was the pilot-in-command.

With Eric at the controls, we were circling and searching at low altitude, enjoying the beauty of the lush green East Texas forest. We were comfortable in our air-conditioned helicopter.

Suddenly, smoke began to bellow into the cabin from the air-conditioner vents, accompanied by an electrical burning smell. We went on full alert, bolting upright in our seats.

All pilots fear an in-flight fire. I had located a missing airplane once that had plowed into the ground at night while the pilot was being burned alive as he tried to land. He had been transporting camera film, which is highly flammable. Eyewitness reports and evidence at the scene indicated that the boxes of film stashed in the pilot's cabin caught fire. The pilot was trying to land quickly, anywhere—just to get it on the ground.

Eric shouted, "Fire!" While looking for a place to land, I grabbed the helicopter controls from Eric, who grabbed the fire extinguisher. Both of us were scared. Analyzing the source of the smoke and smell, I quickly determined it had to be the air conditioner. I turned it off. The smoke stopped coming out of the vents.

I landed in a nearby farmer's field and asked Eric to keep the engine running. I got out. No signs of smoke or fire outside. I opened the engine cowling and confirmed the compressor had locked up and would not turn. With the air conditioner turned on, the pulley from the engine was turning against the drive belt, causing the drive belt to become very hot. The smoke was being sucked into the cabin by the air conditioner fan. Eric and I were relieved. If we had continued to fly with the air conditioner on, the drive belt would have continued to burn and finally break apart, possibly wrapping around the tail-rotor drive shaft. Under this scenario we would have had a real emergency.

I said, "Eric, we should cut and remove the belt, and as long as we don't use the air conditioner, I believe it will be safe to fly. We'll go to the Jasper Airport, which is only ten miles from here, call our mechanic, and see what he says."

At the airport I called our mechanic in Austin. He said, "No problem. Just cut the belt so it doesn't come apart and cause other problems. However, you won't have an air conditioner, and you'll be pretty uncomfortable without it."

I felt proud that I had properly diagnosed the problem and taken the proper action. Eric appeared to be impressed by my knowledge of the helicopter systems, and complimented me.

Proudly, I walked over to the helicopter, raised the engine cowling, and with my knife I sliced through the belt. As the belt fell away from the pulleys, I uttered the usual expletive that is common to disgust and frustration. It just came out. Eric looked puzzled. *Oops!* I had mistakenly opened the wrong cowling and cut the belt to the hydraulic pump. Now we were grounded. Can't fly without hydraulics.

I felt like crawling into the engine compartment and closing the cowling door in an effort to hide from Eric. I also knew that the DPS pilot grapevine was alive and well, and when I called the mechanic again, as I must, every DPS pilot in Texas would know what a stupid thing I had done.

"You did *what?*" asked the mechanic. I repeated my story to him. "Well," he said, "I'll have to get one of our pilots here in Austin to fly me 250 miles to Jasper and put another belt on for you."

As Eric and I waited, I tried to salvage my pride by explaining to him that the air conditioner belt and compressor looked the same as the hydraulic pump and belt except the hydraulic pump and belt is smaller and located on the opposite side of the helicopter. I knew that he thought it was a pitiful excuse.

The mechanic finally showed up and replaced the hydraulic belt as well as the air conditioner compressor and belt. I thanked him, and we took off to continue our marijuana search. The air-conditioned cabin felt good.

Later the other pilots accused me of purposely cutting the wrong belt so the mechanic would have to replace the air conditioner compressor. Man . . . that *co-o-o-l* air sure felt good.

THE LOST AMMO BELT

Long before any official SWAT teams were established in the Texas Department of Public Safety, Texas Ranger Capt. G. W. Burkes decided to create one. It was composed entirely of Texas Rangers from Company B in Dallas. Helo-101, my partner Billy Peace, and I were part of the team. We trained with "Burkes' Bad Boys," as I called them, and we did our training at Camp Maxie, an abandoned WWII military base near Paris, Texas. They were all good shots. As a sniper, one ranger could hit a one-inch target with his scoped sniper rifle at 300 yards. I did okay, too, with the weapons, but my main job was to fly this unique bunch of Texas Rangers.

The rear seats and doors of the helicopter were removed during shooting exercises to make more room for a better field of fire for the shooter inside the chopper. Nothing was allowed to be lying loose in the rear passenger area while the doors were off. For quick reloading, the Rangers carried a military-type cloth belt with pockets that contained fully loaded clips

*Captain Burkes' Ranger SWAT team
("Burkes' Bad Boys").*

of ammunition. They soon became proficient at shooting from above at 60 MPH. In fact, they were terrific at this unique firing exercise.

One morning after a long session of training and shooting from the helicopter, I took off alone to the Paris Airport for fuel. For some reason I looked back at the rear passenger area. There was a cloth ammo belt lying on the floor. It was slowly being sucked out of the helicopter by the wind through the open door. It fell into space. I banked sharply, trying to keep my eyes on the belt. It took a long time to hit the ground, landing in a large grove of trees. I tried to remember nearby landmarks.

After refueling, I returned to the training area and landed. Approaching a group of the Ranger/SWAT team, I asked, "Anybody missing an ammo belt?"

"I am," said a Ranger.

"Well," I said, "it bailed out through my open door about two miles southeast of here, landing in some woods."

He didn't say much. I think he had a mental picture of that belt sailing through space.

Ranger SWAT team in practice firing exercise.
Note extended weapons.

STARTLED BY A CAMERA

I was on an aerial photo mission with a narcotics officer who had a very sophisticated camera. We had just finished taking pictures of a "drug house." The photos would be used for strategy planning on a raid the next day.

On the way back to our home airport there was little conversation. I was concentrating on flying our new Bell Jet Ranger. The engine was humming along smoothly. Suddenly, *"BANG!"*—a loud noise startled me. I sat upright in my seat. Preparing mentally for a quick emergency landing, I checked my instrument and engine gauges. Everything showed normal. We were still flying. I looked at the "narc" and said, "What in blue blazes was that?" He was looking at me with an embarrassed look on his face. I looked down and saw his very expensive camera lying on the Plexiglas "shin bubble" (window) under his feet. It was apparent the camera had knocked a large hole in the Plexiglas, and the camera was lying precariously close to it, on the very edge of falling into space. I slowed the helicopter down and the narc gingerly picked it up and apologized.

"That's okay," I said, suppressing my frustration. "I always wondered how a helicopter's flight characteristics would be affected by a large hole in the shin bubble. This proves that our new ship can still fly level with a large rupture in the Plexiglas shin bubble."

I think the narcotics agent later told his fellow officers that I was a super nice pilot. My mechanic gave me an incredulous look when I explained how the damage occurred.

DERRING-DO!

There are impressive reasons why police helicopter pilots live on the "edge" with danger as a daily companion. One can have an engine failure or other mechanical problems. Or be shot at by rifle fire from a criminal below who doesn't take kindly to being observed from above. Occasionally a helicopter pilot gets into a dangerous situation by getting a little cocky and trying some kind of "cute" maneuver.

I confess. I did this. Thought I was a pretty "hot" pilot. In my late mother's words, God bless her, maybe I just momentarily got "too big for my britches." I survived the risky maneuver okay, but later felt like I had been spanked.

To appreciate the danger I placed myself in, you must understand the auto-rotation maneuver, which is meticulously taught by DPS aircraft instructors. The maneuver is calculated to land a helicopter safely after an engine failure or tail rotor failure.

A practice auto-rotation in a Bell Jet Ranger helicopter is performed by the pilot rolling the throttle to flight (engine) idle. A 65-MPH airspeed is established by lowering the collective stick (rotor blade pitch) and establishing the correct descent attitude of the helicopter. The helicopter will glide down at a rather steep attitude. At approximately fifty feet above the ground the pilot then flares by raising the nose of the helicopter, which decreases forward momentum. As the helicopter settles toward the ground, pulling up on the collective handle increases the rotor blade pitch, holding the helicopter up long enough to softly land with no forward speed. Real emergency auto-rotations and practice auto-rotations are done the same way. A 360-degree circling auto-rotation should be started at an altitude of 1,000 feet above the ground. A sharp, coordinated, and continuous descent is required.

Years ago I was a flight proficiency check pilot for other DPS helicopter pilots. I gave check flights during which we did lots of auto-rotations. I became very proficient at them. This was a good thing, because my proficiency was really tested one day after I had finished giving a check-ride to another pilot. He had done pretty good. Flying home alone, I began to get somewhat overcome with my own flying skills. I had thoroughly mastered the auto-rotation maneuver and was sharing my skills with others!

As I approached my home base airport at 500 feet above ground, I asked myself, "I wonder if I could do a 360-degree auto-rotation from as low as 500 feet?"

I decided to try it. Did the devil make me do it? No. It was me—my decision.

I lined up with the airport runway, closed the throttle, and went into auto-rotation configuration. I made a steep, sharp bank to the right, tightening up my turn as much as possible so as not to lose any more altitude than was necessary, to again line up with the runway. It was going to be close, but I still felt confident. As I turned from base to final approach I was lower than I should have been. I was committed and was then too low to increase engine power and hover or to go around. I uttered the usual word of despair. Calling on all my experience and proficiency, I did a quick steep flare, immediately leveling the helicopter, touching down softly, and sliding on the skids straight down the runway approximately 100 yards before coming to a stop.

It had been close. I had almost failed to make it. I let out a deep sigh and thought, *Now I know why the flight instructors at Bell Helicopter insist on pilots starting the maneuver at 1,000 feet above ground.*

And I was reminded of a saying that had long prevailed among our pilots: "Being good leads to being cocky . . . being cocky leads to errors in judgment . . . errors in judgment are sometimes salvaged by proficiency."

Included in the mental spanking I gave myself was a resolution that I would never try that bit of "derring-do" again!

Helicopter coming down and "flaring."

CHAPTER 28

The eagle has landed

On August 31, 1998, I retired from the Texas Department of Public Safety with thirty-nine and a half years of loyal and faithful service to the people of the State of Texas. My first nine and a half years were as a state trooper in traffic law enforcement. The last thirty years I served as a state police pilot/investigator.

I was blessed to have been chosen to be a part of the Texas DPS, one of the finest law enforcement agencies in the United States and well known for its professionalism in many other parts of the world. To become a police pilot for the DPS was a boyhood dream beyond all my imagination.

I was fast approaching age sixty-two when my beautiful wife Dolores, also a state police officer with the Texas Alcoholic Beverage Commission, began encouraging me to retire, saying that I had earned some peace in my life. I had not given retirement much thought as I was still a dedicated, aggressive warrior against crime, a "police pilot."

Dolores reminded me often of the long days and nights of flying into unknown situations that were filled with danger. The 3:00 A.M. call-outs. The long hours of flight, sitting behind the cyclic (control) stick of the helicopter in a prenatal position with my knees bent with both feet on the tail-rotor pedals, unable to shift position or stretch because it took both hands and feet to fly the helicopter. The pilot seat that became as hard as concrete after many hours of flight. The painful crick in my neck after long hours of looking out my side window, searching for dangerous criminals. I often joked to observers who flew with me that because I had had my head turned looking out the side window for so long, the pain in my neck was so bad that we would have to fly home in overlapping circles to the right. My neck hurt too badly to try to turn my head and look straight ahead.

I have many privileged memories: adrenaline rushes during the excitement of the moment, that invincible feeling as I pressed my luck to catch a dangerous criminal, warm feelings after saving a life. The total experience of the wonder of flight, including the beauty of God's creation as I looked down from 10,000 feet and felt as insignificant on this earth as a grain of sand in a sandbox. The beauty of the morning sunrise shining brightly through the misty morning clouds, reminding me of God's glory. My flight suit flapping in the wind as if to remind me that the wind was my friend. On the ground the sound of the wind whistling through the metal aircraft hangar, rattling the sheet metal as if ghosts of pilots past were comforting me, telling me that there were even more beautiful things to see on my final flight from earth.

After beholding all of this beauty for a third of a century and not knowing what exciting things awaited me the next day, I was not sure that retirement was for me. I had served the people of Texas to the best of my ability. No one had had a more rewarding career. In my little corner of the world I knew that I had made a difference in protecting the weak and preserving the rights and property of those I served. I was a part of the "thin blue line."

I knew that there were other capable and dedicated troopers standing in line waiting for the opportunity to serve as a police pilot. I hoped that when they were selected as DPS pilots they would appreciate all of the beautiful and exciting things that were in store for them.

Dolores needed to work a short time longer before she would be eligible to retire. If I retired, I would be free to enjoy being with her when she was off duty. There would be no more conflicting schedules. But I had feelings of insecurity. The DPS had been my life. I had spent more of my waking hours working than at home.

However, Dolores was right—it was time to retire. To the surprise of many of my fellow officers, I announced my retirement date. Of all the officers in the Department of Public Safety, I was number three in seniority. I was already a veteran officer when most of my fellow officers were trooper trainees; I helped train a few. During my career, I saw many officers come and go. Some left by choice, and a few left not by choice. My personnel record was without blemish, containing many pages of citizen commendations, with no complaints.

My last flight and last landing in DPS Helo-101 was a sad moment. I had used that call sign for so many years. It was as if a relationship with an old friend had just ended.

I called the DPS dispatcher on the radio: "Helo-101 to Dallas."

"Go ahead, Helo-101," replied the dispatcher.

"Helo-101 with pilot 123 is 10-42 (off duty), permanently."

Silence from the dispatcher. Then she asked, "Is this for real?"

Helo-101 with pilot 123, "off duty, permanently."

Helo-101, you were a good partner!

"Ten-four," I said.

Silence. "Ten-four, 123, good luck on your retirement," she said.

As I walked away from Helo-101, I paused. "You've been good to me, partner," I said aloud. She truly had been very good to me. I had pushed her to the maximum many times. With my hands on the controls, she and I became one.

Another moment of sentimental reflection came the next night when I delivered my state-issued car to the hangar. It was just before midnight, the end of my last duty day. As I drove it into the hangar at 10:30 P.M. that night, the sky was overcast, with lots of moisture in the air. Visibility was not too good and barely acceptable for night helicopter flying. I remembered nights like this when I had been called out at a late hour to search for a lost person or dangerous criminal suspect. The usual thoughts confronted me: the night sky was minimum flying weather, but what about the area between the airport and my destination? Would I encounter fog or rain? Relief swept over me. I wouldn't have to worry about the weather anymore.

I parked the car inside the hangar beside Helo-101. As I

walked past the helicopter, I gently wiped my hand across her nose, walked into the office, placed all my keys on my lieutenant's desk, turned, locked the door, and walked out. The airport was so quiet you could hear a pin drop, as if it, too, was paying respect to this tired old warrior. Dolores had just arrived to pick me up and take me home. I climbed into our car and looked at her. She was looking at me, probably reading my mind. With the tip of her finger she wiped away a small tear that had gathered in the corner of my eye. I smiled and she smiled. It was another special moment.

My number-one goal in my career with DPS was to retire with dignity and respect. Dolores assured me that I had accomplished that goal.

After my retirement, the Texas Department of Public Safety honored me with a commission as a "Special Texas Ranger." My "Ranger Badge" is made from the traditional Mexican silver cinco peso coin given to me by my friend, Capt. W. D. Vickers, Company B, Texas Rangers. I carry it with pride. I am a charter member of the Airborne Law Enforcement Association, am still an associate member, and was the last line pilot charter member to retire.

My fellow pilots and co-workers gave me the best retirement party that I had ever attended—or maybe it seemed the best because it was mine. It was held at the Texas Ranger Hall of Fame and Museum in Waco, Texas, which was built on the very spot of old Fort Fisher, a Texas Ranger fort from the late 1800s. It is still headquarters for Texas Ranger Company A. About 130 of my friends and co-workers attended. An Elvis Presley show was staged by my lifelong friend, Tommy Munselle, a professional Elvis Presley impersonator, who is well known in Dallas for his excellent talent.

I was expecting the traditional "roast" of the honored guest—me. There were a few that roasted me, but I was also honored with many accolades and gifts: a Texas flag that had flown over the State Capitol with a letter of authenticity from Texas State Representative Elvira Reyna, certificate of retirement from the Texas Department of Public Safety, including a Pilot/Investigator Retirement Badge. There was also a special gift from all of the DPS pilots—my duty pistol mounted in a custom wooden box and presented by my chief pilot and ex-partner, Bill Isbell—and a letter of special recognition from Dallas Mayor Ron Kirk thanking me for my service and dedication to the city of Dallas. Other awards were a congratulatory plaque and other gifts from Bell Helicopter, and personal gifts from many friends, which included my pilot buddies with whom I had worked and helped train. Also, a beautiful gold bracelet was presented to my wife, Dolores. She and I were overwhelmed by it all.

Poems were read and presented to me by Dolores, my son Mike (DPS pilot), and my daughter Pam. These poems and letters were written by the hands of those I love. Please grant me permission to share them.

MY CHOPPER WARRIOR
by Dolores Creech

My love has silver wings
Drifting ever upward, toward dawn's early rays,
Protect him from all harmful things,
Give him tailwinds throughout the days.

The clouds are his amusement park
His airspace well protected,
As he gazes below, free as a lark
Crooks fear for his presence detected.

He's quite a man, proud and strong
Yet compassionate, kind and caring.
He searches out those who choose to do wrong,
Low to rooftop and woodland, with skill and daring.

His command performance is at his arrival,
All look to his powerful winged force above.
His true test is that of endurance and survival
For isn't all this a police pilot's real love?

Lord, shield he who lives by badge and gun
Though his eyes have so much pain,
Keep him safe for me 'til the job is done
Bringing home my chopper warrior once again.

LETTER TO DAD
by Pam Creech

Well, what do you know, the day finally came,
Your hectic schedule is about to change.

From stressful days to late night flights,
To fun-filled days and restful nights.

Now we all know how you say, "There's not enough time."
From reports and flying and fighting crime.

Your retirement is here, and doesn't it feel great
That you no longer have to work for the State?

And your job as a pilot we know that you loved it,
But doesn't it feel good to say, "Take this job and shove it?"

So now there's no excuse for not having fun,
Your work at DPS is finally done.

And as you've gone up the ladder of success,
It's been an uphill climb at ol' DPS.

So reward yourself and buy a plane or new automobile,
'Cuz from now on, Dad, it's all downhill.

So sit back and relax and do what you do best,
From huntin' and fishin' to getting lots of rest.

Now we hope you have fun on your permanent vacation,
Resting and relaxing on your pecan plantation.

Well, now that you've retired there's lots of time to kill.
Now go to work on your farmhouse in Colmesneil!!!

Now hang up your wings and gather up your stuff,
'Cause we all know, Dad, it's retirement or bust!!!

LETTER TO DAD
by Mike Creech, DPS Pilot

Dad, it's hard to imagine how the years have gone by. To tell you how much they have meant to me, I wouldn't know where to begin. We've shared so many good times and memorable moments together.

I want you to know how much fun it's been and how

much of an honor it was to work alongside you, sharing the wind and being there when I need you the most.

I want you to know how much we appreciate that you had the courage to take a stand as a peace officer and to uphold the laws to protect our family and the people in this great state of Texas.

I want you to know as a young man, I knew you were out there in the night, protecting us in harm's way; working the wrecks, writing the tickets and facing death on those lonely stretches of highway.

I want you to know that as it came time to move on, your calling to serve took you in the air where you have served many years and have served well.

I want you to know that your dedication to the Department, the people of Texas, and our country enables us to live a better life and still have hope because of your service.

I want you to know that you will be missed greatly, and your contributions, experience and professionalism will never be forgotten.

Now as you go on to your new life, I want you to know that:

A pair of aces with wings made of gold,
    We're two of a kind; one young and one old.

Hand in hand, my father, your son,
    We soared together with badge and a gun.

For you I followed, admiration you see,
    Your guidance and love rubbed off on me.

The wisdom you shared and knowledge I gained,
    Forever will guide this never-ending chain.

A pair of aces, you and me,
    Sharing the wind eternally.

Maybe poetry runs in this family. I wrote a poem, too. I read it at the retirement party, and dedicated it to my fellow police pilots.

TIME TO RETIRE
by Paul Creech
April 15, 1959–August 31, 1998

Phase three of my life has finally begun,
As I give up my badge and hang up my gun.

I'm depending on you guys to keep us all safe,
I'll pray for your safety, always, leave an escape.

For 39 years I've carried a gun,
My badge flashed bright in the morning sun.

Silver wings flexing to keep the peace,
Making my corner safe, for those who sleep.

Never knew when that phone might ring,
A lost child, surveillance, all kinds of things.

Arriving at the scene, wings flexing overhead,
Bad guys look up in desperation and dread.

The officers on the ground look with awe and admiration,
It's airborne hope, they've searched in desperation.

With eyes of the eagle we search the ground,
If the bad guy's well hidden, we'll keep him pinned down.

He will be caught today or tonight,
We will not leave 'til the end of the fight.

Whatever you do, whenever you fly,
My spirit is with you in that beautiful sky.

I will grow older and time will sail,
My body will wither and health will fail.

I've served with honor and dignity,
Seen things that most will never see.

Been called out on cold winter nights,
To catch the bad guys and settle the fights.

Sometimes I felt I was doing no good,
Always performing the best that I could.

When my life is over and I stand at the gate,
I will look to St. Peter and await my fate.

"Enter the gate, you've earned golden wings,
Fly around Heaven, see magnificent things."

I'll praise my LORD and give Him thanks,
As I dive and loop and turn in steep banks.

I retired for a short while, but the sky beckoned me. I began working as a part-time news pilot for television station KDFW Channel 4 in Dallas, flying a Bell Long Ranger helicopter. Dolores and I purchased our own airplane and enjoy the freedom of flight together, flying whenever or wherever we please. We especially enjoy the peace and solitude of flying at night in the moonlight with no destination or time restraints. Together, as I hold the hand of my best friend Dolores, we behold the beauty of the night sky and feel the wind, this gift to us, created by the "Great Architect of the Universe."

Now I am home from the war against crime. As others carry on this war, I am back in the home of my youth, drinking in the quietness of the forest, hearing only the soft sighing of the wind wafting through the tall pine trees. Near me is the little town of Colmesneil. The graves of my parents and the little church I first attended are nearby. Here, people come when you're sick, and grieve when you die.

From my farmhouse porch is a view of the woods where the tall oak tree once stood, where I "played pilot" as a boy. I know that past and present, I am truly blessed.

CPSIA information can be obtained
at www.ICGtesting.com
Printed in the USA
LVHW082005071020
668251LV00013B/220